T0340383

CHARITY MARKETING

Charities operate within an increasingly challenging environment, with competition for public engagement, funding and volunteers intensifying. High-profile scandals have knocked public trust and the recent Covid-19 pandemic has illustrated how important it is for charities to provide support in times of need and fill the gap left by inadequate public sector provision. Across 12 chapters a diverse group of academics and deep-thinking practitioners present contrasting perspectives and the latest thinking on the challenges within the charity sector.

The approach of the book contributes to the growing phenomenon of Theory + Practice in Marketing (TPM) presenting different perspectives and theoretical lenses to stimulate debate and future research.

Charity Marketing provides a bridge between the practice of contemporary nonprofit organisations, charity marketing and recent academic insight into the charity sector. Using exemplar case studies of nonprofit and charity brands, this edited volume will be of direct interest to students, academics, marketing practitioners and researchers studying and working in charities, public and nonprofit management, and marketing.

Fran Hyde is Deputy Dean of Suffolk Business School, University of Suffolk, UK. She was previously a marketing practitioner before moving into marketing lecturing. Her interest in nonprofit marketing began during a presentation to a group of students by the marketing director of a hospice who highlighted the challenges of marketing a hospice. Seeing first-hand the disconnect between how marketing theory can be taught and how this translates into practice, this encounter is what began her examination and interest in nonprofit marketing practice.

Sarah-Louise Mitchell is Senior Lecturer in Marketing at Oxford Brookes University, UK. She holds a PhD from Henley Business School and an MBA from London Business School. Her primary area of research focuses on providing academic insight for the nonprofit sector, particularly understanding the role of brand for nonprofit organisations through mapping stakeholder decision-making behaviour, decoding nonprofit brand storytelling and exploring charity brand touchpoints. Previously, she worked extensively for consumer goods, food retail and nonprofit organisations, in senior roles including strategic marketing, category insight and new product development.

ROUTLEDGE STUDIES IN MARKETING

This series welcomes proposals for original research projects that are either single or multi-authored or an edited collection from both established and emerging scholars working on any aspect of marketing theory and practice and provides an outlet for studies dealing with elements of marketing theory, thought, pedagogy and practice.

It aims to reflect the evolving role of marketing and bring together the most innovative work across all aspects of the marketing 'mix' – from product development, consumer behaviour, marketing analysis, branding, and customer relationships, to sustainability, ethics and the new opportunities and challenges presented by digital and online marketing.

Brand Management in a Co-Creation Perspective
Communication as Constitutive of Brands
Heidi Hansen

New Consumer Culture in China
The Flower Market and New Everyday Consumption
Xi Liu

Information Asymmetry in Online Advertising
Jan W. Wiktor and Katarzyna Sanak-Kosmowska

Evaluating Social Media Marketing
Social Proof and Online Buyer Behaviour
Katarzyna Sanak-Kosmowska

Charity Marketing
Contemporary Issues, Research and Practice
Edited by Fran Hyde and Sarah-Louise Mitchell

For more information about this series, please visit: www.routledge.com/Routledge-Studies-in-Marketing/book-series/RMKT

CHARITY MARKETING

Contemporary Issues, Research and Practice

Edited by Fran Hyde and Sarah-Louise Mitchell

Routledge
Taylor & Francis Group

LONDON AND NEW YORK

Cover image © Aleksandr Zubkov / Getty Images

First published 2022
by Routledge
4 Park Square, Milton Park, Abingdon, Oxon OX14 4RN

and by Routledge
605 Third Avenue, New York, NY 10158

Routledge is an imprint of the Taylor & Francis Group, an informa business

British Library Cataloguing-in-Publication Data
A catalogue record for this book is available from the British Library

Library of Congress Cataloging-in-Publication Data
A catalog record has been requested for this book

ISBN: 978-0-367-65202-9 (hbk)
ISBN: 978-0-367-68089-3 (pbk)
ISBN: 978-1-003-13416-9 (ebk)

DOI: 10.4324/9781003134169

Typeset in Bembo
by Taylor & Francis Books

CONTENTS

FIGURES

CONTRIBUTORS

Ahmed Al-Abdin is a Senior Lecturer in Marketing and Programme Director for BA Marketing/BA Marketing at the University of Liverpool Management School. He specialises in branding, services research and health marketing. Over the past few years, he has completed projects investigating consumption practices in conflict/disaster zones and how consumers manage the 'new normal'. He has also researched widely into service experiences in end of life care and as part of a team, and has worked with hospices/palliative care units across the country and internationally.

Alison Body is a Lecturer with the Centre for Philanthropy at the University of Kent and the Director of their MA Philanthropic in Studies programme. Before this she worked as a CEO of a leading children's charity and as a lead Commissioning Officer for early intervention services, and has significant experience of working closely with voluntary sector organisations and funders to deliver essential services which achieve maximum impact for children, families and communities. Her research focuses on philanthropy, children and education.

Beth Breeze worked as a fundraiser and charity manager for a decade before co-founding the Centre for Philanthropy at the University of Kent in 2008. Her books include *Richer Lives: Why Rich People Give* (2013), *The Logic of Charity: Great Expectations in Hard Times* (2015), *The Philanthropy Reader* (2016), *The New Fundraisers: Who Organises Generosity in Contemporary Society?* and her latest book entitled *In Defence of Philanthropy* was published in 2021.

Chris Chapleo is Associate Professor in Societal Marketing and former Head of the Department of Marketing at Bournemouth University. He has published widely in international journals on marketing and branding, particularly in non-profit organisations and the education sector. He has also presented keynotes and conference papers at many conferences, and has combined this with consultancy and enterprise work for leading organisations. Current work focuses on charity branding and marketing's role in influencing positive societal change.

Athanasia Daskalopoulou is Senior Lecturer in Marketing at the University of Liverpool Management School. Athanasia's interpretive research programme focuses on market dynamics, consumer culture theory, gender and arts marketing. Athanasia's work has been published in international peer-reviewed journals such as *Sociology, European Journal of Marketing, New Technology, Work and Employment, Journal of Services Marketing,* and *Advances in Consumer Research.*

Iain Davies is Professor of Marketing at the University of Strathclyde. He lectures, researches and consults in Marketing Ethics, Social/Sustainable Enterprise and Customer Management. Following careers in both the Fairtrade sector and strategy consultancy, Iain now dedicates his work to exploring how to make markets operate more ethically and sustainably. With a particular focus on foods, fashion and luxury goods, he works closely with third sector organisations as they try to change the market from within.

Max du Bois has over 25 years of charity, health, education and commercial brand-building experience. He builds brands for social change and brands that challenge attitudes, change minds and inspire action. He is currently Executive Director of award winning brand consultancy Spencer du Bois.

David J. Hart is an Associate Professor in Marketing in the Department of Marketing, Operations and Systems at Northumbria University. His primary research interests are charitable marketing, customer loyalty and customer complaint behaviour.

Philippa Hunter-Jones is a Professor of Marketing and Interim Subject Group Head for Marketing in the University of Liverpool Management School. Over the last 30 years she has engaged in research seeking inclusion and social justice for different marginalised consumers. She has explored this most often within the context of health and wellbeing, researching the service experiences of those facing life-limiting illnesses. Her work has been published in a variety of publications including *Journal of Service Research, Journal of Business Research, Annals of Tourism Research* and *Tourism Management.*

Zoe Lee is Senior Lecturer in Marketing at Cardiff Business School, University of Cardiff. Her current research focuses on three main areas: corporate branding/identity, sustainable luxury and activism. Her latest research explores the internal perspective of corporate (re)branding and corporate identity change, in particular nonprofit employees' emotional resilience. Dr Zoe Lee is currently conducting research in understanding brand activism in nonprofit rebranding. Her research has been published in *Journal of Business Research, Journal of Business Ethics, European Journal of Marketing* and *Journal of Marketing Management*.

Robert Longley-Cook had a 25-year international career with a major multi-national corporate working in commercial, marketing, branding and strategy roles. In 2006, he moved into the charity sector as Executive Director of Fundraising & Marketing, Policy & Communications, and Volunteering at (W)RVS. Between 2010 and 2019, he was Chief Executive of the learning disability charity Hft. Robert is currently Vice Chair of the circular economy and resource efficiency charity WRAP and provides advice and support to other charities.

Ian MacQuillin, MCIoF(Dip) is the Director of the international fundraising think tank Rogare, which he founded in 2014. Rogare aims to help fundraisers better use theory and evidence by translating academic ideas into professional practice and building fundraising's knowledge base. He's recognised as a leading thinker on fundraising ethics, presenting regularly at fundraising conferences around the world and writing for the charity sector press.

Helen O'Sullivan is a Chartered Marketer and Senior Fellow of the Higher Education Academy. She has worked within higher education for the past 17 years. Helen is the Deputy Head of the Department of Marketing, Strategy & Innovation, part of Bournemouth University Business School. Her research is in the fields of societal marketing, branding for NPOs, student learning gain and consumer behaviour. Helen is the Co-Chair for the Academy of Marketing's Marketing of Higher Education Special Interest Group. Helen is passionate about education and marketing and committed to giving people from all backgrounds the access to education they deserve.

Chloe Preece is a Senior Lecturer in Marketing at Royal Holloway, University of London. Her research focuses on marketing within the arts and creative industries and how this translates into social, cultural and economic value. She is currently Chair of the Arts, Heritage, Nonprofit and Social Marketing Special Interest Group of the Academy of Marketing.

Emma Reid is a Lecturer and Programme Leader in Digital Marketing at the University of the West of Scotland (UWS). She holds a PhD in Marketing from the University of Strathclyde. She is responsible for teaching digital marketing, and has research interests in digital marketing, charity marketing, arts marketing and audience development. Prior to taking on the role at UWS, Emma worked for a digital agency, specialising in social listening and social media monitoring.

Andrew J. Robson is a Professor in the Department of Marketing, Operations and Systems at Northumbria University. His teaching focuses on data analysis and associated quantitative methods and modelling, with research interests spanning across marketing, information management and learning and teaching.

Andrew Ryde is Chief Executive of Oakhaven Hospice, based in Hampshire for the past 15 years. Prior to this, Andrew was Chief Executive of Sobell House Hospice Charity (based in Headington, Oxford) for over five and half years. Andrew has a Master's in Business Administration (MBA) from Durham Business School and also a Master's (MSc) in Hospice Leadership from Lancaster University.

Joe Saxton is founder and driver of ideas at nfpSynergy, a research consultancy for charities. He was co-founder and chair of CharityComms, the professional body for not for profit communicators from 2005 to 2013. He was chair of the Institute of Fundraising for three years till July 2008, and co-founder and chair of CharityComms for seven years. For six years till June 2020 he was chair of Parentkind, the umbrella body for PTAs. He also sits on the board of two small grant-makers. He was in the top ten of the most influential people in UK fundraising every year for its first decade, being top of the poll on four occasions. He was named one of the most influential people in voluntary sector communications by PR Week, and has twice been named as one of the 1000 most influential people in London by the *Evening Standard* newspaper. He was given the Lifetime Achievement award by the Institute of Fundraising, and was highly commended in the Chair of the Year category in the Third Sector excellence awards. Away from charities, he is a double award winner for his first novel *Secrets of the Flock*.

Lucy Smith is Director of Patient Services at Oakhaven Hospice. Lucy has held several other positions at Oakhaven including Head of Nursing and Head of Education. She is also a lecturer/practitioner at the University of Southampton and teaches palliative care and end of life care education development, strategy as well as provision and support in both university and practices settings. Lucy has a Post Graduate Certificate in Academic Practice from the University of Southampton and a Master's (MSc) in Advanced Practice: Cancer and Palliative Care from Buckinghamshire New University.

Lynn Sudbury-Riley is a Senior Lecturer in Marketing and Director of Education for Marketing at the University of Liverpool Management School. With its central focus on improving quality of life for vulnerable consumers, her research examines ways in which marginalised consumers face difficulties in access to and consumption of products and services. Her recent research in health emphasises the ways in which service needs to be refined in order to improve access and experience for vulnerable consumers. Lynn has published extensively on older and marginalised consumers, receiving recognition through several international research awards including two Emerald Literati Awards.

Kati Suomi, DSc (Econ. and Bus. Adm.), works currently as a Lecturer in Marketing at the Turku School of Economics at the University of Turku (Pori Unit), Finland. She holds a title of Docent (Adjunct Professorship) at the Tampere University Faculty of Management and Business, Finland. Her current research interests include topics such as branding in the nonprofit sector, as well as brand co-creation and extreme brand relationships. Her research has been published in the *Journal of Business Research, International Journal of Public Sector Management* and *Tourism Management*, among others.

Walter Wymer is a Professor of Marketing at the University of Lethbridge (Canada). His primary areas of research include nonprofit marketing, nonprofit brand management, social marketing and higher education marketing. He is an Associate Editor for the *European Journal of Marketing* and the *International Review on Public and Nonprofit Marketing*, and serves on the editorial review board of several other journals.

FOREWORD

It's not easy doing good. It's not easy to run an organisation where the sources of income can be entirely unrelated to the services run. It's not easy to manage people like volunteers who do their work for love not money. It's not easy to manage an organisation when you want to be professional, but you can't ever get caught being professional by the public or the media. It's not easy running an organisation where so many of the ways of doing things look like those in the for-profit world, but in fact they can be deceptively different.

It's for these reasons that the development of a separate and distinct strand of non-profit management ideas is so important. All too often charities get the ill-fitting intellectual hand-me-downs from the commercial world, and all too often people who come from the commercial world believe those ideas can be neatly put into practice in the not-for-profit world. The challenge for managers and trustees is not that mainstream management theory is not ever applicable. I remember reading Philip Kotler's *Marketing Management* early in my career with a sense of intellectual euphoria Here were ideas that had so many potential applications for the nonprofit world.

The challenge for nonprofit managers is to understand which ideas are useful and relevant, which are useful when adapted to the nonprofit context and which ideas are specific only to the nonprofit context.

This is why this book has a treasure trove for those who want to manage and develop charities and other nonprofits. Its content covers three very useful areas: those ideas from the commercial world which have direct relevance for nonprofit management but need to be adapted and tweaked. Those ideas which are unique to the challenges of running charities. And lastly some great case studies which show the reality of putting management ideas into practice.

Brand and marketing are two key mainstream management practice ideas comprehensively covered in this book. Robert Longley Cook and Max du Bois explore how the use of brand and brand management techniques have grown in importance over the last few decades. Charities have come to realise that brand shouldn't be a dirty word, but a critical way that a nonprofit organisation can punch above its weight. Similarly, Zoe Lee and Iain Davies look at rebranding in charities and the importance of continually keeping an image fresh and up to date. Lastly Chris Chapelo and Kati Suomi explore the often-neglected area of internal marketing and brand perspective with a particular emphasis on the importance of getting structure right.

Volunteering is a management discipline which simply doesn't exist in the commercial world, while many nonprofits are wholly or heavily dependent on volunteers. Sarah-Louise Mitchell explores the development of volunteer management through the comparison with consumers, and calls for the introduction of B2V marketing and management. Ian MacQuillan analyses the challenges of fundraising ethics, both from a theoretical point of view and also by reference to specific examples where the ethics of donations have been challenging. Alison Body and Beth Breeze address another area unique to charities which is the way that some causes are 'unpopular' while others thrive. They set out some best practice guidelines for helping charities ask for donations no matter their cause. Athanasia Daskalopoulou and Chloe Preece develop the thinking about the challenges of raising funds with specific examples from the arts sector.

Alongside the theoretical ideas the chapters in this book are rich with practical examples. Emma Reid looks at how one Scottish mental health charity struggled with reaching particular audiences, and how it enlisted students to help create new marketing ideas. Fran Hyde shows how the ideas of relationship marketing worked for one charity in Suffolk addressing rural loneliness. A case study from Oakhaven Hospice in the palliative care sector changes the focus from many of the other chapters and looks at how good marketing ideas were used to better understand the needs of current and potential service users. Helen O'Sullivan changes the focus yet again with a case study on marketing the nonprofit sector to students and helping them to get a better practical understanding of the challenges of charity management.

The joy of a book like this is that not only do the chapters cover a breadth of issues and topics, but they weave together theory and practice. The authors are an excellent blend of practitioners and academics. The structure of chapters by this breadth of authors encourages readers to dip in and out to gain more food for thought. I have no doubt that this book will build a bridge between nonprofit management theory and practice and will be a source of insight to readers for years to come.

Joe Saxton

INTRODUCING CHARITY MARKETING

Contemporary issues, research and practice

Fran Hyde and Sarah-Louise Mitchell

This exploration of the unique nature of non-profits and how key stakeholders differentiate, evaluate, and choose to enter into a relationship with such organisations is an important and under-researched area.

(Venable et al., 2005, p. 296)

Our motivation for developing this new book on charity marketing was to address a gap in knowledge. We had some questions. What is it that makes the nonprofit context distinctive? How does theory inform real-life practice and vice versa? What role can higher education play in addressing some of the challenges that charities are currently facing?

What constitutes nonprofit marketing, how or indeed if it is different to marketing in for-profit organisations is a key question to consider. Araujo and Kjellberg (2009, p. 196) note that 'there is no stable set of practices or theories that we can unequivocally call "marketing"'; instead they suggest we see marketing practice as interconnected and routinised behaviour. Thus, it must be through case studies and drawing from those who are actively engaged in the sector that we can explore how nonprofit marketing 'is done' (Hyde, 2020). To meet the challenges for this sector we need to not only advance the understanding of the practice of marketing by illuminating the processes, actors and tasks – the 'inner workings' (Zwick & Cayla, 2011, pp. 4–5) of marketing practice – but also consider how we are educating a future generation of marketing practitioners.

Now more than ever we need to equip individuals to be able to practice marketing appropriately and successfully within this unique sector. Drawing from a diverse group of academics and deep-thinking practitioners this book will present contrasting perspectives and the latest thinking on the challenges with the aim of stimulating classroom debate and future research. The approach of the book contributes to the growing phenomenon of Theory + Practice in Marketing (TPM).

DOI: 10.4324/9781003134169-1

Despite the recent theoretical development of the 'strategy-as-practice' construct and special journal editions focusing on TPM, the charity sector has been largely absent from the debate. This is an oversight given the importance of the sector to the jobs, economy and social fabric of our country. The book provides a bridge between the practice of contemporary nonprofit organisations, charity marketing and recent academic insight into the challenges, culture and communication and exemplar case studies of nonprofit and charity brands.

Through bringing together leading experts in the field, the book identifies the key activities of charities such as attracting and retaining stakeholders including donors, volunteers and corporate supporters. At each stage, the academics draw on industry examples to illustrate their points and, in turn, identify implications for practice. It considers the enormous impact of cause – what motivates people to give, how the arts sector is distinctive, and what happens when your cause is unpopular. Through three live examples, it demonstrates the impact that collaborative working can deliver, including between universities and charitable organisations. The book starts with an introduction to underpinning theory followed by a practitioner/agency perspective on charity brands.

Audience

This book is for students, charity marketeers and fellow academics. There are an increasing number of postgraduate and undergraduate courses at universities that focus on nonprofit and charity marketing and management, as well as students studying for professional marketing and management qualifications, such as with the Chartered Institute of Marketing and Chartered Institute of Management, who are required to extend reading beyond core texts for certain modules and their final projects. Charity and nonprofit practitioners will also find this book helpful in seeking to find new ways of thinking to improve the effectiveness of their organisation's marketing. Finally, for academics researching the nonprofit sector, we hope the book will be a useful update on the latest thinking in the sector.

Acknowledgements

The editors would like to thank the Academy of Marketing for its support for our work, including hosting the nonprofit workshop at their conference in 2019 at which many of our co-authors presented and the idea for the book was born.

References

Araujo, L. & Kjellberg, H. (2009). Shaping exchanges, performing markets: The study of marketing practices. In P. Maclaran, M. Saren, B. Stern & M. Tadajewski (eds), *The Sage Handbook of Marketing Theory*. Sage.
Hyde, F. (2020). Harry's most important work. *Marketing Theory*, 20(3), 211–218.

Venable, B.T., Rose, G.M., Bush, V.D. & Gilbert, F.W. (2005). The role of brand personality in charitable giving: An assessment and validation. *Journal of the Academy of Marketing Science*, 33, 295–312.

Zwick, D. & Cayla, J. (2011). *Inside Marketing: Practices, Ideologies, Devices*. Oxford University Press.

THEORETICAL FOUNDATIONS FOR EXPLORING CHARITY MARKETING

Sarah-Louise Mitchell

Introduction

This chapter introduces the reader to some of the core constructs underpinning our thinking about charity marketing: symbolic consumption, social exchange and market orientation (or not). This is followed by a practitioner/agency perspective on brand. We hope they work well together to provide a foundation for exploring the key issues of charity marketing in theory and practice.

Context definition and distinctiveness

One starting point for understanding a new context is considering the language used. Widespread variation in terminology adds complexity to the 'charity' context, with labels including charity, voluntary organisations, social enterprise, not-for-profit, independent sector and third sector. For ease, this book uses charity and nonprofit interchangeably, as descriptions of nonprofit organisations (NPOs) that exist

> to provide for the general betterment of society, through the marshalling of appropriate resources and/or the provision of physical goods and services.
>
> *(Sargeant, 2009, p. 8)*

This fundamental difference in purpose to commercial organisations is at the heart of the distinctiveness of the sector, combined with an anchoring of non-profit brands in the values and beliefs of their stakeholders, both external and internal (Frumkin & Andre-Clark, 2000). NPOs that are founded upon, and consistent with, their values enable trust to be built with their stakeholders (Sargeant & Lee, 2004).

DOI: 10.4324/9781003134169-2

There are three additional, clearly observable, differences between nonprofit and for-profit organisations.

- The first is the complexity of the multivalent stakeholder relationships (Mitchell & Clark, 2019), where the person directly paying for the service is rarely also the beneficiary of the service – purchase and consumption are detached.
- The second concerns a tension around competition, where NPOs with similar missions may practically compete for resources such as donations and volunteer time but also collaborate to achieve a wider societal impact, such as Breast Cancer Awareness Week or the Disaster Emergency Committee (DEC).
- Finally, many NPOs are characterised by a reliance on volunteer resource to deliver services. Given the natural churn in volunteering, without effective volunteer recruitment and retention strategies, the very sustainability of the NPO is under threat. Together these characteristics make the nonprofit sector distinct, despite increasing professionalism and adoption of 'business-like practices' (King, 2016; Maier et al., 2016).

Theory 1: Symbolic consumption

Traditional theories of consumption describe a person buying, using and disposing of a tangible product. However, this definition has been broadened to include a person's choices about how they consume

> services, activities, experiences and ideas such as going to the dentist, attending a concert, taking a trip and donating to UNICEF.
>
> *(Hoyer et al., 2012, p. 3)*

Choice of NPO has been defined as consumer behaviour: a consumption decision (Wymer & Samu, 2002). Bagozzi (1975) argues consumer behaviour can be indirect and involve intangible and symbolic factors such as social or psychological benefits. He builds on the work of Levy (1959) in his 'Symbols for sale' article:

> People buy things not only for what they can do, but also for what they mean.
>
> *(Levy, 1959, p. 118)*

Hoyer et al.'s (2012) work in deconstructing the symbolic consumption concept is particularly relevant to understanding the meaning stakeholders give to NPOs. They describe the four components of symbolic consumption as emblematic, role acquisition, connectedness and expressiveness. With the emblematic function, they argue:

> Consciously or unconsciously we use brands and products to symbolise the groups to which we belong (or want to belong).
>
> *(Hoyer et al., 2012, p. 446)*

With the role acquisition function the choice of brand reflects the role that person feels they are occupying at that moment in time. Role acquisition has been shown to be a positive effect of volunteering, particular for older people post-retirement (Chambre, 1984). Our choice of brand may also reflect a personal connection to a specific person, group or event in our lives (Michel & Rieunier, 2012). Finally, with the expressiveness component of symbolic consumption, buying a brand says something about us as individuals, how we are different and what we stand for (Hoyer et al., 2012; Randle and Dolnicar, 2011). In this way, the emblematic, role acquisition, connectedness and expressiveness components of symbolic consumption link the NPO choice to work on self-identity, values and social groups.

Jundong et al. (2009) in their work on the role of brand equity with Chinese donors state:

> Empirical results indicated that two dimensions of non-profit brand equity – brand personality and brand awareness could strengthen individual donors' self-concept, which in turn influenced on individual giving directly and significantly.
>
> *(Jundong et al., 2009, p. 225)*

Likewise Bennett (2003) argues:

> The finding that the favourability of a person's overall impression of a charity exerted a strong effect on his or her selection of that charity underscores the need for charities to devote substantial resources to image building and reputation management.
>
> *(Bennett, 2003, p. 27)*

The importance of developing and managing that brand image and reputation is developed in the next chapter on practitioner perspective, as well as within the chapters on CSR, rebranding, fundraising and volunteering.

Theory 2: Social exchange

The second important theoretical construct within the nonprofit context is social exchange theory (Blau, 1964; Emerson, 1976). It argues that the 'voluntary actions of individuals are motivated by the rewards they are expected to bring' (Blau, 1964, p. 91). Venable et al. (2005) argue that although there may be social benefits from buying commercial brands, such as status and security, they are more salient amongst nonprofit brands.

> Because of the intangible, service-orientated nature of non-profit organisations, we posit that social exchange and trust play an important role in consumer's decisions of whether to donate money, time, or in-kind goods and services to such organisations.
>
> *(Venable et al., 2005, p. 296)*

Stakeholders consider the rewards of action at an abstract level – including personal satisfaction, social approval or humanitarianism. The prospective benefits of achieving those personally important goals are weighed against the cost of volunteering, donating or other forms of engagement.

Five propositions of social exchange theory have been identified by Homans (1961). Three of these propositions can be interpreted as being anchored in repeat purchase behaviour, relevant for donors or customers of nonprofit goods and services. For example, the success proposition argues that the more often a person is rewarded for a behaviour, the more likely they are to do it. Likewise, with the stimulus proposition, if a person is rewarded for behaviour with a particular stimulus, when those stimuli happen again, so the behaviour will also happen. Finally, the deprivation-satiation proposition argues the more often a person has received a reward, the less valuable it is to that person in the future. For the volunteer stakeholder group, although there is some evidence of serial volunteering (Low et al., 2007), the decision to volunteer is more likely to be an infrequent decision. However, the remaining two of Homan's propositions do have greater relevance to these nonprofit stakeholders. The more valuable the results of that action are to the person making the decision, the more likely it is they will make the decision, known as the value proposition. The implication is that when a person is considering the decision to support a charity, if they perceive there to be significant personal rewards from their support for a specific organisation, then they are more likely to make the decision. Likewise with the rationality proposition, when choosing between alternative potential support opportunities, following Homan's (1961) logic, the person will choose the one where the value of the result combines with the likelihood of the support role happening (Emerson, 1976).

Therefore, the social exchange construct involves an evaluation of perceived costs and benefits of involvement by stakeholders in NPOs. It implies a conscious decision-making process and an evaluation of alternatives, whether they are other charities or other uses of time and money. As the cost benefit exchange is salient and explicit, it can be recalled by supporters, which might explain its prominence in both national volunteering and donor surveys (Cabinet Office, 2013) and academic studies (Clary et al., 1998).

When an NPO understands this social exchange, they are in effect considering the needs of their customers, their stakeholders. They understand that in order to sustain the multiple stakeholder relationships needed to deliver their mission, as an organisation they must fulfil their side of the exchange. Long-term stakeholder relationships will not be established if the stakeholders are purely viewed as a source of resource, whether funding or manpower. The NPO must understand what each stakeholder group requires in return. In theoretical terms, they need to be market orientated.

Theory 3: Market orientation

The increasing market orientation (MO) of charities has brought a growing recognition of the importance of developing brand differentiation and stakeholder engagement to attract resources within this increasingly competitive environment (Balabanis et al., 1997; Macedo & Carlos Pinho, 2006; Randle et al., 2013).

Jaworksi and Kohli (1993) define MO as:

> organisation-wide generation of market intelligence pertaining to customers, competitors and forces affecting them, internal dissemination of the intelligence and reactive as well as proactive responsiveness to the intelligence.
>
> *(Jaworski & Kohli, 1993, p. 54)*

As a theoretical construct, MO is anchored in customer focus: where an organisation bases decision-making on current and future customer needs. It is not simply the generation of market intelligence that identifies it as market orientated but also the dissemination of and responsiveness to that insight. Narver and Slater (1990) operationalise MO as an organisational culture that creates superior value for customers through customer orientation, competitor orientation and interfunctional coordination. At the heart of both definitions is the customer.

MO delivers mission-based goals, as it has been shown to drive financial performance in commercial sectors (Baker & Sinkula, 1999; Slater & Narver, 1994). However, for nonprofit organisations it is driven indirectly through three dimensions: customer satisfaction (where customers are defined as beneficiaries and other stakeholders), peer reputation and resource attraction (Shoham et al., 2006). An MO culture not only predicted a growth in resources and higher levels of customer satisfaction within the nonprofit context, but also a strengthening of reputation amongst peers (Gainer & Padanyi, 2002). However, there is also evidence of mission drift away from community building and advocacy towards service provision (Maier et al., 2016), so the relationship between MO and achievement of mission-based goals needs further exploration.

Perhaps it is for this reason that, despite the widespread observation of increasing MO of NPOs, there remains unease within the sector. The dominant observed relationship is between the brand and donor stakeholder group. Strengthening the gathering and dissemination of market intelligence about donors has a clear and measurable impact. It also concerns NPO behaviour, that is *what* they do, rather than mission, which speaks to *who* they are (McDonald, 2007). It is less threatening, in contrast, to debate about NPO brand as a competitive lever. However, this is changing in the face of increasing pressure on resource acquisition and lack of differentiation within a cluttered operating environment (Dato-On et al., 2015).

MO resides within the broader environment of increasing professionalism within society (Hwang & Powell, 2009). The nonprofit sector is no exception. The transition from amateur to paid professional, from volunteer founder led to executive leadership, is well underway as NPOs become major service providers (Bennett, 1998; Chad, 2014). The resultant changes in structure can include 'the use of managerial and organisation design tools developed in for-profit business settings, and broadly framed business thinking to structure and organize activity' (Dart, 2004, p. 294).

The impact on ways of working within NPOs has been identified in four distinct dimensions: programme goals, organisation of service delivery, organisation management and organisation rhetoric (Dart, 2004). From a resource perspective, professionalisation can strengthen the ability of the NPO to attract and retain qualified staff (Guo, 2006). Enhanced and formalised support structures may drive overall volunteer participation, although they may potentially alienate grassroots activists. (Maier et al., 2016). Increased fundraising capability through importing strength and depth has a direct and positive impact on net income for the NPO (Betzler & Gmür, 2016). However, the impact on the culture and identity of the NPO is not only due to the incoming expertise but also the 'integration of professional ideals into the everyday world of charitable work' (Hwang & Powell, 2009, p. 268).

The translation of the MO construct from the commercial to the nonprofit context must consider two situational differences – the complexity of customer relationships and the mission delivery goals, rather than the financial goals, of the organisation. Three distinct customer relationships are identified and illustrated in Figure 0.1.

Service companies may demonstrate pure 'dyadic' customer relationships or 'mediated dyadic', through a third party such as a booking agent. However, 'identifying who an organisation's customers are is even more complex when service is provided to one party, but payments are received from another' (Kohli & Jaworski, 1990, p. 4). Nonprofit organisations have multiple 'customers', including service beneficiaries, individual donors, retail customers, volunteers, service funders and opinion formers. This moves beyond dyadic to what can be described as 'multivalent' relationships.

Each stakeholder group is defined as a set of customers, particularly given the importance of social exchange theory and symbolic consumption theory observed within the nonprofit sector. The level of MO will not be uniform across these relationships (Padanyi & Gainer, 2004); in effect the NPO needs to manage each of these 'multivalent' relationships, all with a distinct impact on performance and culture, through understanding and fulfilling the 'exchange' that customers require.

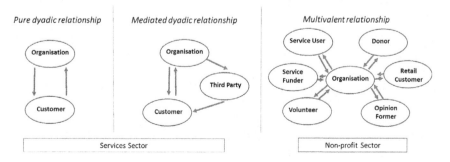

FIGURE 0.1 Market orientation relationships

A new lens: customer engagement framework

Therefore, it is the engagement between the NPO and its stakeholders that reflects its phase of organisational development. Moderating that relationship is the level of MO of the organisation, particularly towards customers/stakeholders and the level of social exchange that those customers/stakeholders desire from the organisation in return for money, goods and time offered. The theoretical model describing these relationships is shown in Figure 0.2.

In situations where the organisation is highly market orientated and understands the need for focus on the customer, and those customers have a strong desire for social exchange, where personal needs are met through donation of time, goods or money, then there will be high levels of engagement between the two.

The level of MO the NPO exhibits is in turn influenced by three factors: the strength of organisational ambition, the competitive context and the internal capabilities within the organisation. Not all NPOs need or desire customer engagement. Some are funded purely by central government grants where the need for social exchange is not only less but also focused on fewer stakeholders. Others exist to fulfil a specific and time-bound mission, such as fundraising for an event; once achieved the NPO will cease to exist. However, for the majority of NPOs, the level of MO is determined by the level of strategic ambition within the organisation, how far they want the organisation to progress in delivering its mission. This will also in part depend on the competitive context. The more competitive that specific cause category or broader civic participation environment, the greater the need to be differentiated and customer focused. The ability to deliver that opportunity will therefore also be determined by the capabilities within the organisation. The skills and expertise needed at each phase will evolve. The challenge is whether the NPO recognises that requirement and can harness the opportunity through actively ensuring those required capabilities are in place.

In turn, the level and form of social exchange required by the customers, the stakeholders, depends on their sense of self, congruence with the values of the organisation and reaction of friends and family. The concept of self is important to the customer: it affects the choices they make directing behaviour towards enhancing self-concept through the consumption of goods as symbols. In this way, people gain or reinforce their sense of self through the services or goods they buy

FIGURE 0.2 Theoretical model of NPO–stakeholder relationships

and what it says about them (Belk, 1988). The construct of self has been divided into four categories – ideal self, actual self, actual-social self, and ideal-social self. Actual self is how a person sees themselves in reality whereas ideal self is how the person would like to perceive themselves in an ideal world. Social self is how we present ourselves to other people (Champniss et al., 2015; Sirgy, 1982). Research by Achouri and Bouslama (2010) demonstrated that people look for opportunities that enhance their identities, and when they find them that relevant identity is reinforced. The more salient self-concepts have been identified as being the ones that are more likely to affect behaviour than those that are not so important (Arnett et al., 2003). The implication is that the stronger the congruity between the consumer's actual or ideal self and those of the product or service brand, the stronger the preference for that brand (Brunsø et al., 2004; Malholtra, 1988). Finally, the choice of and level of engagement with a specific NPO is made within a wider psycho-social context, one where the opinions of family, peers and community play a role. This is well described within the expressive and emblematic constructs of symbolic consumption theory (Hoyer et al., 2012) where people choose to associate themselves with a brand in part due to what it says about them to other people, or to associate themselves with a particular group, such as a faith community or local residents.

References

Achouri, M.A. & Bouslama, N. (2010). The effect of the congruence between brand personality and self-image on consumer's satisfaction and loyalty: A conceptual framework. *IBIMA Business Review*, 2, 34–49.

Arnett, D.D., German, S.D. & Hunt, S.D. (2003). The identity salience model of relationship marketing success: The case of nonprofit marketing. *Journal of Marketing*, 67, 89–105.

Bagozzi, R.P. (1975). Marketing as exchange. *Journal of Marketing*, 39, 32–39.

Baker, W.E. & Sinkula, J.M. (1999). The synergistic effect of market orientation and learning orientation on organisational performance. *Journal of the Academy of Marketing Science*, 27, 411–427.

Balabanis, G., Stables, R.E. & Phillips, H.C. (1997). Market orientation in the Top 200 British charity organisations and its impact on their performance. *European Journal of Marketing*, 31, 583–603.

Belk, R.W. (1988). Possessions and the extended self. *Journal of Consumer Research*, 15, 139–168.

Bennett, R. (1998). Market orientation among small to medium sized UK charitable organisations: Implications for fund-raising performance. *Journal of Nonprofit & Public Sector Marketing*, 6, 31–45.

Bennett, R. (2003). Factors underlying the inclination to donate to particular types of charity. *International Journal of Nonprofit and Voluntary Sector Marketing*, 8, 12–29.

Betzler, D. & Gmür, M. (2016). Does fundraising professionalization pay? *Nonprofit Management and Leadership*, 27, 27–42.

Blau, P.M. (1964). *Exchange and Power in Social Life*. Transaction Publishers.

Brunsø, K., Scholderer, J. & Grunert, K.G. (2004). Closing the gap between values and behavior: A means–end theory of lifestyle. *Journal of Business Research*, 57, 665–670.

Cabinet Office. (2013). Community life survey. TNS BRMB. Available at: www.gov. uk/government/publications/community-life-survey-2013-to-2014-data (accessed 7 September 2021).

Chad, P. (2014). Organizational change within charities: Improved performance via introduction of market orientation and other strategic orientations. *International Review on Public and Nonprofit Marketing*, 11, 89–113.

Chambre, S.M. (1984). Is volunteering a substitute for role loss in old age? An empirical test of activity theory. *The Gerontologist*, 24, 292–298.

Champniss, G., Wilson, H.N. & Macdonald E.K. (2015). Why your customer's social identities matter. *Harvard Business Review*, 93(1/2), 88–96.

Clary, E.G., Ridge, R.D., Stukas, A.A., Snyder, M., Copeland, J., Haugen, J. & Miene, P. (1998). Understanding and assessing the motivations of volunteers: A functional approach. *Journal of Personality & Social Psychology*, 74, 1516–1530.

Dart, R. (2004). Being 'business-like' in a nonprofit organisation: A grounded and inductive typology. *Nonprofit and Voluntary Sector Quarterly*, 33, 290–310.

Dato-On, M.C., Keller, E.D. & Shaw, D. (2015). Adapting for-profit branding models to small nonprofit organizations: A theoretical discussion and model proposition. In C.L. Campbell (ed.), *Marketing in Transition: Scarcity, Globalism, & Sustainability*. Springer.

Emerson, R.M. (1976). Social exchange theory. *Annual Review of Sociology*, 2, 335–362.

Frumkin, P. & Andre-Clark, A. (2000). When missions, markets, and politics collide: Values and strategy in the nonprofit human services. *Nonprofit and Voluntary Sector Quarterly*, 29, 141–163.

Gainer, B. & Padanyi, P. (2002). Applying the marketing concept to cultural organisations: An empirical study of the relationship between market orientation and performance. *International Journal of Nonprofit & Voluntary Sector Marketing*, 7, 182.

Guo, B. (2006). Charity for profit? Exploring factors associated with the commercialization of human service nonprofits. *Nonprofit and Voluntary Sector Quarterly*, 35, 123–138.

Homans, G.C. (1961). *Human Behavior: Its Elementary Forms*. Harcourt Brace.

Hoyer, W., Macinnis, D. & Peiters, R. (2012). *Consumer Behaviour*. South-Western Cengage Learning.

Hwang, H. & Powell, W.W. (2009). The rationalisation of charity: The influences of professionalism in the nonprofit sector. *Administrative Science Quarterly*, 54, 268–298.

Jaworksi, B.J. & Kohli, A.K. (1993). Market orientation: Antecedents and consequences. *Journal of Marketing*, 57, 53.

Jundong, H., Lanying, D. & Zhilong, T. (2009). The effects of nonprofit brand equity on individual giving intention: Mediating by the self-concept of individual donors. *International Journal of Nonprofit & Voluntary Sector Marketing*, 14, 215–229.

King, D. (2016). Becoming business-like: Governing the nonprofit professional. *Nonprofit and Voluntary Sector Quarterly*, 46, 241–260.

Kohli, A.K. & Jaworksi, B.J. (1990). Market orientation: The construct, research propositions, and managerial implications. *Journal of Marketing*, 54, 1–18.

Levy, S.J. (1959). Symbols for sale. *Harvard Business Review*, 37(4), 117–124.

Low, N., Butt, S., Ellis Paine, A. & Davis Smith, J. (2007). *Helping Out: A National Survey of Volunteering and Charitable Giving*. Cabinet Office/UK Government.

Macedo, I.M. & Carlos Pinho, J. (2006). The relationship between resource dependence and market orientation: The specific case of nonprofit organisations. *European Journal of Marketing*, 40, 533–553.

Maier, F., Meyer, M. & Steinbereithner, M. (2016). Nonprofit organizations becoming business-like: A systematic review. *Nonprofit and Voluntary Sector Quarterly*, 45, 64–86.

Malholtra, N.K. (1988). Self-concept and product choice: An integrated perspective. *Journal of Economic Psychology*, 9, 1–28.

McDonald, R.E. (2007). An investigation of innovation in nonprofit organizations: The role of organizational mission. *Nonprofit and Voluntary Sector Quarterly*, 36, 256–281.

Michel, G. & Rieunier, S. (2012). Nonprofit brand image and typicality influences on charitable giving. *Journal of Business Research*, 65, 701–707.

Mitchell, S.-L. & Clark, M. (2019). Reconceptualising product life-cycle theory as stakeholder engagement with non-profit organisations. *Journal of Marketing Management*, 35, 13–39.

Narver, J.C. & Slater, S.F. (1990). The effect of a market orientation on business profitability. *Journal of Marketing*, 54(4), 20–35.

Padanyi, P. & Gainer, B. (2004). Market orientation in the nonprofit sector: Taking multiple constituencies into consideration. *Journal of Marketing Theory and Practice*, 12, 43–58.

Randle, M. & Dolnicar, S. (2011). Self-congruity and volunteering: A multi-organisation comparison. *European Journal of Marketing*, 45, 739–758.

Randle, M., Leisch, F. & Dolnicar, S. (2013). Competition or collaboration and quest: The effect of non-profit brand image on volunteer recruitment strategy. *Journal of Brand Management*, 20, 689–704.

Sargeant, A. (2009). *Marketing Management for Nonprofit Organizations*. Oxford University Press.

Sargeant, A. & Lee, S. (2004). Trust and relationship commitment in the United Kingdom voluntary sector: Determinants of donor behavior. *Psychology & Marketing*, 21, 613–635.

Shoham, A., Ruvio, A., Vigoda-Gadot, E. & Schwabsky, N. (2006). Market orientations in the nonprofit and voluntary sector: A meta-analysis of their relationships with organizational performance. *Nonprofit and Voluntary Sector Quarterly*, 35, 453–476.

Sirgy, M.J. (1982). Self-concept in consumer behavior: A critical review. *Journal of Consumer Research*, 9(3), 287–300.

Slater, S.F. & Narver, J.C. (1994). Does competitive environment moderate the market orientation-performance relationship? *Journal of Marketing*, 58(1), 46–55.

Venable, B.T., Rose, G.M., Bush, V.D. & Gilbert, F.W. (2005). The role of brand personality in charitable giving: An assessment and validation. *Journal of the Academy of Marketing Science*, 33, 295–312.

Wymer Jr, W.W. & Samu, S. (2002). Volunteer service as symbolic consumption: Gender and occupational differences in volunteering. *Journal of Marketing Management*, 18, 971–989.

BUILDING POWERFUL CHARITY BRANDS

An inside perspective

Max du Bois and Robert Longley-Cook

If only actions spoke louder than words

The focus of a charity should be about making, or maintaining, change. Brand plays a central and vital role in delivering this.

Jeff Bezos is widely quoted as saying 'Your brand is what people say about you when you are not in the room'. And while this may seem quite simplistic, what it underlines is that your brand is not about a name, a logo or a colour pallet, it's about what you do, how you do it and how that impacts on your audiences. Fundamentally, it is about the building of trust between organisation and audience, and it is this that informs the next decision that audience makes about them. All those feelings are then imbued into your name and logo in the minds of your audience and become the shortcut through which you can reach them.

What this also emphasises is that brand is not some standalone activity that can be delegated to your communications team or outsourced to an agency. It sits at the very heart of what you do and must be engrained in your culture and strategy. Everyone in the organisation needs to own and live the brand through their actions and behaviours to deliver its promise. A quote that sums this up, attributed to Maya Angelou and used by Charles Saatchi, is: 'People won't remember what you say. They won't remember what you do. But they will remember how you make them feel'. David Aaker echoes this: 'A brand is built through deeds more than words – it is how your customers experience what you do'. So, the bottom line is that building your brand is everyone's job!

One way of visualising this is to think of your brand as the microscope through which you invite your audiences to view your organisation. Your brand values are the lenses and, when viewed through these, your actions and behaviours need to be both clear and truthful if your brand is to be truly authentic. And to be authentic, a brand may express aspiration but needs to be grounded in current reality.

DOI: 10.4324/9781003134169-3

One of the challenges in this media-noisy world is that everyone wants attention, be it to sell something, monetise their clicks, gain a donation or get you to do something for them. It's also a world in which many organisations – including charities – do similar things, so differentiation becomes hard. This demands that your brand is distinctive, and to achieve this, charities need to develop deep, fact-based insights into themselves in order to clearly articulate the challenge they are addressing, the action they uniquely take and the transformation this action brings to their beneficiaries. The organisation needs to be able to express this clearly and consistently to all their audiences. To quote David Aaker again: 'Until everyone from your CEO to your receptionist can accurately and consistently articulate your brand promise, how do you expect your customers to?'

The benefits of getting brand right are significant. Strong brands are thought of first, they are thought of more favourably, and they are given the benefit of the doubt. At the same time the stronger the brand the more likely they are to polarise opinion – which should not be seen as a negative. If only actions spoke louder than words, you wouldn't need a brand. But they don't. So, it's not good enough to set up a great charity, with a great vision, great people and great processes. To be successful you need to be known to be great.

The point of it all

So, let's step back a moment: why do charities exist? Simply put, charities exist to make the world a better place: campaigning, researching, innovating and delivering services where founders, staff and funders, including governments, feel there is a need to make change at an individual, local, regional, national or international scale. They operate where the state chooses not to directly or indirectly operate, where the state cannot effectively engage a group of people or to go beyond minimum state provision, providing 'vital additionality'. This is all called 'public benefit' and charities are expected to be able to demonstrate this.

If you asked people to name the five largest charities, they would probably say Cancer Research UK, British Heart Foundation, Macmillan, Oxfam and the Royal National Lifeboat Institution (RNLI). All famous brands – even compared with commercial ones. Actually, Sightsavers is now number three in many lists but is not as well-known as a brand (Fundraiser, 2020).

In fact, of the charities listed above, only Cancer Research UK – at £634 million in income a year – is in the top ten largest charities, as there are a range of charitable organisations that are far bigger but their brands are not known to the general public as charities. The biggest is The British Council at nearly £1.2 billion in income, followed by Nuffield Health at £950 million, Lloyds Register Foundation at £891 million and the Arts Council of England at £728 million. Only then do we get to Cancer Research. Others in the top ten include The Christian Aid Foundation, The National Trust, Cardiff University Trust, The Wellcome Trust and the Capricorn Foundation (GiveSuper, 2019): none of these brands tends to be front of mind for the public when talking about charities.

What this highlights is that public perception of a charity brand is shaped by a combination of the fundraising profile (CRUK Race for Life, Macmillan Coffee Mornings, British Legion Poppy Appeal, Oxfam, Scope and BHF shops), awareness of the public-facing activity (RNLI at beaches and along the coast, Macmillan in hospitals), and cause-related promotional activity (Prostate Cancer's Bob Monkhouse 'beyond the grave' campaign in the London Underground[1] or Leonard Cheshire's Aardman Animation 'Creature Discomforts' campaign[2]).

Beyond the headline charities, the context in which charities operate is pretty complex and often hard for the public to easily understand. Firstly, the sheer scale and diversity of the sector is huge. In 2019 there were about 169,000 registered charities in England and Wales with an overall income estimated at £83 billion but with an average of £490,268 and a median of £17,290 (so half of all charities have an income of less than £17,290).

There are a vast array of objectives and activities. The best known are around health (e.g. CRUK, Great Ormond St, BHF, Mind, Alzheimer's), animals (RSPCA, PDSA, Dogs Trust), children (Save the Children, NSPCC, Action for Children), disability (Guide Dogs, RNID, Leonard Cheshire, Mencap), poverty and homelessness (Shelter, St Mungos, Crisis), times of crisis (RNLI, Red Cross, St John Ambulance), international aid (Oxfam, Unicef, MSF), environment (Greenpeace, WWF, Ellen MacArthur Foundation) and the military (British Legion, Help for Heroes, SAFFA), however there are a raft of regional and local charities delivering great grassroots projects and services throughout the country.

In each sector there are a multitude of charities, many with closely overlapping – perhaps even competing – objectives and often with similar names and few differentiating characteristics. Where you would see 'value' driven consolidation within the commercial sector in order to increase scale and efficiency, the charity sector tends to resist mergers due to (claimed) differing 'values', which tends to leave the sector increasingly fragmented and open to accusations of inefficiency and wasted funds.

There is also a large array of charities whose main income is not public donations. Many of the biggest charities get their income from government funding (as in the British Council or Arts Council England) or government contracts (Turning Point, Mencap, RVS or United Response in the social care sector), from endowments (Wellcome Trust or Garfield Weston Foundation), or from running a business (as with Nuffield Health). While many of these don't look for donations, those charities in this category that do want to raise funds will often find that their large statutory income inhibits individual donations – and those dependent on contracts may often be inhibited from taking a strong stand on issue if they feel that doing so would put contracts at risk.

A particular claim for charities is that, unlike businesses, they are driven by public benefit and values, not shareholder value. But even that distinction becomes blurred when you see many charities almost operating along commercial lines (in fact many charities talk about 'getting more commercial') and many businesses in the same sector demonstrating strong values through corporate social responsibility (Charity Benchmarks, 2021[3]).

The public has some fairly well-developed preconceptions around charities. They don't expect the people who run charities to be paid – well not to any great extent. And at the same time, they expect charities to be run very efficiently. Given the size, scale and complexity of many charities, in particular the larger ones, public perception and the reality of recruiting high-performing executives are at odds with each other, which can lead to some reputational challenges when the public is asked to put their hands in their pockets, given how transparent charity pay is.

One real strength of the charity sector is the level of trust the public have in it when compared to many other institutions such as government, media or corporate – though corporate is not that far behind (Edelman, 2021). The downside of being on this pedestal is that the public hold charities to higher standards of behaviour and react strongly to any breach of this trust and tend to let this impact on how they perceive the whole sector. Examples are the public response to issues such as those at Oxfam, Save the Children and Alzheimer's/Samaritans – often driven by individual behaviours at a senior level that then reflect on the perception of the whole charity. They also think charities are inefficient, though it's not always clear where these perceptions come from.

Whilst organisations can draw upon deep and strong sector foundations of trust and goodwill to build a charity brand, it is important to take into account the complex nature of the sector and the interactions within it, and be aware how this can trip-up or dilute efforts to build strong brands.

As the focus of a charity is about making, or maintaining, change this 'all in' approach gives them their right to operate and should give a competitive point of difference and advantage in service delivery markets. However, all too often this quest for change becomes obscured by the grind of day-to-day operations, funding worries or is replaced by a desire to grow, sometimes for its own sake.

One key caveat for those looking to rebrand or build a charity brand: the very act of doing this is often seen by the public and media as a frivolous waste of donations – and they love shouting about it. The quickest way to get challenging headlines is to tinker with a beloved charity brand! (Boycott-Owen, 2021) Having said all that, building a strong charity brand can bring huge benefits in terms of delivering objectives and driving income. Delivering a new brand whilst keeping key stakeholders and the public on side is a tight needle for a charity's CEO and chair to thread.

This all goes to the heart of what brand is and, more importantly, what brand does.

Brand: its role and value

Brand's core role is as an 'enabler' for delivering a charity's vision of change. It's the way you build and focus a charity's reputation to reach out to the people a charity needs and to inspire them to act in ways that achieve a charity's goals by changing habits, giving money, volunteering, changings laws, etc.

Brand lets people know you're here and that what you do matters to them. It answers the question 'Why': why choose to act, rather than turn away, why choose me rather than the competition, why choose my cause, my service, my way of doing things. It is the mechanism to challenges attitudes, change minds and inspire action. And this is also where the greatest difference to commercial brands currently sits, although with the rise of 'purpose brands' the boundaries are blurring and the remit 'to do good' is being hijacked.

Effective brands share three key characteristics:

- Distinctive: To stand out in a noisy world and differentiate, especially in crowded areas.
- Relevant: Locking into your audiences' needs, hopes and aspiration as the best vehicle for their generosity or their desire for change.
- Capturing the imagination: To reach into hearts and minds and inspire action.

As well as providing a clear and engaging articulation of what your charity's about, brand also pulls together all your activities and actions; it is the lens through which people both see and experience the organisation. It acts as the glue for all interactions, in terms of communications and behaviours. By focusing your collective strengths, you stand out more. People can see and understand the depth and breadth of what you offer. You get the credit for what you do.

And getting credit for what you do, proving your impact and effectiveness, is key to a charity's existence. It is the proof of delivering on the promise of change that funders, 'users' and stakeholder have entrusted a charity with. This is made all the more acute as, in many areas, the lines between state and charity provision are blurred in the public's mind, and because charities often compete with other charities and, in the provision of care, with private providers. However, charities appear to be failing to get the credit they deserve. Worryingly, despite an upswing in the sector's size and increased demand for their services, from 2008 to 2020, public trust in charities has fallen from 72% to 55% (Charity Commission, 2020).

Distilling this down, brand can also be divided into two major components: preference and trust. Preference contains the 'why choose me', the 'what I've got for you that others haven't' – your competitive difference. Trust underpins your claims. It fuses impact, track record and promise and makes them credible. It says 'I can deliver'. As charities are a channel for altruism or bulwark against fear, without trust brands are worthless, ignored words.

Effective brands in high-performing charities also act as a powerful enabler for other parts of the organisation, helping amplify their focus, performance and effectiveness:

- In fundraising it promotes awareness and trust, allowing the 'ask' to be more single minded and cost effective.
- In campaigning and policy it justifies why you should be heard and why your point should be taken seriously, it gets you influence.

- In service delivery, it adds additional value to the service being pitched to local authorities and funders.
- In information provision, it proves authority and wins trust often for people in difficult times.
- In PR it provides a platform for promotion and resilience in a crisis.
- For volunteers, it creates the sense of movement and belonging.
- For frontline service delivery staff it reinforces the wider value of what they do and inspires them to be their best professional selves.
- For recruitment, it attracts the better candidates in the highly competitive battle for talent and persuades people to seek careers in their areas.
- For boards and decision-makers, it keeps the 'mission' front and centre of decisions.
- For all staff, supporters, trustees and volunteers, it turns their individual voices and actions into a collective roar.

Nor are brands the domain of big, high-spending charities, although the rates of growth they enjoy and their investment in their brand are no accident. It's doubly important for small and medium charities to carve out their space, to maximise each opportunity and to compete and operate effectively.

Simply said, a brand's role and greatest value is as an agent for action.

Measuring and assessing brands

In the charity sector, brand can be said to operate at three levels:

- As a 'wrapper' to coherently pull together complex operations: this is brand at its most simplistic and least useful.
- As a focused 'lens' to communicate its vision and how it's achieving this. This is the most common use across the sector and while useful, limits it to a communications tool.
- As a charity's 'DNA'. This is brand at its most powerful, as a motivating and inspiring tool for change at every level.

It is relatively straightforward to measure and monitor a brand's impact on its audiences by external bespoke research and by subscription services[4] or by monitoring response to a charity's activities, such as fundraising response rates, services tendering success, social media engagement,[5] website visits and volunteering rates. The problem with the latter category is that brand is rarely a means for its own ends, it 'enables' other activities and is combined with these, and has to be viewed with balance.

These tools tell you how your brand is performing at the end point. They don't tell you how, where or why brand drives these results. To understand this, eight 'brand levers' can be assessed, looking at:

1.   How well brand drives the delivery of *corporate strategy*.
2.   The part brand makes in *decision-making* across the charity.
3.   How brand engages core audiences and drives desired actions.
4.   How fully brand has been *adopted* across the organisation.
5.   How effectively the charity's *verbal and visual* brand works.
6.   How well the visual and verbal brand is *applied* across all touchpoints.
7.   How well can the brand work in the near future in terms of technical channels (digital) and audience trends (decay or loyalty and rise of spontaneity)?
8.   How *loved* is the brand? A technically floored but loved brand will outperform a technically good but ambivalent brand.

Depending on results for each, a charity's brand can be classified into one of five 'states' to understand how it is performing and where improvements need to be made. In declining order of excellence and impact:

A *Brilliant Brand* is a powerful brand that maximises on all opportunities to achieve its clearly focused goals.

It is a brand that understands its stakeholders. Its work is grounded in comprehensive and thoughtful research into its different audiences and their needs. Its brand and branding wrap around existing and new audiences, and promote a coherent, relevant and consistent message across all of its channels.

The brand is integral to decision-making throughout the charity. The executives understand its value and use it to drive strategic decisions and evaluation across the organisation. The internal departments know how to use the compelling central idea to execute impactful actions.

The brand is well positioned on all channels, excellently managed and coherently implemented visually and verbally. As a result, it is flexible enough to support relationships with all its key audiences.

Brilliant Brands are the change makers.

A *Bright Brand* is a brand that shines and makes the most of its opportunities. It is working well and delivering for the charity but there is scope for improvement.

The brand performs well because it is driven by a focused corporate strategy and is grounded in audience insight. The charity has spent time understanding its stakeholders to ensure it can deliver a distinctive and relevant brand that meets their needs, reaches its business goals and benefits the wider cause.

However, while it is coherently implemented and tailored to each audience, there are opportunities to drive the brand forward. For example, the brand messages communicated to audiences might not be consistent, or there might be room to push the brand and branding to make it more effective and engaging.

Bright Brands are well defined, grounded in insight, coherent and support a clear corporate strategy.

A *Flickering Brand* is either on the edge of igniting to become a Bright or even Brilliant Brand, or showing early signs of decline. It's doing a serviceable job for the moment but is finding it difficult to make ground and there are questions about its ability to make the most of opportunities as things change over the next few years.

The brand is guided by the corporate strategy and there are tangible examples of where it is delivering benefits and impact in key areas of the organisation. However, the wider environment has changed and the corporate strategy is feeling dated or less relevant.

The brand is starting to creak under the strain. It works well in places, but is feeling patchy. It is only used to inform some of the decisions and actions, not others, largely in the marketing and communications teams.

With this type of brand there is the opportunity to evolve the brand, develop more impactful audience-targeted messaging founded in research, and create more differentiating branding.

A *Dull Brand* is lacklustre and unloved. It holds the charity back and is in need of urgent attention.

The brand isn't closely aligned to the organisation's corporate strategy and cause and is failing to make an impact. It is rarely considered or used as part of decision-making across the organisation and is largely seen as a communications tool or something that doesn't apply to other departments.

Fatally, it's failing to engage with its audiences. Its donors, volunteers and partners see it as fairly generic and uninspiring due to the undifferentiating and untailored messages it promotes. New initiatives often ignore the brand and create their own messages in an attempt to bridge this engagement gap, leading to inconsistency and confusion.

There is inconsistency across the branded activities and channels, with many poorly connected sub-brands or initiatives starving the core band of salience or relevance.

The brand is more of a hindrance than a help, made serviceable only by a disproportionate investment of time, effort or money.

At the bottom of the scale is the *Void Brand*. The charity is successful in spite of, rather than because of, the brand. The brand isn't helping the charity now and it definitely won't in the future.

There might be a vision but this isn't being communicated. If there is anything that can be identified as a brand, it doesn't meaningfully align to the corporate strategy and is never taken into consideration when decisions are made in any part of the organisation. It is usually highly generic, unfocused and unengaging, using the same untailored messages for all of its audiences.

It's putting the future of the charity at risk, failing the organisation, the cause and the people it wants to help.

This scale, developed by charity brand agency Spencer du Bois (2019), was made publicly available and gathered data on over 550 charities (2019 to March 2020) and found that only 6% were Brilliant Brands and 57% needed significant and urgent improvement (Keller, 2000).

The agony and ecstasy: getting brand right

Getting brand right is a thoughtful and multi-dimensional task, and the authors in this book look at this in detail. However, there are a few basic pitfalls that it's worth looking out for as you enter into the process.

'We are all experts': it's funny how everyone believes that they are experts in brand and marketing. Because we come across it every day as the focus of other organisations' brand and marketing interventions… and since we know what impacts on us and what we like, we therefore assume we are experts. In reality, most of us aren't, but that has never stopped people from expressing strong opinions: the more senior someone is, the stronger their self-belief and the more damaging this can be. So, make sure you get experts into the room (from within your organisation or an agency) and listen to them, become fact based, think like your audiences not yourself, be objective. Just remember, a Lynx Africa advertisement may be irritating to you at 65, but to a 16-year-old who wants to have a good time, it's spot on!

Think of ALL your audiences. A particular challenge for charity marketing is that positioning your beneficiaries as victims can get the money rolling in from fundraising. So that's good! How do your beneficiaries feel? If your campaign takes off as you want it to, it's likely that your beneficiaries will see it too, and if they feel you are patronising them or disempowering them this could undermine your ability to deliver impact. So, think audience and think balance. Can you use your fundraising campaign to empower beneficiaries? That's the big prize and its worth striving for.

Having said that, don't try to appeal to everyone as you risk becoming a vanilla brand. Keep in mind that a powerful brand will often polarise. So, accept that some people will not buy into your brand and what you stand for: that's worthwhile if those you do want to take on the journey find your case even more compelling. Do all this knowingly, which demands that you understand all your audiences.

Visionary brands are energising and exciting – but if they fail to deliver, it becomes just hubris. Your charity's brand and marketing can express vision and aspiration but they also need to be grounded in reality. As with all good targets, what you say about yourself needs to be a stretch but also to be achievable; they need to acknowledge that almost every underlying issue a charity sets out to tackle is challenging and may have bumps along the way.

It's important not to see rebranding as a shortcut to organisational or culture change within a charity. A new brand should be the outward manifestation of change that has happened or is happening within an organisation: the narrative arc of that change should provide a compelling foundation for the brand positioning. Rebranding without change risks being lipstick on a pig – and that's when you get stakeholder outcry against it.

Brand and marketing can risk becoming a technical process, and communication a pile of facts and anecdotes. But people engage with, and become invested in, stories. Wherever you look, a compelling narrative arc draws in audiences – from TV, books and films, to products and campaigns. So what's your story? As an organisation, you need a consistent and powerful story that everyone can tell, and your chief executive and chair need to be storytellers-in-chief. It needs to be grounded in facts and data but woven with emotion and passion. The upside in this is that a good story is easier to remember and tell than a pile of facts and anecdotes.

Finally, never take your brand for granted, never rest on your laurels: the world keeps moving so always make sure that you keep selling the brand narrative – internally as well as externally, keeping it relevant, looking to improve and incorporate new and fresh stories. It's also good to use fads and fashion at the tactical level but be cautious about getting carried away with them at the strategic level.

Some things change, some stay the same: the question is which?

We could not end this chapter without looking at the future and thinking about future trends. Many great brands achieve success by resonating with an emerging zeitgeist and this is often put down to better understanding of trends and foresight. In fact success can be as much down to being in the right place at the right time as having better insight; however, failure to understand trends and being open to change will almost certainly lead to failure.

The analysis of future trends in charity brands would be a book on its own, so what we have looked to do here is highlight a few 'thought starters'.

Blurring: Historically, charities have held a distinct place in society: they were seen as doing good with freely donated money rather than making profits. As such, they could be trusted to do the right thing for society – going above and beyond what was provided by the state and commerce. Now there is an increasing blurring of the boundaries: both with public sector service provision, with more public services looking to raise more donated money (e.g. NHS Charities Together) and with growing numbers of corporates developing a 'purpose culture' where the organisations business models are based on achieving positive societal objectives and tapping into ethical consumers (Lewis, 2020). At the same time, charities have looked to address the perception of being inefficient by looking to be more business orientated or commercial, looking to recruit people from business in order to drive that change.

Blurring the boundaries risks others stealing charities' reputational thunder, and with it, their resources, mindset and money.

Charities need to get clear on what they stand for and why they are different. They need to go beyond making an assumption that they have the moral high ground and start actively positioning themselves to defend it.

Agility and adaptability: Doing more with less… and faster: It is highly likely that, following the current pandemic, the world will be confronted by a huge range of social crises. This is likely to result in donors and supporters being confronted with a huge array of competing causes and 'asks'. At the same time there are a number of emerging trends in donations: there is a move away from the steady direct debit culture – driven by GDPR and recruiting methodology falling out of favour – exacerbated by Millennials and Gen Z preferring to give spontaneously and focusing on a cause rather than a charity. There has also been a societal move from cash to contactless, accelerated by the pandemic. While giving loose notes and change as spontaneous donations will be a thing of the past, average donations (pre-pandemic) were higher for contactless than cash so those who adapt are likely to benefit.

As well as a change in donor attitudes, there are also changes in terms of how causes are supported. Shorter attention spans and the wealth of distractions has led to a great response to short stimuli (e.g. TikTok, Instagram posts and other memes) vs long reads and infomercials. There is also a sense that there is a rise of the armchair clicktivist vs the on-the-march activist, the former believing that they have created change through signing a petition or 'liking' a post. Transitioning someone from superficial engagement to deep support becomes a growing challenge.

On the upside, there is a dramatic rise in youth volunteering, driven as an integral part of personal development and desire to 'contribute', focused around community and personal benefits. But as with the armchair activism, during the Covid crisis RVS has found that many people signed up as volunteers but a significant proportion remained inactive. So, the challenge is around engagement and activation.

Bringing in consistent levels of funds and attracting and activating supporters will demand that charities are agile and adaptable and are able to make their limited funds stretch further. They will also need to ensure that in a crowded marketplace, they stand out as a clear and distinctive 'champion of the cause': they will need strong and distinctive brands.

Brand and marketing were often seen as large set piece exercises which required both investment and time. Whilst strong brands do require investment (just like any other asset an organisation owns, it needs regular maintenance at the very least) audiences have changed and are now much more accepting of more spontaneous, response and 'low-tech' engagement. Millennials and Gen Z will follow spontaneous movements, engaging through posts from friends and influencers rather than engaging with large set piece centrally run campaigns: so more TikTok than big ads, citizen journalist than editorial content. The upside is that smart use of viral, ambush, guerrilla and buzz marketing is both agile and value-for-money, but it does demand a change of approach for many traditional charities: and whilst collateral production values may change, organisational values need to remain deep and strong.

Brave collaborations: Along with the blurring of the clear line between charities, the state and corporates, the public has a strong perception that charities would be more effective if they worked in partnership with other institutions (Edelman, 2021, pp. 25–34, Business: Catalyst for Change). This view provides support for charities to move beyond the traditional corporate partnerships of 'they give: we do' into the space of genuine coproduction of outcomes. This will demand a more entrepreneurial mindset where charitable goals are achieved through joint-ventures and commercial partnerships, ones where a corporate may even profit from delivery of those outcomes. Moving into this space demands organisational confidence, both for ensuring a balanced partnership with a corporate or state partner and in addressing potential criticism for 'sleeping with the enemy' by both internal and external stakeholders.

Some things don't change: Getting brand right, getting your brand well known and getting your organisation aligned around a brand are still critical.

When it comes to brand and marketing, corporates will often outspend charities as they see brand and marketing as 'investment' whereas charities tend to see it as 'cost', unless it's directly related to fundraising. Charities need to get better at valuing the non-fundraising benefits of investment in brand, ultimately, relating it to their ability to deliver change. If not, the charity will wither into obscurity and irrelevance, and the wrongs they sought to change will continue to blight lives.

Brand doesn't have to cost the earth. Take the words of Ernest Rutherford to heart: 'We haven't got any money, so we must think', and think hard. We have far more valuable currencies in our inspiration, vision and drive. 'Bottle' them carefully and thoughtfully in your brand and see the difference you can make.

Notes

1 Successful 2008 London Underground campaign where Bob Monkhouse's estate allowed is image and humour to be used to raise awareness of Prostate cancer.
2 Launched in 2008, this animation-driven campaign series, created by the studio that produced 'Wallace and Gromit', challenged perceptions held about people with disability.
3 The last few years have seen a sudden rise of social enterprises and 'purpose-led' commercial activity. Whereas once there was a clear divide between the commercial and the charity sector, businesses are increasingly presenting themselves in terms of achieving positive social and environmental impact.
4 External subscription services:

> nfpSynergy's Charity Awareness Monitor, and Charity Brand Evaluator
> YouGov's Charity Brand Index
> Third Sector/ Harris Interactive's Charity Brand Index
> Eden Stanley's Charity Tracker

5 Social media 'buzz' monitors Pulsar Brandwatch.

References

Boycott-Owen, M. (2021). Royal British Legion accused of losing touch, *The Telegraph*, 24 January. Available at: www.telegraph.co.uk/news/2021/01/24/royal-british-legion-accused-veterans-losing-touch-charitys (accessed 6 September 2021).

Charity Benchmarks. (2021). Charity Benchmarks: Insight for the UK charity sector. Available at: www.charitybenchmarks.org (accessed 6 September 2021).

Charity Commission. (2020). Trust in charities 2020. Available at: https://assets.publishing. service.gov.uk/government/uploads/system/uploads/attachment_data/file/897204/ Public_Trust_in_Charities_2020_overview_of_findings.pdf (accessed 6 September 2021).

Edelman. (2021). Edelman trust barometer 2021. Available at: www.edelman.com/trust/ 2021-trust-barometer (accessed 6 September 2021).

Fundraiser. (2020). Top 100 fundraisers spotlight April 2020. Available at: www.charity choice.co.uk (accessed 6 September 2021).

GiveSuper. (2019). The 50 biggest charities by income in the UK in 2019. Available at: http s://givesuper.co.uk/blog/the-50-biggest-charities-in-the-uk-in-2019 (accessed 6 September 2021).

Keller, K.L. (2000). The manager's tool kit: The brand report card. *Harvard Business Review*, 78(1), 147–158.

Lewis, P. (2020). Why good ethics are now big business – and how to embrace them. *Forbes*, 14 October. Available at: www.forbes.com/sites/phillewis1/2020/10/14/why-good-ethics-are-now-big-business-and-how-to-embrace-them/?sh=56988c2c4748 (accessed 6 September 2021).

Spencer du Bois, with du Bois, M., Watson, M., Dryer-Gough-Wilson, A. & Bacon, J. (2019). Brand effectiveness scorecard. Available at: https://spencerdubois.co.uk/brand-effectiveness-score-card/ (accessed 6 September 2021).

1

CHARITY MARKETING AND CORPORATE SOCIAL RESPONSIBILITY

Walter Wymer

Overview

Charity marketing activities and tactics are ultimately aimed at attracting (and retaining) support for a charity so that the charity can further its mission (Faulkner & Romaniuk, 2019). Charities receive support from individual donors and volunteers. Charities also receive support as grant recipients from government agencies and foundations. A growing source of support comes from the business sector. Charities may view donations and other forms of business support as a new source of revenue which can be valuable in offsetting government funding reductions or in funding new programmes (Himmelstein, 1997).

Just as charities are increasingly interested in learning more about how to better market to businesses to attract their support, business's interest in supporting charities is also growing (von Schunurbein et al., 2016). Supporting charities is one way in which a business can demonstrate its corporate social responsibility (CSR). CSR refers to ways in which businesses demonstrate to society that they are interested in being a positive influence in the world and not solely concerned with their own interests (Dahlsrud, 2008; Weeden, 1998).

How do charities attract and retain business/commercial support?

Charity marketing activities directed at attracting support from the business sector need to be adapted to the needs and motivations of the potential business supporter. After the business support has been cultivated, the relationship between the charity and business must be maintained in order to retain the business support (Sagawa & Segal, 2000).

A brand orientation and brand management culture in the charity is particularly efficacious in helping the charity to be an attractive organisation that businesses

DOI: 10.4324/9781003134169-4

want to support (Wymer et al., 2015). Increasing brand remarkability – that is, acquiring a reputation for being an excellently managed and exceptional charity – is fundamental. Communicating that brand remarkability to stakeholder groups on a regular basis increases brand familiarity; that is, the level of knowledge target audiences have about the charity. As brand remarkability and brand familiarity increase over time, the charity as a brand gets stronger. As the brand gets stronger, more businesses want to support the charity (Wymer & Casidy, 2019; Wymer et al., 2016).

As the charity becomes more widely known as an exceptional organisation, the charity's marketing efforts can be directed at targeting, or identifying businesses likely to respond positively to the charity's donor cultivation efforts. Identifying a potential business supporter begins with looking for potential partners that appear to be a good fit for a relationship or alliance (Wymer & Samu, 2003). Mission fit, or a fit between the charity's mission and business's operations, might indicate a good match. Target market fit, or a similarity between those helped by a charity and a business's customers, might also indicate a good match (Austin, 2000; Drumwright et al., 2000; Sagawa & Segal, 2000).

Appropriate selection of a business supporter is not the only prerequisite for a good charity relationship with a business donor/supporter. It is essential that the charity and business supporter are clear and open about their expectations from the relationship. Take, for example, the charity partnership between Breast Cancer Care and Marks & Spencer (M&S). Breast Cancer Care's clients often had difficulty in finding appropriate bras after having a mastectomy. M&S partnered with Breast Cancer Care and created bras specifically for women who had been through breast cancer (Gilbert, 2019). Clearly communicating expectations about how the relationship will proceed, desired outcomes, and each partner's responsibilities will guide the formation of the most useful type of supportive relationship. Some businesses may desire their support in the form of discrete events. Other businesses might want more enduring relationships (Wymer & Samu, 2003). Forming the type of relationship that helps charity and business supporter meet their expectations provides a strong foundation for a successful relationship. The typical charity–business relationships will be discussed later in the chapter.

Cultivating business/corporate support is akin to traditional donor cultivation activities. Once potential business supporters have been identified, charity marketing activities should focus on informing prospective businesses about the charity and its work. Introducing business owners/managers to the charity's leadership, key staff, board members and key donors can also be helpful. Bringing prospective business supporters to the charity for a site visit can make more tangible the important work of the charity. The guiding principle in the early phase of donor cultivation is to make the prospective business partner more familiar with the charity and to emphasise the good work of the charity.

After the prospective business supporter becomes more familiar with the charity, the foot-in-the-door technique can be useful in attaining an initial modest level of support. The executive could be asked for advice on a managerial issue faced by the charity. The business owner could be asked to help sponsor an event. The goal in this phase of donor cultivation is to gain compliance for an initial modest level of support. Managers should not be made to feel like only their money is wanted by the charity. The charity should seek to build a relationship with the business in which the business's investment in the charity's mission is sought (Harrow et al., 2011; Leonhardt, 2011; Wymer et al., 2006).

Retaining a business's support once it has been acquired requires purposeful relationship marketing activities from the charity. This will require a long-term approach to relationship cultivation and management through regular communication and engagement (Polivy, 2013; Waters, 2009a, 2009b). One way for charities to strengthen their corporate relationships is through enhancing corporate employee involvement. Microsoft's CSR programme includes a volunteer grant programme. Microsoft donates $25 per hour for each hour one of its employees' volunteers for a charity. The donation goes to the charity in which the employee volunteered. ExxonMobil has an employee matching gift programme as part of its CSR activities. The corporation donates up to $3 for each $1 employee donation to a charity, up to a specified limit.

Implications of CSR on charity marketing to individual donors

Corporations are increasingly demonstrating their commitment to CSR through community or social philanthropy programmes (Sasse & Trahan, 2007). Not a great deal is known, however, about the effects of corporate donations to a charity on the donation behaviours of individuals to those recipient charities. This is an important issue. For many charities, individual donors account for most donations (compared to grants or corporate donations) (Chaudhry & Heiss, 2020, Giving USA, 2019). Hence, the effects on individual donations from corporate support could have important consequences for charities. This is especially true given the potential threat of corporations withdrawing their support in the future (Himmelstein, 1997).

Paljug (2018) supports donations from corporate philanthropy as an effective means of showing a corporation's commitment to a charity. Matunhu (2011) argues that corporate philanthropy has a negative effect on a charity's ability to attract individual donations. Reid (2016) argues, however, that corporate support for charities enhances those charities' ability to attract individual donations. Corporations often publicise their charitable giving to realise public relations benefits from their philanthropy. Corporate public relations communications to audiences to inform them of the corporations' good works also has the effect of promoting the recipient charities. Hence, those charities become better known to the public. Those charities' brand familiarity increases. Charities that are better known to the public are more likely than relatively lesser known charities to receive favourable responses in fundraising campaigns (Wymer & Akbar, 2019; Wymer et al., 2020).

Another argument for a positive influence of corporate donations on individual donations is that publicised corporate donations to a charity are essentially an endorsement of the charity (Finley et al., 2020). By its philanthropy, a company is vouching for the importance and worthiness of the charity. According to this argument, the corporate donation acts like an endorsement, which has a positive influence on individuals' attitudes toward the recipient charity as well as a positive influence on the recipient charity's trustworthiness (Randle et al., 2019).

Those who suspect corporate charitable donations have a negative effect on individual donations argue that when individuals learn of the large sums a corporation donates to their charity, their individual donations, by comparison, seem paltry. The perceived lower magnitude of their individual donations concomitantly lowers the perceived intrinsic rewards individual donors may experience. Hence, individual donors are less motivated to give to charities that receive corporate donations (Wymer et al., 2014).

Implications of CSR on charity reputation

There has been some research on the effects of corporate charitable donations on the donating corporation's reputation (Hogarth et al., 2018; Xia et al., 2019), but little is known about the influence of corporate donations on the charity's reputation. One longstanding concern about the potential negative influence of corporate donations on a charity's reputation occurs in the wake of a scandal involving the corporate donor (Himmelstein, 1997). For example, when Volkswagen was involved in a scandal in 2015, we know little about the effects on the reputations of charities it supported like the Martin Luther King Jr. National Memorial (Cohen, 2015).

A charity should carefully consider accepting corporate support from a corporation wishing to use its support to repair its reputation, which is a popular strategy for reputation repair (Peterson, 2018; Wu et al., 2020). A charity that associates or collaborates with a disreputation corporation risks sullying its own reputation (Bergkvist & Zhou, 2019). Since a charity's ability to attract donations is influenced by its reputation (Crettez et al., 2020; Wymer et al., 2020), it is unwise to make a decision which would result in the worsening of a charity's reputation.

Another way in which a charity's association with a corporate supporter can weaken the charity's reputation occurs with there is a mission misfit between the two organisations. A mission misfit might exist when the corporation's operations seem oppositional to the charity's purpose. An extreme example might exist when an oil company donates to an environmental organisation, or a tobacco company donates to a cancer-prevention organisation. Another factor to consider is the degree to which the corporation or the charity exemplifies its purpose. For example, an animal rights organisation with a single-minded objective (e.g. all animals are entitled to the same rights as humans) may be less tolerant of corporate support than a more moderate animal welfare organisation (e.g. donations help to pay for the care of unwanted pets awaiting adoption to reduce euthanasia).

Latest theory

This section will begin by discussing a business's motivations for engaging in CSR. Then the manifestations of CSR will be discussed.

Motivations for CSR

For a charity to effectively market to businesses interested in demonstrating their social responsibility through charitable support, the charity needs to understand company motivations. Motivations for CSR usually fall into a blend of self-serving or egoistic motives or society-serving or altruistic motives (Graafland & Mazereeuw-Van der Duijn Schouten, 2012). Generally, the preponderance of motivations leans toward egoistic motives, but motivations are often laced with a desire to benefit others (Kim, 2014; Skarmeas & Leonidou, 2013).

A major business motivation for CSR is public relations (Kim & Choi, 2012). The business may want to enhance its brand image, to improve its reputation or simply to improve consumer attitudes toward the company or its brands (Groza et al., 2011; Mazodier et al., 2020). In 2011, Rise Against Hunger, an international charity working toward ending world hunger, received support from Kraft Heinz. The corporation developed a CSR programme, Huddle to Fight Hunger, as their vehicle to support Rise Against Hunger. Kraft Heinz agreed to donate an amount needed to fund a meal each time someone liked the Huddle to Fight Facebook page.

Another motivation for CSR is meeting evolving expectations (Mohr et al., 2001). For example, a Cone Communications study reported that 90% of consumers expect companies to practice CSR (Post, 2017). Prior consumer research indicates that consumers view businesses that are involved in CSR favourably (Schooley, 2020).

Consumer perceptions of business motives

There has been an interest in the management research community in consumer perceptions of corporate motives for engaging in CSR. Generally, consumers understand that businesses are primarily self-serving. However, businesses may also be society-serving. Research shows that consumers tend to be less sceptical of business CSR motives when the business acknowledges its self-serving motives as well as its society-serving motives (Kim, 2014). When businesses with negative reputations emphasise only their society-serving motives, consumers' attitudes toward those businesses may worsen (Kim, 2014). When consumers perceive corporate motives to be solely self-serving, the negative outcomes can include reduced equity, acceptance of negative information about the corporation, and negative word-of-mouth comments (Skarmeas & Leonidou, 2013).

Consumers intuitively understand that business motives are self-serving but can also be public-serving. If consumers believe that firms are sincere in their desire to serve public interests, they can accept a company's self-serving CSR motives without negative responses (Kim & Lee, 2012). If consumers have a high level of trust in a company, however, consumers do not appear to attribute corporate motives to their CSR activities. When public trust in a company is high, its CSR efforts tend to have positive outcomes (Zasuwa, 2019).

In addition to the potential positive effects on consumers from CSR, Story and Neves (2015) found potential positive effects on a company's employees. When employees perceived the company's motives for its CSR initiatives to be society-serving in addition to the assumed self-serving motives, employees worked with more effect and their task performance increased. The influence of CSR on employees is moderated by employees' perceptions of society-serving motives for engaging in CSR by the company and its managers (Boddy et al., 2010).

This section has discussed most of what we know from the existing research on company motivations for CSR. The next section will discuss the various manifestations of CSR. Companies may demonstrate their social responsibility in different ways, depending upon their values, interests and objectives.

Manifestations of CSR

Businesses often emphasise their environmental stewardship as evidence they are socially responsible. Reducing negative environmental impact is a key pathway through which many companies manifest their social responsibility initiatives. Companies or industries may partner with government agencies or environmental organisations in order to show cooperation and transparency and as a means of ameliorating negative publicity (Orlitzky et al., 2011). For example, the Sierra Club endorsed Clorox's Green Works product line and the Wildlife Conservation Society certified forestry products from Congolaise Industrielle des Bois (Boyd, 2014).

Companies may improve their environmental reputations to improve public attitudes, to divert the ire of environmental activists, or to connect with pro-environmental consumers (Wymer & Polonsky, 2015). Clorox brands, for example, evoke consumer associations of a powerful disinfectant and bleach. Clorox brands were not originally concerned with environmental issues. In order to appeal to environmentally concerned consumers, however, Clorox developed the Green Works brand extension (Wymer, 2017). Developing Green Works branded products allowed Clorox to appeal to a different consumer segment while also demonstrating its social responsibility.

Although corporate environmental stewardship is an important facet of CSR, for the purpose of this chapter the emphasis will be on another manifestation of CSR: supporting the efforts of charities and other nonprofit organisations. Supporting charities and community organisations is a means of businesses to demonstrate their regard for issues and communities (Kumar, 2019; Uduji et al., 2019).

Charities should understand the typical ways in which businesses support the charitable sector to better inform their marketing efforts. Next, the typical ways companies support charities will be discussed. These include corporate philanthropy, corporate foundations, licensing agreements, sponsorships and cause-related marketing.

With respect to corporate philanthropy, some businesses make monetary or nonmonetary (i.e. in kind) contributions to nonprofit organisations on an episodic, informal basis (Smith, 1994). For example, Coca-Cola donates 1% of its prior year's operating income. The company supports women entrepreneurship efforts, education and youth development, and the conservation of clean drinking water. Other companies allocate funds to a corporate philanthropy budget, have a manager oversee the disbursement of funds, and earmark these funds as charitable contributions for tax deductions. Corporate philanthropy also includes allowing employees to volunteer for local nonprofit organisations while the volunteers receive compensation from their companies (this is contrasted with those companies that encourage employees to volunteer without compensation) (Wymer & Samu, 2003).

Another way in which firms demonstrate their CSR through supporting charities is by establishing corporate foundations. For example, Coca-Cola established a corporate foundation in 1984. It has donated more than $820 million since. The corporate foundation is a nonprofit entity created by a company to manage its philanthropy objectives. The foundation is responsible to trustees who are usually corporate officers (Himmelstein, 1997). In most cases, the foundation establishes a directive which specifies the types of causes the foundation wishes to fund. Potential grantees submit competitive grant proposals to the foundation, which awards grants based on the merits of the proposals and available funds (Wymer & Samu, 2003). For example, the Target corporation established the Target Foundation as a vehicle to manage the corporate philanthropy portion of its CSR strategy (Target, 2020).

Corporate philanthropy and corporate philanthropy channelled through a corporate foundation are two ways in which companies can demonstrate social responsibility by supporting charities (von Schnurbein et al., 2016). A company's primary motive for this type of support is usually public relations and reputation management (Gardberg et al., 2019). When corporations have a stronger interest in supporting sales and brand management through their charitable support, they may select licensing agreements. In this type of business–charity relationship, charitable organisations allow corporations to use their names and logos in return for a flat fee and/or a royalty. Businesses look for nonprofit organisations with strong, favourable images (e.g. names, brands) in the minds of important market segments (Wymer & Samu, 2003).

Affinity cards are an example of a licensing agreement. They generally take the form of a major credit card printed with the identity of a charity of interest to a target group (Huang & Fitzpatrick, 2018). For example, a university would enter into an agreement with a credit card company to produce credit cards printed with the university's image. The university would receive a nominal percentage of sales charged with the card (e.g. 1%). The university would provide the credit card issuer with a list of alumni or students and endorse the association. Then the card issuer would solicit customers using the provided contact lists (Wymer & Samu, 2003).

In licensing agreements, a business pays a charity for using its images in their advertisements, packaging and so forth. In addition to licensing agreements, another way in which companies can support the charitable sector while furthering their business interests is by participating in sponsorships. In sponsorships, the business pays the charity a sponsorship fee for using the business's brand in the charity's advertisements or other external communications. There are two components of sponsorships: (1) the sponsor pays the sponsee a fee for the right to associate itself with the activity sponsored, and (2) the marketing of the association by the sponsor. Both activities are necessary if the sponsorship is to be a meaningful investment (Cornwell & Maignan, 1998). A business participating in sponsorships is primarily interested in promoting its brand or company name, although sponsors also want to fund/promote the event (Cornwell, 2013).

There are several types of sponsorships. Abratt et al. (1987) present eight types of sponsorships. There are sports sponsorships (five types of sports sponsorships), book sponsorships, exhibitions, education sponsorships, expeditions, cultural activities, local events and documentary films. While businesses are motivated primarily by the opportunities to associate their name/brand in a favourable way before their target markets, charities are motivated to enter into sponsorship agreements to attain additional funding. The desired funding may be generated to support an event (e.g. Special Olympics), or the sponsored event may be a fundraiser for the charity (Wymer & Samu, 2003).

Another way in which a company can support a charity while furthering its business interests is through cause-related marketing. Cause-related marketing or CRM is defined by Varadarajan and Menon (1988, p. 60) as 'the process of formulating and implementing marketing activities characterised by an offer from the firm to contribute a specified amount to a designated cause when customers engage in revenue-providing exchanges that satisfy organizational and individual objectives'. A key characteristic of CRM is that a business's contribution to the charity is linked and proportional to sales. CRM became popular in 1983 when funds were being solicited to restore the Statue of Liberty. American Express created a campaign and contributed a few cents each time its customers used their American Express cards in a transaction (Wymer & Samu, 2003).

The major ways in which companies demonstrate their social responsibility through charitable support have been discussed. Next, the limitations of CSR will be presented.

Limitations of CSR

There are natural limits on the benefits CSR can provide. This is due to the inherent nature of CSR. CSR is a compromise strategy. That is, CSR is a company's demonstration of its regard for the interests of society in as much as CSR also furthers the company's own interests.

To further explain the preceding paragraph, keep in mind that the purpose of a publicly traded corporation is to increase the wealth of its owners. The vehicle for increasing shareholder wealth may be beneficial (a private hospital corporation) or harmful (a tobacco company). Executives may allow their decisions to be influenced to varying degrees by ethical considerations. In all cases, however, executives have fiduciary duties to shareholders. Executives are also rewarded or punished based on performance criteria that will invariably have some financial facets. While engaging in CSR activities, whether motivated by self-interest or other-interest, the degree to which corporations will alter their activities will be influenced by those activities' financial impact. The tax-deductible expenses associated with philanthropy for public relations purposes may be considered marketing expenses. Expenses related to operational changes to reduce a company's environmental harm might have greater implications for the company's profits.

While any action a company voluntarily takes to reduce its harm to the environment is good for society, companies' willingness to improve their environmental performance is extended as far as what is profitable. An executive who makes decisions that reduce corporate profits may find a board of directors who view those decisions as harming shareholder interests. What is in shareholders' interests may not coincide with societal interests. Indeed, it is in society's interest to reduce, reuse and recycle. It is in business's interest to promote consumerism and consumption (Wymer & Polonsky, 2015).

Corporations are primarily interested in advancing their own interests and secondarily interested in promoting society's interests. This explains why most of the literature on CSR is concerned with how companies can use CSR (including green marketing) to advance their own interests (Peloza & Shang, 2011; Rhou et al., 2016). Corporations do not appear to be altruistic but egoistic, looking out for their self-interests – always. This truism is tacitly acknowledged in the practical literature that promotes CSR, encouraging companies to engage in CSR because of what doing so can do for the companies (Epstein-Reeves, 2012).

Charities that are marketing to corporations to attract support such as corporate philanthropy are often advised to help businesses achieve their objectives from that support as a means of maintaining the relationship (Sagawa & Segal, 2000). It is naïve to wish to make fundamental changes to society through ethical consumption or CSR initiatives because of the natural limitations of business involvement in areas that do not support their self-interests (Rhodes & Bloom, 2018).

Effects of CSR on charities

One effect of CSR on charities is increased funding. According to the Giving USA Foundation (2020), in the US in 2019, corporate giving was approximately $21.09 billion and corporate foundation giving was approximately $75.69 billion. In the UK, for 2018, corporate giving was £0.5 billion and individual giving was £12.8 billion (Pharoah & Walker, 2019). Compared to individual giving, corporate giving is a relatively minor proportion of total donations funding charities. However, because corporate giving is increasing and becoming an important part of CSR initiatives, corporate giving represents an important addition to charities' revenue streams.

Another positive effect of CSR on charities is increased charity brand familiarity. For corporations to attain the benefits of CSR that motivate them to engage in CSR, they must communicate their CSR activities to target audiences. Company promotions about their CSR activities have the side effect of familiarising audiences with the charities the company is supporting. As more audiences become familiar with the charities, the charities' brand familiarity increases. This increases the effectiveness of the charities' own marketing efforts (Wymer & Casidy, 2019; Wymer et al., 2016).

As more companies become active in supporting charities through their CSR programmes, charities learn more about company motives for their charitable support. Charities learn more about how to manage relationships with corporate supporters. This experiential learning can help charities better attract and retain support from other businesses as well as major individual donors and foundations (Haddad, 2018).

A potential disadvantage to a recipient charity of CSR is a dependence upon that support. Because corporate support may be relatively new compared to a history of core support from individual donors, charities may assign the corporate support a high level of importance. Should that corporate support continue for a prolonged period, charities can grow to depend upon that corporate support for their operations and programmes. This dependency contains a risk, however. Due to a variety of possible reasons, corporations can discontinue their support, which may create a funding shortfall for the charity (Himmelstein, 1997).

Another potential disadvantage to the recipient charity of CSR is the potential negative effects on individual donors. Corporations promote their CSR activities to attain the benefits that motivated them to engage in CSR. As a result of corporate promotion of their charity support, individuals learn about the charity and they learn about the corporate support of the charity. Individuals who do not donate to the charity do not seem to be influenced negatively when learning about corporate giving to the charity (Wymer et al., 2014). In fact, as more individuals become familiar with the charity more of them may be willing to donate to the charity. (Future research is needed to understand this issue.) However, the influence of corporate donations to a charity on the charity's current donors is not well understood. (Future research is needed here as well.) It could be that corporate giving acts as an endorsement of the charity, reinforcing individual donors' commitment to the charity. However, it could be that corporate giving may be perceived by the charity's current donors as diminishing the importance of their individual donations. Clearly, this is an issue which needs more investigation. It is, however, a potential disadvantage of CSR for charities.

Charities that benefit from CSR

Corporate CSR programmes vary from the simple to the complex. They may have multiple motivations for their development as well as multiple expected outcomes. CSR activities should not be thought of as pure acts of altruism. Rather, they are, in part at least, acts serving company interests. Given this, it is likely that corporations will channel their charitable support to charities that are instrumental in helping them to attain their CSR goals and objectives (Porter & Kramer, 2002). If this reasoning is sound, then it also follows that companies will not find all charities suitable targets of their support. Some charities are more attractive recipients of corporate support than other charities (Falconer, 2017). From a charity marketing viewpoint, if a charity can make itself a more attractive partner for CSR programmes without compromising its values, strategy and purpose, then it may be advisable to do so. Next, the qualities that make a charity an attractive corporate CSR partner are discussed.

Since a primary corporate motive in supporting charities as a component of company social responsibility tactics is improving its reputation and image (Bartlett, 2011), it would be valuable to understand the properties of a charity that make it suitable to enhance corporate public relations efforts. First and foremost, a charity that is attractive to a company looking for a CSR partner needs to be well-known to many people. This type of charity is likely to be well-established and be known to a large proportion of the target geographic region's population.

Companies prefer to associate with charities that have excellent reputations. This implies that the charity is a strong brand. That is, an attractive charity is both well-known (high brand familiarity) and is perceived to be exceptional in its field (high brand remarkability). Such a charity would enjoy a favourable reputation and people would have strong positive attitudes toward that charity. Since much of the public relations benefits that accrue to a company through its charity support are from associating with the charity's favourable brand associations, a charity with a strong brand is desirable.

It is reasonable to believe, then, that charities that are attractive recipients of corporate support would have popular missions (Endacott, 2004). Charities with controversial missions or strategies that are perceived to be radical would be undesirable to companies.

It is becoming more common for corporations to also support charities that are favoured by influential political leaders (Lin et al., 2015). Charities that employee political leaders' family members or charities that are supported and endorsed by political leaders are attractive to companies that want to be supported by those political leaders.

Though the most well-known charities with the best reputations will be desired targets of companies looking for charities to support in their CSR programmes (Barrett, 2020), companies may be advised to avoid supporting a charity that is already associated with other corporations. Charities that are closely associated with a corporate supporter would not be the ideal partner.

It is apparent from this discussion that many charities may not be attractive CSR partners. These charities would include lesser-known charities, charities that serve a small area, newer charities and charities with less popular missions. Since many charities are not useful to corporations in attaining their public relations goals from CSR, the overall societal effects of CSR are worth considering. While corporate charitable support at first appears laudable, is society better off? Some of these issues will be discussed next.

Societal effects of CSR

Investors are a stakeholder group of society. Corporate executives through their charitable support are manifesting a belief that supporting charities is good for business. The argument may be one of meeting consumer expectations for corporate behaviour or improving brand image. There is also an argument that it is unfair to investors for executives to support charities. When corporations give money to charities, for example, they decide for investors how they want their charitable contributions made (Carson, 1993). Setting aside the philosophical debate about the meaning of corporate social responsibility (Orlitzky, 2015), the issues pertaining to the general public will be discussed next.

Does corporate support of charities benefit society? Without analysing the question, it would appear so. Corporations provide support to charities which use that support to further their missions. Charities benefit society so supporting charities benefits society. Whatever a company's motives may be for supporting charities, the outcomes are prosocial. There is a logic to this argument. After all, how could supporting charities be harmful to society? One way in which there is a potential for corporate charity support to be harmful is when corporations pressure the charities they support to lobby on their behalf for the benefit of the corporations (Rosenman, 2015).

What if corporate donations to charities were not cost-free to citizens? Since charitable donations are tax deductible, are citizens ultimately paying for corporate donations by paying taxes that corporations are avoiding and by paying higher prices? If government needs a specific level of revenue and the corporate portion of that amount declines, the reduced corporate contribution must be offset by reduced government services, increase taxes on individuals, or increase public debt, in all cases representing a cost to society (Sasse & Trahan, 2007). If society effectively pays for corporate charitable support, one could argue that corporate charitable support represents an undemocratic channelling of society support to charities.

If corporations are diverting some resources in society to charities, which charities are benefitting? Because companies are, at least in part, motivated to support charities for public relations purposes, they select charities which will help them attain their CSR objectives. Many non-selected charities that benefit society will be overlooked. Hence, citizens' preferences for supporting charities are not necessarily reflected in corporate preferences (Polonsky & Grau, 2008).

The influence of corporate philanthropy and other forms of corporate charitable support on individual charitable support is not well understood. Little research has been done on this topic, since most research has been concerned with the benefits to corporations. Corporations' promotions of their charitable support may increase public familiarity of the recipient charities. However, since corporations tend to support well-known charities, this effect may not be great. When corporations publicise their charitable support, individuals' perceptions of the comparative worth of their more meagre contributions may decline. There is evidence that individuals may be less willing to donate to a charity that receives corporate support because they feel their contributions will matter less (Bennett et al., 2013).

It is reasonable to believe that corporate charitable support may influence individual charitable support. Insufficient research has been conducted to fully understand this influence. However, it appears that corporate involvement with charities alters individuals' charity support in some ways. This represents a distortion in a society's allocation of resources across the charitable sector. Whether this distortion is prosocial or anti-democratic is not understood. Next, some examples of corporate charitable support will be discussed.

Examples

In 2011, Rise Against Hunger, an international charity working toward ending world hunger received support from Kraft Heinz. The corporation developed a CSR program, Huddle to Fight Hunger, as their vehicle to support Rise Against Hunger. Kraft Heinz agreed to donate an amount needed to fund a meal each time someone liked the Huddle to Fight Facebook page.

Microsoft's CSR program includes a volunteer grant program. Microsoft donates $25 per hour for each hour one of its employees' volunteers for a charity. The donation goes to the charity in which the employee volunteered.

ExxonMobil has an employee matching gift program as part of its CSR activities. The corporation donates up to $3 for each $1 employee donation to a charity, up to a specified limit.

Coca-Cola established a corporate foundation in 1984. It has donated more than $820 million since. Furthermore, Coca-Cola donates 1% of its prior year's operating income. The company supports women entrepreneurship efforts, education and youth development, and the conservation of clean drinking water.

Implications for practice and theory

Implications for practice

Charities use marketing to attract and retain resources such as donations or volunteers in order to further their missions. Support from the business sector may represent a new source of funding or volunteers that can enable a charity to thrive when other charities are facing declining support from individuals and government agencies. Charity marketers should always be mindful of collaborating with companies in a manner that facilitates individual fundraising efforts.

In order to attract corporate support, charity marketers should realise that a company's primary motive is to attain public relations benefits from that support. Charities that are well-known and have an excellent reputation are more attractive recipients of corporate philanthropy and other support. Hence, charities should engage in a long-term marketing strategy that increases the degree to which it is well known and enjoys an excellent reputation. In effect, such a long-term marketing strategy will not only help the charity attract corporate support, it will also help it attract individual support and make the charity's short-term marketing tactics more effective (Wymer, 2017).

Charities should also partner with companies that will enhance the charity's familiarity and reputation. A reputable company supporter will not only promote the charity along with its self-promotion of its CSR programme, its support will serve as an endorsement of the charity's integrity and good work. Charities should avoid associating with companies its individual supporter base would find objectionable. Companies with prior, successful experiences supporting charities and companies with public relations goals rather than sales goals from the charity support will probably make better partners.

Maintaining a successful relationship with a corporate supporter requires understanding the company's motives and establishing realistic expectations regarding the relationship experience and likely outcomes. Relationship management will require open communication and working towards helping the company experience benefits from its charity support (Sagawa & Segal, 2000).

Smaller, community charities will be less attractive to large corporations with a large market reach. Community charities will have to attract support from the local business community. Local business support is best attracted and retained using individual donor cultivation and relationship management tactics charities use for the major individual donors (Leonhardt, 2011; Polivy, 2013).

Implications for theory

A good deal of the academic research has emphasised the benefits to corporations from engaging in CSR activities (Mazodier et al., 2020). There appear to be two primary tacit assumptions that motivate this research. First, consumers expect companies to practice CSR. Second, CSR is good for business. These implicit assumptions need to be explored. Do consumers really expect businesses to engage in CSR? How widespread is this expectation? What is the nature of these consumer expectations? What are the implications of exceeding the expectations or not meeting the expectations?

Future research is needed to better understand the complexity of individual donor responses to corporate donations. The managerial implications for the charity are straightforward. Corporations will continue to promote their charitable donations for public relations benefits. Charities should try to ensure that the way in which their charities are portrayed in corporate public relations campaigns is favourable. Charity communications to individuals should emphasise the importance to the charity of individual donations.

The idea that CSR is good for business needs to be further explored. What type of CSR initiatives provide the greatest benefits to companies? There are many ways in which companies can demonstrate their social responsibility. How can a company know how to optimise its CSR tactical mix? What are the limitations of benefits companies can attain?

While most of the research interest has emphasised business interests, comparatively little has focused on the interests of charities or society. There is an assumption that any corporate support of charities is good for the recipient charities and good for society. Are tax policies, in fact, creating a dynamic in which individual citizens subsidise corporate charity support partially motivated by corporate public relations? Does society really benefit by having corporate involvement in resource disbursement to the charity sector? What are the effects on charities that companies choose not to support?

More needs to be known about the effects of corporate charity support on recipient and non-recipient charities. We need to better understand the conditions in which corporate support benefits charities and the conditions in which the support produces negative outcomes for charities. What effects do corporate support of charities have on individuals' donation decisions? How can charities maximise the positive outcomes for themselves from corporate support?

More needs to be known about how charities can select and attract the optimal corporate support and promote the corporate support in a way that has positive effects on individual donors, non-donors and volunteers. More needs to be known about how charities can arrive at an optimal mix of support from companies. More needs to be known about managing relationships with corporate supporters.

CSR efforts may also include employee volunteering. More needs to be known about the outcomes for charities of corporate-supported volunteering.

Most attention in the CSR/charity marketing area occurs in the context of large corporations supporting large charities. Comparatively little research has examined charity marketing issues for community charities with support from community businesses. Much more needs to be known about the dynamics of community business support of community charities.

Chapter discussion questions

1. Most corporate involvement with charities has occurred within the context of large companies supporting national or international charities. What are the reasons for this history? Do you believe that the trend of advertising from mass media to narrow targeting through social media will provide opportunities for smaller charities to better attract company support?
2. Some corporate charity support is channelled through employee volunteering and employee giving programmes. Since the Coronavirus pandemic, companies have encouraged many employees to work virtually from home. After the pandemic, companies may want to maintain working from home to maintain cost savings. How will the work-from-home trend affect employee volunteering and employee giving programmes?
3. How do you think CSR and corporate philanthropy will change in the future? What are trends that might influence these changes?

References

Abratt, R., Clayton, B.C. & Pitt, L.F. (1987). Corporate objectives in sports sponsorship. *International Journal of Advertising*, 6(4), 299–312.

Austin, J.E. (2000). Strategic collaboration between nonprofits and businesses. *Nonprofit and Voluntary Sector Quarterly*, 29(1), 69–97.

Barrett, W. (2020). America's top charities. *Forbes*. Available at www.forbes.com/lists/top-charities/#5b4167845f50 (accessed 9 February 2021).

Bartlett, J.L. (2011). Public relations and corporate social responsibility. In Ø. Ihlen, J.L. Bartlett & S. May (eds), *The Handbook of Communication and Corporate Social Responsibility*. Wiley.

Bennett, C.M., Kim, H. & Loken, B. (2013). Corporate sponsorships may hurt nonprofits: Understanding their effects on charitable giving. *Journal of Consumer Psychology*, 23(3), 288–300.

Bergkvist, L. & Zhou, K.Q. (2019). Cause-related marketing persuasion research: An integrated framework and directions for further research. *International Journal of Advertising*, 38 (1), 5–25.

Boddy, C.R., Ladyshewsky, R.K. & Galvin, P. (2010). The influence of corporate psychopaths on corporate social responsibility and organizational commitment to employees. *Journal of Business Ethics*, 97(1), 1–19.

Boyd, J. (2014). Business motivations for conservation. *Resources*. Available at www.resour cesmag.org/archives/business-motivations-for-conservation/ (accessed 9 February 2021).

Carson, T. (1993). Friedman's theory of corporate social responsibility. *Business and Professional Ethics Journal*, 12(1), 3–32.

Chaudhry, S. & Heiss, A. (2020). Dynamics of international giving: How heuristics shape individual donor preferences. *Nonprofit and Voluntary Sector Quarterly*. doi:10.1177/0899764020971045.

Cohen, R. (2015). The philanthropy of a corporate cheat: Volkswagen. *Nonprofit Quarterly*. Available at https://nonprofitquarterly.org/corporate-philanthropy-volkswagen-philanthrop y-meaning/ (accessed 9 February 2021).

Cornwell, T.B. (2013). State of the art and science in sponsorship-linked marketing. In S. Söderman & H. Dolles (eds), *Handbook of research on sport and business*. Edward Elgar Publishing.

Cornwell, T.B. & Maignan, I. (1998). An international review of sponsorship research. *Journal of Advertising*, 27(1), 1–21.

Crettez, B., Hayek, N. & Zaccour, G. (2020). Optimal dynamic management of a charity under imperfect altruism. *Omega*. doi:10.1016/j.omega.2020.102227.

Dahlsrud, A. (2008). How corporate social responsibility is defined: An analysis of 37 definitions. *Corporate social responsibility and environmental management*, 15(1), 1–13.

Drumwright, M.E., Cunningham, P.H. & Berger, I.E. (2000). *Social alliances: Company/nonprofit collaboration*. Marketing Science Institute.

Endacott, R.W.J. (2004). Consumers and CRM: A national and global perspective. *Journal of Consumer Marketing*, 21(3), 183–189.

Epstein-Reeves, J. (2012). Six reasons companies should embrace CSR. *Forbes*. Available at www.forbes.com/sites/csr/2012/02/21/six-reasons-companies-should-embrace-csr/?sh= 10ecc0de3495 (accessed 9 February 2021).

Falconer, J. (2017). Top tips for choosing a CSR partner. *HR*. Available at www.hrmaga zine.co.uk/article-details/top-tips-for-choosing-a-csr-partner (accessed 9 February 2021).

Faulkner, M. & Romaniuk, J. (2019). Supporters' perceptions of benefits delivered by different charity activities. *Journal of Nonprofit & Public Sector Marketing*, 31(1), 20–41.

Finley, A.R., Hall, C., Harris, E. & Lusch, S.J. (2020). The effect of large corporate donors on non-profit performance. *Journal of Business Ethics*, 172(1–2), 1–23.

Gardberg, N.A., Zyglidopoulos, S.C., Symeou, P.C. & Schepers, D.H. (2019). The impact of corporate philanthropy on reputation for corporate social performance. *Business & Society*, 58(6), 1177–1208.

Gilbert, P. (2019). How to form great business and charity partnerships. *Goodbox*. Available at www.goodbox.com/2019/07/how-to-form-business-and-charity-partnerships/ (accessed 9 February 2021).

Giving USA. (2019). Giving USA 2019: Americans gave $427.71 billion to charity in 2018 amid complex year for charitable giving. Available at https://givingusa.org/giving-usa -2019-americans-gave-427-71-billion-to-charity-in-2018-amid-complex-year-for-charita ble-giving/ (accessed 16 December 2020).

Giving USA Foundation. (2020). *Giving USA 2020: The Annual Report on Philanthropy for the Year 2019.* Giving USA Foundation.

Graafland, J. & Mazereeuw-Van der Duijn Schouten, C. (2012). Motives for corporate social responsibility. *De Economist,* 160(4), 377–396.

Groza, M.D., Pronschinske, M.R. & Walker, M. (2011). Perceived organizational motives and consumer responses to proactive and reactive CSR. *Journal of Business Ethics,* 102(4), 639–652.

Haddad, F. (2018). Donor cultivation is key to success. *NonprofitPro.* Available at www.nonp rofitpro.com/post/donor-cultivation-is-key-to-success/ (accessed 16 December 2020).

Harrow, J., Jung, T., Pavey, H. & Scott, J. (2011). Donor cultivation in theory and practice: A Centre for Charitable Giving and Philanthropy/Arts & Business Scotland discussion paper. Available at www.cgap.org.uk/uploads/Donor%20cultivation%20in%20theory% 20and%20practice%20Toolkit.pdf (accessed 16 December 2020).

Himmelstein, J.L. (1997). *Looking Good and Doing Good: Corporate Philanthropy and Corporate Power.* Indiana University Press.

Hogarth, K., Hutchinson, M. & Scaife, W. (2018). Corporate philanthropy, reputation risk management and shareholder value: A study of Australian corporate giving. *Journal of Business Ethics,* 151(2), 375–390.

Huang, L. & Fitzpatrick, J. (2018). Lending a hand: Perceptions of green credit cards. *International Journal of Bank Marketing,* 36(7), 1329–1346.

Kim, S. & Lee, Y.J. (2012). The complex attribution process of CSR motives. *Public Relations Review,* 38(1), 168–170.

Kim, Y. (2014). Strategic communication of corporate social responsibility (CSR): Effects of stated motives and corporate reputation on stakeholder responses. *Public Relations Review,* 40(5), 838–840.

Kim, Y. & Choi, Y. (2012). College students' perception of Philip Morris's tobacco-related smoking prevention and tobacco-unrelated social responsibility programs: A comparative study in Korea and the United Stated. *Journal of Public Relations Research,* 24, 184–199.

Kumar, N. (2019). Corporate social responsibility: An analysis of impact and challenges in India. *International Journal of Social Sciences Management and Entrepreneurship (IJSSME),* 3(2), 53–63.

Leonhardt, T.W. (2011). Key donor cultivation: Building for the future. *Journal of Library Administration,* 51(2), 198–208.

Lin, K.J., Tan, J., Zhao, L. & Karim, K. (2015). In the name of charity: Political connections and strategic corporate social responsibility in a transition economy. *Journal of Corporate Finance,* 32, 327–346.

Matunhu, J. (2011). A critique of modernization and dependency theories in Africa: Critical assessment. *African Journal of History and Culture,* 3(5), 65–72.

Mazodier, M., Carrillat, F.A., Sherman, C. & Plewa, C. (2020). Can donations be too little or too much? *European Journal of Marketing,* 55(1), 271–296.

Mohr, L.A., Webb, D.J. & Harris, K.E. (2001). Do consumers expect companies to be socially responsible? The impact of corporate social responsibility on buying behavior. *Journal of Consumer Affairs,* 35(1), 45–72.

Orlitzky, M. (2015). The politics of corporate social responsibility or: Why Milton Friedman has been right all along. *Annals in Social Responsibility,* 1(1), 5–29.

Orlitzky, M., Siegel, D.S. & Waldman, D.A. (2011). Strategic corporate social responsibility and environmental sustainability. *Business & Society,* 50(1), 6–27.

Paljug, K. (2018). How businesses can partner with a charity. *Business News Daily*. Available at www.businessnewsdaily.com/1604-choosing-business-charity.html (accessed 9 February 2021).

Peloza, J. & Shang, J. (2011). How can corporate social responsibility activities create value for stakeholders? A systematic review. *Journal of the Academy of Marketing Science*, 39(1), 117–135.

Peterson, D.K. (2018). Enhancing corporate reputation through corporate philanthropy. *Journal of Strategy and Management*, 11(1), 18–32.

Pharoah, C. & Walker, C. (2019). Foundation giving trends 2019. Association of Charitable Foundations. Available at www.acf.org.uk/downloads/publications/ACF_Foundation_Giving_Trends_2019.pdf (accessed 11 February 2021).

Polivy, D.K. (2013). *Donor Cultivation and the Donor Lifecycle Map + Website: A New Framework for Fundraising*. John Wiley & Sons.

Polonsky, M.J. & Grau, S.L. (2008). Evaluating the social value of charitable organizations: A conceptual foundation. *Journal of Macromarketing*, 28(2), 130–140.

Porter, M.E. & Kramer, M.R. (2002). The competitive advantage of corporate philanthropy. *Harvard Business Review*, 80(12), 56–68.

Post, J. (2017). What is corporate social responsibility? *Business Daily*. Available at www.businessnewsdaily.com/4679-corporate-social-responsibility.html (accessed 9 February 2021).

Randle, M., Kemperman, A. & Dolnicar, S. (2019). Making cause-related corporate social responsibility (CSR) count in holiday accommodation choice. *Tourism Management*, 75, 66–77.

Reid, R. (2016). Does philanthropy do good or harm? Available at www.linkedin.com/pulse/does-philanthropy-do-good-harm-bob-reid (accessed 9 February 2021).

Rhodes, C. & Bloom, P. (2018). The trouble with charitable billionaires. *The Guardian*, 24 May. Available at www.theguardian.com/news/2018/may/24/the-trouble-with-charitable-billionaires-philanthrocapitalism (accessed 19 December 2020).

Rhou, Y., Singal, M. & Koh, Y. (2016). CSR and financial performance: The role of CSR awareness in the restaurant industry. *International Journal of Hospitality Management*, 57, 30–39.

Rosenman, M. (2015). Calling the piper's tune: Corporate funders and charity endorsements. *Huffpost*. Available at www.huffpost.com/entry/calling-the-pipers-tune-c_b_7161616 (accessed 9 February 2021).

Sagawa, S. & Segal, E. (2000). Common interest, common good: Creating value through business and social sector partnerships. *California Management Review*, 42(2), 105–122.

Sasse, C.M. & Trahan, R.T. (2007). Rethinking the new corporate philanthropy. *Business Horizons*, 50(1), 29–38.

Schooley, S. (2020). What is corporate social responsibility? *Business News Daily*. Available at www.businessnewsdaily.com/4679-corporate-social-responsibility.html (accessed 9 February 2021).

Skarmeas, D. & Leonidou, C.N. (2013). When consumers doubt, watch out! The role of CSR skepticism. *Journal of Business Research*, 66(10), 1831–1838.

Smith, C. (1994). The new corporate philanthropy. *Harvard Business Review*, 72(3), 105–114.

Story, J. & Neves, P. (2015). When corporate social responsibility (CSR) increases performance: Exploring the role of intrinsic and extrinsic CSR attribution. *Business Ethics: A European Review*, 24(2), 111–124.

Target. (2020). Corporate responsibility. Available at https://corporate.target.com/corporate-responsibility/philanthropy (accessed 9 February 2021).

Uduji, J.I., Okolo-Obasi, E.N. & Asongu, S.A. (2019). Multinational oil companies in Nigeria and corporate social responsibility in the HIV/AIDS response in host communities. *Local Environment*, 24(5), 393–416.

Varadarajan, P.R. & Menon, A. (1988). Cause-related marketing: A coalignment of marketing strategy and corporate philanthropy. *Journal of Marketing*, 52(3), 58–74.

von Schnurbein, G., Seele, P. & Lock, I. (2016). Exclusive corporate philanthropy: rethinking the nexus of CSR and corporate philanthropy. *Social Responsibility Journal*, 12 (2), 280–294.

Waters, R.D. (2009a). The importance of understanding donor preference and relationship cultivation strategies. *Journal of Nonprofit & Public Sector Marketing*, 21(4), 327–346.

Waters, R.D. (2009b). Comparing the two sides of the nonprofit organization–donor relationship: Applying coorientation methodology to relationship management. *Public Relations Review*, 35(2), 144–146.

Weeden, C. (1998). *Corporate Social Investing: The Breakthrough Strategy for Giving & Getting Corporate Contributions*. Berrett-Koehler Publishers.

Wu, B., Jin, C., Monfort, A. & Hua, D. (2020). Generous charity to preserve green image? Exploring linkage between strategic donations and environmental misconduct. *Journal of Business Research*. doi:10.1016/j.jbusres.2020.10.040.

Wymer, W. (2017). *Brand Management: Creating and Maintaining a Strong Brand*. CreateSpace.

Wymer, W. & Akbar, M.M. (2019). Brand authenticity's influence on charity support intentions. *Journal of Nonprofit & Public Sector Marketing*, 31(5), 507–527.

Wymer, W. & Casidy, R. (2019). Exploring brand strength's nomological net and its dimensional dynamics. *Journal of Retailing and Consumer Services*, 49, 11–22.

Wymer, W. & Polonsky, M. (2015). The limitations and potentialities of green marketing. *Journal of Nonprofit & Public Sector Marketing*, 27(3), 239–262.

Wymer, W. & Samu, S. (2003). Dimensions of business and nonprofit collaborative relationships. *Journal of Nonprofit & Public Sector Marketing*, 11(1), 3–22.

Wymer, W., Knowles, P. & Gomes, R. (2006). *Nonprofit Marketing: Marketing Management for Charitable and Nongovernmental Organizations*. Sage.

Wymer, W., McDonald, K. & Scaife, W. (2014). Effects of corporate support of a charity on public perceptions of the charity. *Voluntas: International Journal of Voluntary and Nonprofit Organizations*, 25(6), 1388–1416.

Wymer, W., Boenigk, S. & Möhlmann, M. (2015). The conceptualization of nonprofit marketing orientation: A critical reflection and contributions toward closing the practice–theory gap. *Journal of Nonprofit & Public Sector Marketing*, 27(2), 117–134.

Wymer, W., Gross, H. & Helmig, B. (2016). Nonprofit brand strength: What is it? How is it measured? What are its outcomes? *Voluntas: International Journal of Voluntary and Nonprofit Organizations*, 27(3), 1448–1471.

Wymer, W., Becker, A. & Boenigk, S. (2020). An exploratory investigation of the antecedents of charity trust and its influence on volunteering and donating. *International Journal of Nonprofit and Voluntary Sector Marketing*. doi:10.1002/NVSM.1690.

Xia, X., Teng, F. & Gu, X. (2019). Reputation repair and corporate donations: An investigation of responses to regulatory penalties. *China Journal of Accounting Research*, 12(3), 293–313.

Zasuwa, G. (2019). Do consumers really care about organisational motives behind CSR? The moderating role of trust in the company. *Social Responsibility Journal*, 15(8), 977–991.

2

NONPROFIT BRAND AND MANAGING NONPROFIT REBRANDING STRATEGY

Zoe Lee and Iain Davies

Overview

In contemporary society, brands play an important role in bringing significant value to organisations to remain relevant in consumers' minds (Keller, 1993). In the nonprofit sector, strong brands are equally important in fundraising and achieving organisational missions (Hankinson, 2001; Lee, 2013; Sargeant et al., 2008; Stride & Lee, 2007; Wymer et al., 2016). In the UK, many people recognise the great work by household charity brands such as Cancer Research UK, Comic Relief, Macmillan Cancer Support, British Red Cross and others. Many of these nonprofits pay attention to investing in and nurturing their brands. To stay competitive, nonprofits (just like business corporations) need to rebrand to create a distinctive identity and image, and to meet the changing needs of their beneficiaries and different stakeholders. In some cases, the mission needs to be refreshed, adapted and reimagined (Miller et al., 2014). For example, Prostate Cancer UK changed its name in 2012 to avoid a perceived association with 'well-intentioned amateurs' and estimates its income to have increased by 30% in a year as a direct consequence (Allchin, 2012). However, the rebranding exercise is risky as it often fails.

This chapter provides a strategic view on the role of branding beyond fundraising, to illuminate why and how nonprofits engage in rebranding strategies, and explore what the potential pitfalls are and how they may counter them. Moving away from an external perspective (product level) of managing brands, this chapter provides a more nuanced understanding of the tensions in managing the process internally (organisational level), and highlights key elements of what makes a good nonprofit rebrand. It calls for nonprofit organisations to balance both the internal and external perspectives when considering a rebrand strategy. It promotes nonprofit managers prioritising the internal perspective when following a rebranding

DOI: 10.4324/9781003134169-5

strategy. In particular, considering the implications for employees and volunteers, who have to live out the new 'values' associated with the new branding.

Nonprofit brand relating to supporters

A brand is a name, term, sign, drawing or any combination of these that serves to identify a firm's goods or services and differentiate them from those of competitors (Aaker, 2009). Given the ever-increasing number of nonprofit organisations and the subsequent competition for donations, a strong nonprofit brand is key to differentiation and survival (Boenigk & Becker, 2016; Wymer et al., 2016). The sector is huge with more than 160,000 charities in the UK alone (NCVO, 2020). In 2017/2018, the public continued to be the largest income stream for nonprofits, representing for 83% of all income growth and a total of £25.4 billion.

Historically, nonprofit researchers viewed brands as logos and images, designating branding as a tool for differentiation to manage the external perception of the organisation. Following this view, several studies have been conducted identifying attractive brand images and personalities that would appeal to donors' needs and expectations (Bennett & Gabriel, 2003; Michel & Rieunier, 2012; Sargeant et al., 2008; Venable et al., 2005). For example, Venable et al. (2005) show that nonprofit brand personality explains 30–40% of intention to give, whereas Sargeant et al. (2008) show that personality traits such as being exciting, heroic, innovative and inspiring can evoke an emotional response in donors, encouraging them to give more money. The Royal National Lifeboat Institution (RNLI), which has been patrolling the waters off the coast of Great Britain since 1824, found that advertisements that use bearded men in lifeboats remains the organisation's most effective recruitment device, because the image best reflects the rugged personality of the organisation, and creates a focus for donations. Similarly, animal nonprofits rely on 'warm' and 'caring' personality traits to align themselves with potential donors (Neumayr & Handy, 2019; Sargeant et al., 2008).

Despite the vast resources spent on brand communications, however, many managers remain disappointed with the return on investment in terms of increasing reach and impact. This external view of branding causes many nonprofits to view their brands as something that they have to manage and control to drive income generation, rather than as an internal tool to drive better alignment with mission, vision and values. As different stakeholders hold different expectations and demands, the ability of the nonprofit brand to flex and meet those needs can be a challenge.

Paradigm shift and nonprofit rebranding at an organisational level

Contemporary research shows that nonprofit organisations increasingly use rebranding strategies to generate value, as well as enhance brand relevance and internal efficiency (Melewar et al., 2012; Miller et al., 2014; Vallaster & Lindgreen, 2011). There is growing interest in building a strong organisational brand to achieve greater social impact and tighter organisational cohesion, in addition to fundraising benefits (Ewing & Napoli, 2005; Kylander & Stone, 2012; Sepulcri et al., 2020). However, nonprofit rebranding exercises are risky, as they often require considerable investment and can be viewed as wasteful in relation to the nonprofit's mission (Stuart, 2018). For example, one drug and alcohol charity changed its name from 'Addaction' to 'We Are With You' in a £140,000 rebrand, causing a blacklash as staff went on strike over pay (Cipriani, 2020). Besides reputational risk, internal stakeholders such as staff and supporters need to buy into the new brand strategy for it to succeed. The rebrand of the British Royal Legion caused great anger amongst its supporters for costing £100,000 that could otherwise have been spent on the beneficiaries (Boycott-Owen, 2021).

Research on nonprofit rebranding draws on the domain of corporate branding literature where brands are regarded as strategic assets, linked to reputation and identity (Balmer, 2001; Hatch & Schultz, 2003). Corporate branding generally refers to the overall articulation and expression of the corporate brand, and so a corporate rebranding refers to organisational change from one corporate brand formulation to another (Gotsi & Andriopoulos, 2007; Lee, 2013; Merrilees & Miller, 2008). Such a broad definition includes cosmetic minor changes, such as to a logo, colours and symbols, through to major radical changes such as a name change or shifts in values or mission (Chad, 2015; Muzellec & Lambkin, 2006).

There are several schools of thought regarding how rebranding works, in particular, the external perspective based on visual identity management, and the internal perspective based on internal branding (see Table 2.1). According to the external perspective, the focus of rebranding is to develop a strong and distinctive visual identity, to differentiate one organisation from another, and to define how the new identity and image aligns with current service/work. Many organisations engage in some level of alteration to logo, colour palette and symbols on a regular basis to better align their image with external stakeholder perceptions (Kaikati & Kaikati, 2003; Kalaignanam & Bahadir, 2013; Muzellec & Lambkin, 2006). According this approach, corporate brand is an image that managers aim to control to influence audience perceptions. For instance, since its rebrand in 2006; which included a new logo and a new palette, Macmillan Cancer Support's brand awareness among its core audience – people diagnosed with cancer and their families/friends – increased from 41% and 38% to 65% and 66% respectively from 2006–2011 (CharityComms, 2012). Fundraising income also increased from £97 million in 2006 to £141 million in 2011 on the back of the rebrand.

The internal perspective of corporate rebranding, on the other hand, postulates that a corporate brand is socially constructed (Melewar et al., 2012). According to this approach, successful corporate rebranding is not only formed by senior management's vision, but also through the influence of organisational culture and image amongst stakeholders. In other words, internal and external stakeholders, together with the organisation, co-create meanings attributed to the new corporate brand (Hatch & Schultz, 2003). These meanings are driven by internalised brand values, combined with individuals' motivations and beliefs. Following this approach, several studies have focused on the notion of employee 'buy-in' to the revised corporate brands, managing multiple stakeholders' expectations (Hankinson, 2002; Lomax & Mador, 2006; Miller & Merrilees, 2013) and the significance of cultural change in the process (Gotsi & Andriopoulos, 2007). The cultural change is particularly complex for nonprofit employees, who have invested heavily in the brand and are often committed to the vision and mission. Any changes to the purpose, mission and vision would require significant effort in engaging with these stakeholders to achieve a strong alignment and maintain a powerful brand image.

Why rebrand?

Before we can determine how best to manage a nonprofit rebrand, we must first step back and understand why it is crucial for nonprofits' growth. Nonprofit rebranding typically follows an organisational-wide change. Hence, the new brand strategy needs to align with corporate strategy and organisational mission. For example, the aim of the aforementioned rebrand at Macmillan was to reposition the brand away from being seen as only about palliative (end of live) care, to becoming a 'life force' that supports everyone affected by cancer (living with or caring for). The rebrand aligns with a strong ambition to work with broader audiences and partners in achieving impact.

However, before any rebrand can be implemented, branding teams need to get full support from the senior management teams and trustees. So, what are the factors that prompt nonprofit managers to consider rebranding? Here are five factors that could trigger a rebrand:

- *Low brand awareness.* While many nonprofit organisations are doing good work, it is somewhat surprising that the level of brand awareness is still relatively low, particularly with their target audience. This is particularly true for smaller nonprofit organisations that may not have the budget to invest in brand communications.

TABLE 2.1 External and internal perspectives of rebranding

	External perspective (product level)	Internal perspective (organisational level)
Rebranding belief	Managers control and manage brand's expression, brands as static	A social construction of meaning that has a relational nature; and is constantly constructed by individuals; brands as dynamics
Frame of analysis	Brand perceived as an exchange, driven by fundraising income	Internalised values, meanings and contradictions that justify and legitimise the individual's commitment; discourse analysis; greater social impact
Practices	Creating labels to ensure consistency across multiple touchpoints	Use cultural resources such as brand values training to embed the new values in everyday practices

- *Lack of reach*: Nonprofit brands can find themselves unable to engage with a younger audience as many Millennials and Gen Z do not associate themselves with the nonprofit brand identity.
- *Discrepancy between brand image and what the organisation does*: Nonprofit organisations evolve over time and some services are added and others dropped. Hence, the old brand may not represent what they stand for today. Many people think Barnardo's still run orphanages, even though the last one closed 50 years ago, and that the Scouts is all about the uniforms and badges. Such discrepancies can act as a barrier for nonprofit organisations to achieve their mission.
- *Reduced income*: Many nonprofit organisations are looking to diversify their income. Those who rely on government and statutory funding are interested in developing a brand that would be attractive and distinctive in the fundraising market. For example, Prostate Cancer UK's bold rebrand attracted attention from corporate partners with a shared vision. The charity launched a successful campaign with a football club called 'Men United v Prostate Cancer' to raise awareness as well as income.
- *Merger and acquisition*: When two similar charities merge, there is a need to decide whether the new nonprofit will adopt a new brand name and visual identity to signal the new direction of the organisation, or a combination of attributes from both organisations. For example, Help the Aged and Age Concern merged to form Age UK.

Managing nonprofit rebranding

Managing a nonprofit rebranding can be a complex process. Unlike corporations, nonprofits need to balance both the social mission and income generation, both of which may require different pathways and strategies. In analysing ten cases of British charity rebranding, Lee (2013) found that there are three common themes in terms of tensions in managing nonprofit rebrands:

Tension 1: Alignment between old image (heritage identity) and new identity. During the rebranding process, there are many instances where managers recognise the struggles between the old image and new identity. Managers also face the dilemma of embracing the 'new' identity and/or defending the 'old' identity. For nonprofit organisations with strong heritage, any changes to the nonprofit's brand can cause a sense of identity loss and defensiveness. Nonprofit employees who often develop strong emotional bonds to their organisation may react in negatively. For example, Macmillan Cancer Relief has an ambition to help everyone affected by cancer. However, their brand name was not aligned with the ambition and acted as a barrier to reach wider audiences. The word 'relief' has a strong association with cancer pain as well as the iconic Macmillan nurses with palliative care. In their 2006 rebrand, the word 'relief' was replaced with 'support' to shift the nonprofit's image as 'end of life' to being a 'life force' identity. Internal stakeholders have to take time to accept and embrace the new identity.

On one hand, the distinct image of Macmillan nurses is crucial for fundraising purposes, and this clashed with the service team who wanted to move away from the image exclusively related to the end of life care and focus on living well after cancer. Therefore, managers have to think of creative ways to balance both the old and new identity, whilst also finding ways to maintain consistency of message that is still relevant to a wider audience (Lee & Davies, 2019). For further details, please refer to the Macmillan Cancer Support brand transformation case study below.

Tension 2: Difficulties in engaging key stakeholders and embedding values. An important aspect of the nonprofit rebrand is to find an effective way to engage with core and potential audiences. In some cases, the new vision and ambition of the nonprofit organisation can clash with supporters' and beneficiaries' expectations, or even evoke negative reactions. As a rebrand strategy is resource intensive, supporters and beneficiaries could feel frustrated to see monies donated being spent on a new visual identity instead of helping the cause. In other cases, supporters questioned the decision of the new symbol or colour used. For example, in the Prostate Cancer UK rebrand, supporters were questioning the use of the colour black in the new identity, as they associated black with death. Such reactions show the lack of awareness amongst external stakeholders about the reasons for rebranding (e.g. to stand out) and reveal the deep beliefs that nonprofit brands are simply a logo. Also, different audiences may require a different tone of voice and messaging and such divergence complicates the engagement in the nonprofit's brand communication. For example, younger (potential) audiences expect a more active and direct tone of voice, whilst traditional supporters and corporate partners expect a warmer tone.

In addition to the potential backlash from external stakeholders, many nonprofits may also underestimate the process of embedding the new values amongst their employees and frontline staff. Rebranding typically results in some level of cultural change, whether it is about changing mindsets or behaviours. Whilst employees may be briefed about why change was necessary, the way to bring the brand to life internally is often overlooked due to other priorities in the process. This can cause confusion and frustration if the road map is not clearly articulated to internal stakeholders. Simply creating a badge and banner with new values is not sufficient. It is important to recognise the role of employees' identification with nonprofits, and to identify relevant brand champions who can advocate and act as a strong voice for change internally.

Tension 3: Balancing fundraising's and communications' needs. Nonprofit organisations organise their communications and fundraising functions differently. For some nonprofits, both functions sit within the same section and work together harmoniously under a director of branding and communications. However, in many nonprofits, both functions are separated and typically work in a silo. In a rebranding process, such organisational structures can cause friction if they are not managed properly. For example, Guide Dogs refreshed their brand when they identified a need to maintain the warmth (crucial for fundraising) and get spiky (campaigning as a central part of the new positioning). The nonprofit was a much-loved British charity but wanted to increase understanding of their campaigning work, especially in breaking down barriers which prevent the blind and partially sighted from getting out and about on their own terms. Their research showed that guide dogs were increasingly coming under attack from other dogs. Hence, they were campaigning for a review of the Dangerous Dogs Act as they wanted an attack on an assistance dog to be seen as an attack on the person. Such a new strategy brings to light the tensions in developing a brand story that could potentially hinder fundraising income. Would the current disruptive campaign help or hinder the fundraising income, even though it is the right thing to do? To minimise such tensions, nonprofits need to find ways to integrate both fundraising and communications so that they can have common interest.

Negotiating tensions in rebranding strategy and managerial implications

Understanding the dynamic tensions in the rebranding process enables managers to take a balanced approach in negotiating the external and internal perspectives affecting the change process. Once managers realise that nonprofit brands are not static, they can begin to put in place strategies to move stakeholders who tend to resist change towards embracing it for their benefits. Here is how this can work:

- *Build a strong business case and commitment from CEO and trustees.* Managers leading the rebrand strategy need to engage CEOs and trustees early on in the process. The early engagement is crucial to establish a sense of common understanding, especially the rationale for change. The strong commitment from the CEO is important – as we highlighted before, the rebranding strategy does not sit in the communication department and typically it would require some changes to organisational culture and the approach to achieving its mission. If not, the rebrand may be seen as a 'rebadge' exercise. More importantly, any rebrand would require significant and continuous investment.
- *Aligning the brand strategy with the corporate strategy.* Brand reviews may typically follow a corporate strategy change or may happen in parallel. A strong alignment is important to ensure a clear understanding among staff and supporters of the new direction. The new brand should enable managers to deliver the corporate/business strategy and galvanise change. This alignment could strengthen integration across domains. Current research shows that instead of compromising between different identities (national, cultural role and social role), nonprofits can create a virtuous understanding between different stakeholders of the inter-relationship between fundraising, core and peripheral service activities. Hence, this re-emphasises the need for the branding strategy to run through the whole organisation, from services to policy, from campaign to fundraising, and include securing financial sustainability and growth.
- *Rethink brand architecture.* One of the common tensions in the rebrand process is to increase reach, but managers don't want to antagonise or alienate core supporters. As seen in the Macmillan case, the nonprofit was very successful in developing new sub-brands by selectively compartmentalising relevant

identities for different target audiences, allowing for unique communications for target groups that does not undermine the core heritage identity (Lee & Davies, 2019). Compartmentalising and having the ability to flex the parent brand in a meaningful way opens up opportunities to grow and achieve the mission. This is effectively an example of nonprofit brand architecture. In the rebranding process, managers need to use architecture to balance consistency so that it is instantly recognisable, yet relevant to specific audiences in terms of the key message and tone of voice. Another successful example is practiced in Cancer Research UK with its Weekly Lottery, Race for Life and Kids and Teens campaigns each setting a different tone.

- *Engage authentically with multiple stakeholders.* Nonprofit rebrands can create lots of positive as well as negative emotions amongst its stakeholders, especially employees who show commitment and similar values to the organisation. Recent research shows that it is important to acknowledge that some employees can be either 'heritage defenders' (institutional defenders) or 'service innovators' (institutional entrepreneurs) (Lee & Davies, 2019; Levy & Scully, 2007). Here, they identify institutional entrepreneurs as important and valuable protagonists in overcoming the conservative and backward thinking defenders in ensuring progressive development. Nonprofit managers must embrace such differences and find balance in engaging in with these stakeholders in an authentic way. In this way, nonprofit can transform the negative feelings in reshaping the meaning of the new brand to keep it meaningful for the future.

- *Use the rebrand to inspire action.* Nonprofit rebranding should not be narrowly viewed as to diversity and increase income. Branding has the ability inspire action amongst people with shared values. There are many examples regarding how social movements have been instrumental in sparking difficult conversations and debates such as #MeToo campaign, Black Lives Matter and Charity So White. More importantly, the change process was driven by a strong purpose and dedication to make things better (Dufour, 2020). Hence, managers need to use the collective power to push forward and make a difference and inspire action.

In the nonprofit rebrand context, some charities have adopted such a mindset succesfully to tap into shared beliefs and emotions. Macmillan Cancer Support uses an open access 'BeMacmillan' brand portal to show inclusiveness and invites supporters to create branded material for fundraising. Another great example is Fight for Sight. The 50 years old nonprofit rebranded to make fight for sight a movement (Kantaria, 2019). In the process, the nonprofit wanted to tackle the negative perception that sight loss cannot be prevented or cured. Co-creating with scientists, people living with sight loss as well as existing and potential supporters, they inspired a social movement that combines the power of revolutionary science with warmth to reveal exciting new breakthroughs in tackling sight loss.

Balancing both the external and internal perspectives: two cases

Macmillan Cancer Support: a bold brand transformation

Macmillan Cancer Support, a large British cancer charity, was ranked first in the Charity Brand Index in 2013 and later awarded Brand of the Year 2014 by the Marketing Society, against other brands including O2 and Easyjet. This is a clear testament that a nonprofit brand can be as strong as a corporate brand. This success followed a successful rebranding exercise in 2006. To understand the transformation, one needs to examine their brand journey.

Macmillan Cancer Support was founded by a civil servant, Douglas Macmillan, in 1911 after his father died from cancer. Historically, it was known as the Society for the Prevention and Relief of Cancer. It was the first charity dedicated to preventing cancer and to bringing relief to those with the disease. The vision of its founder was to transform how cancer care was delivered in the UK. Unlike other cancer charities that lead on medical research to fight the disease, Macmillan Cancer Support positioned itself as improving the lives of people with cancer. Early on, Douglas Macmillan realised that to care for patients and their families with cancer required more than medicine, drugs, radiotherapy and surgery (Ross, 2009). However, the real impact of their work began when they embarked on palliative care via home visits and hospices by developing a partnership with the NHS, funding the first Macmillan nurses in 1975. Macmillan nurses are uniquely trained for dealing with end of life, palliative care for those with terminal cancer.

However, the mid-2000s witnessed a shift in cancer care. As more people survived cancer, people wanted and needed better cancer care. For example, there was a growing demand for people needing care in their homes and the community, and not just hospitals. Yet Macmillan were best known for their nurses and the end of life care they provided. Their behaviour and communications felt institutional, which limited their scope. In 2006, the charity changed its name from Macmillan Cancer Relief to Macmillan Cancer Support, dropping the word 'Relief' to align more closely with their changing activities related to living with cancer, rather than providing palliative care. With the help of branding agency Wolff Olins, they developed a new ambition to reach and improve the lives of everyone living with cancer. In this process, the agency coached all levels of the organisation up to the CEO and emphasised the internal aspect of the rebrand to own and live the change. Although there was some initial resistance, such as Macmillan nurses disapproving of the new brushstroke brand identity as too 'childish' and not reflecting their professionalism, they were soon brought into a sense of understanding and acceptance. Within two years of the rebrand, Macmillan's fundraising increased by £26 million – a 6% year-on-year growth (Wolff Ollin, 2020). Additionally, the number of callers to the Macmillan Support line increased by 35%, and 50% more people had found the benefits they were entitled to.

Such a bold and successful rebrand provided further energy for Macmillan to continue to innovate to achieve its mission. Macmillan then went on to engage in several brand refresh exercises. In the recent refresh in 2019, the nonprofit organisation aimed to attract a more diverse audience of volunteers with a brand proposition of 'live life as fully as you can'. The new platform enabled different audiences to come together, for example with the 'World's Biggest Coffee Morning' – one of Macmillan's most recognised fundraising events – targeting at its core audience such as elderly women, as well as a younger, male-oriented fundraising product 'Brave the Shave'. This shows Macmillan's rebrand helps the brand to stretch and reach different audiences with a clear brand architecture (Rouge, 2020).

Prostate Cancer UK: embedding new values via cultural change

Until 2012, Prostate Cancer Charity (PCC) was a relatively unknown UK charity compared to other bigger cancer charities such as Cancer Research UK and Save the Children. Yet prostate cancer is the most common cancer in men, killing nearly as many men as breast cancer kills women. The condition is practically invisible and men did not like to talk about it. This meant PCC had a huge challenge ahead of them.

Despite generating £20 million income with their award-winning communications, PCC's brand did not stand out. The brand had only 7% prompted awareness, and 50% of men did not know what the prostate was. Similarly, the brand image looked like the NHS and the colour 'baby blue' was perceived as 'distant, indirect and patriarchal, muffled and apologetic'. Such disconnects meant that the charity was actively bypassed by men. Instead, the charity relied on asking women to prompt the men in their lives to go to the doctor. Competition from other charities on prostate cancer is also intense. There are smaller charities with bigger voices such as Prostate Action, which has a more masculine brand and is very active in engaging men to get tested.

Such challenges prompted the nonprofit to change. PCC decided that a revolutionary change was required. The nonprofit aimed to put 'men' at the centre of what they do, with a strong brand proposition of 'men deserve better'. The rebranding process took about seven months. The nonprofit worked with design agency Hat-Trick, and many staff were involved from the very beginning. For example, there were three one-day workshops and interviews. Unlike other rebrands, PCC used Linguistic Landscapes (a discourse analysis) to review the language used internally and the culture that it fostered (Koller & Ereaut, 2020). Through this research, they identified that the nonprofit's culture was overly polite and apologetic. Hence, a key part of the rebrand process was to change their name to Prostate Cancer UK: they believed the word 'charity' was holding them back.

The rebrand was an immediate success. Brand name awareness increased and, eight years later, it is still going strong. What are the reasons underlying Prostate Cancer UK's success? The rebrand did not start by trying to find a way to diversify their income. The charity genuinely felt the disconnection from their target audience – men. By using a discourse analysis approach, they uncovered the internal culture of the organisation. How employees think and talk has a huge impact on the brand when employees communicate with their audience. The decision to change the culture, to be bolder and more direct, is the crux of the success.

Conclusion

Nonprofit rebrands are not the same corporate rebrands. This is because there is a deeper level of attachment to the brand both internally and externally. To effectively steward nonprofit brands, we must first understand what the brand means in relation to the mission, the employees and the beneficiaries. In contemporary society, nonprofit brands play an important fundraising role, as well as galvanising change through employees, frontline staff and volunteers. Moving away from an external brand perspective at the product level, this chapter provides a more nuanced internal understanding of the challenges of managing a nonprofit rebrand at an organisational level.

Highlighting key tensions and strategies in negotiating these tensions, the chapter shows two successful nonprofit rebrands that have been navigated through strong leadership from the top, producing a new brand identity that is relevant to beneficiaries and new values being culturally embedded by employees. Therefore, managers should take a long-term view when managing their brands. Rebranding strategies should be a continuous exercise, dynamic and evolutionary, always pushing boundaries to reach a greater audience and create bigger impacts for their causes.

Chapter discussion questions

1.   What are the paradigm shifts in managing a nonprofit brand? What are the implications for managing brands inside-out?
2.   Why do nonprofits engage in a rebranding strategy?
3.   What factors define a strong nonprofit rebranding?
4.   Evaluate a recent charity rebrand. How did the organisation align the vision, culture and image? Was the alignment successful? Why?

References

Aaker, D.A. (2009). *Managing Brand Equity*. Simon and Schuster.
Allchin, J. (2012). How Prostate Cancer UK politicised its brand. *Marketing Week*, 30 October. Available at www.marketingweek.com/how-prostate-cancer-uk-politicise d-its-brand/ (accessed 22 February 2021).
Balmer, J.M. (2001). Corporate identity, corporate branding and corporate marketing: Seeing through the fog. *European Journal of Marketing*, 35(3/4), 248–291.
Bennett, R. & Gabriel, H. (2003). Image and reputational characteristics of UK charitable organizations: An empirical study. *Corporate Reputation Review*, 6(3), 276–289.
Boenigk, S. & Becker, A. (2016). Toward the importance of nonprofit brand equity: Results from a study of German nonprofit organizations. *Nonprofit Management and Leadership*, 27(2), 181–198.
Boycott-Owen, M. (2021). Royal British Legion accused by veterans of 'losing touch' over charity's £100,000 rebrand. Available at www.telegraph.co.uk/news/2021/01/24/roya l-british-legion-accused-veterans-losing-touch-charitys/ (accessed 13 February 2021).
Chad, P. (2015). Utilising a change management perspective to examine the implementation of corporate rebranding in a non-profit SME. *Journal of Brand Management*, 22(7), 569–587.

CharityComms. (2012). Best practices guide: Branding inside out. Available at www.charity comms.org.uk/branding-inside-out-a-best-practice-guide?gclid=CjwKCAjw1JeJBhB9EiwA V612y6t0mPlerFTJNi02AcQqvLyaBmFD6XKWJp9TzaRvCQ0Pv7TFqiOSpRoClcQQA vD_BwE (accessed 10 January 2021).

Cipriani, V. (2020). Addaction staff strike over pay dispute as rebranding launches. *Civil Society*, 27 February. Available at www.civilsociety.co.uk/news/addaction-workers-re turn-to-strike-over-pay-dispute-as-rebranding-launches.html (accessed 28 February 2021).

Dufour, D. (2020). What can charities learn from social movements? Available at www.charity comms.org.uk/what-can-charities-learn-from-social-movements (accessed 27 March 2021).

Ewing, M.T. & Napoli, J. (2005). Developing and validating a multidimensional nonprofit brand orientation scale. *Journal of Business Research*, 58(6), 841–853.

Gotsi, M. & Andriopoulos, C. (2007). Understanding the pitfalls in the corporate rebranding process. *Corporate Communications: An International Journal*, 12(4), 341–355.

Hankinson, P. (2001). Brand orientation in the top 500 fundraising charities in the UK. *Journal of Product & Brand Management*, 10(6), 346–360.

Hankinson, P. (2002). The impact of brand orientation on managerial practice: A quantitative study of the UK's top 500 fundraising managers. *International Journal of Nonprofit and Voluntary Sector Marketing*, 7(1), 30–44.

Hatch, M.J. & Schultz, M. (2003). Bringing the corporation into corporate branding. *European Journal of Marketing*, 37(7/8), 1041–1064.

Kaikati, J.G. & Kaikati, A.M. (2003). A rose by any other name: Rebranding campaign that work. *Journal of Business Strategy*, 24(6), 17–23.

Kalaignanam, K. & Bahadir, S.C. (2013). Corporate brand name changes and business restructuring: Is the relationship complementary or substitutive? *Journal of the Academy Marketing Science*, 41(4), 456–472.

Kantaria, P. (2019). Fight for sight rebrands as movement not a remote body. *Civil Society*, 17 October. Available at www.civilsociety.co.uk/news/fight-for-sight-rebrands-as-a movement not a remote funding body html (accessed 2 March 2021).

Keller, K.L. (1993). Conceptualizing, measuring, and managing customer-based brand equity. *Journal of Marketing*, 57(1), 1–22.

Koller, V. & Ereaut, G. (2020). Culture change and rebranding in the charity sector: A linguistic consultancy approach. In L. Mullany (ed.), *Professional Communication*. Palgrave Macmillan.

Kylander, N. & Stone, C. (2012). The role of brand in the nonprofit sector. *Stanford Social Innovation Review*, 10, 35–41.

Lee, Z. (2013). Rebranding in brand-oriented organization: Exploring tensions in the nonprofit sector. *Journal of Marketing Management*, 29(9–10), 1124–1142.

Lee, Z. & Davies, I. (2019). Navigating relative invariance: Perspectives on corporate heritage identity and organizational heritage identity in an evolving nonprofit institution. *Journal of Business Research*, 129, 813–825.

Levy, D. & Scully, M. (2007). The institutional entrepreneur as modern prince: The strategic face of power in contested fields. *Organization Studies*, 28(7), 971–991.

Lomax, W. & Mador, M. (2006). Corporate re-branding: From normative models to knowledge management. *Journal of Brand Management*, 14(1), 82–95.

Melewar, T.C., Gotsi, M. & Andriopoulos, C. (2012). Shaping the research agenda for corporate branding: Avenues for future research. *European Journal of Marketing*, 46(5), 600–608.

Merrilees, B. & Miller, D. (2008). Principles of corporate rebranding. *European Journal of Marketing*, 42(5/6), 537–552.

Michel, G. & Rieunier, S. (2012). Nonprofit brand image and typicality influences on charitable giving. *Journal of Business Research*, 65(5), 701–707.

Miller, D. & Merrilees, B. (2013). Rebuilding community corporate brands: A total stakeholder involvement approach. *Journal of Business Research*, 66(2), 172–179.

Miller, D., Merrilees, B. and Yakimova, R. (2014). Corporate rebranding: An integrative review of major enablers and barriers to the rebranding process. *International Journal of Management Reviews*, 16(3), 265–228.

Muzellec, L. & Lambkin, M. (2006). Corporate rebranding: Destroying, transferring or creating brand equity? *European Journal of Marketing*, 40(7/8), 803–824.

NCVO. (2020). UK civil society almanac 2020. Available at https://data.ncvo.org.uk/ (accessed 3 March 2021).

Neumayr, M. & Handy, F. (2019). Charitable giving: What influences donors' choice among different causes? *VOLUNTAS: International Journal of Voluntary and Nonprofit Organizations*, 30(4), 783–799.

Ross, P.N. (2009). *Fighting Cancer with More than Medicine: A History of Macmillan Cancer Support*. The History Press.

Rouge, D. (2020). Macmillan Cancer Support rebrand: Creating a brand transformation with true purpose. Available at www.theoystercatchers.com/posts/58912-macmillan-cancer-support-rebrand (accessed 14 February 2021).

Sargeant, A., Ford, J.B. & Hudson, J. (2008). Charity brand personality: The relationship with giving behavior. *Nonprofit and Voluntary Sector Quarterly*, 37(3), 468–491.

Sepulcri, L.M.C.B., Mainardes, E.W. & Belchior, C.C. (2020). Nonprofit branding: A bibliometric analysis. *Journal of Product & Brand Management*, 29(5), 655–673.

Stride, H. & Lee, S. (2007). No logo? No way. Branding in the non-profit sector. *Journal of Marketing Management*, 23(1–2), 107–122.

Stuart, H. (2018). Corporate branding and rebranding: An institutional logics perspective. *Journal of Product & Brand Management*, 27(1), 96–100.

Vallaster, C. & Lindgreen, A. (2011). Corporate brand strategy formation: Brand actors and the situational context for a business-to-business brand. *Industrial Marketing Management*, 40(7), 1133–1143.

Venable, B.T., Rose, G.M., Bush, V.D. & Gilbert, F.W. (2005). The role of brand personality in charitable giving: An assessment and validation. *Journal of the Academy of Marketing science*, 33(3), 295–312.

Wolff Ollin. (2020), Macmillan case study. Available at: www.wolffolins.com/case-study/macmillan/ (accessed 9 September 2020).

Wymer, W., Gross, H.P. & Helmig, B. (2016). Nonprofit brand strength: What is it? How is it measured? What are its outcomes? *Voluntas: International Journal of Voluntary and Nonprofit Organizations*, 27(3), 1448–1471.

3

MARKETING CHARITIES TO ATTRACT VOLUNTEERS

Time for B2V

Sarah-Louise Mitchell

Introduction

The mandate for charities to support the most vulnerable in our society has rarely been more pressing, given the recent cuts in benefits and rising numbers of people needing help (Clifford, 2017). However, for many nonprofit organisations, the provision of these services is dependent on attracting *new* volunteers. In the UK, 22% of people volunteer formally at least once a month and 27% informally. One example, 'parkrun', the weekend community sport phenomenon, has nearly 280,000 volunteers in England and Wales (Clark, 2021). Encouraging people to 'donate time' requires effective marketing of the charity to potential volunteers – enabling them to believe in the cause, trust in the brand, but also meeting their needs in terms of intangible benefits received. Those roles can be regular, infrequent or one-off. They can be time-bound or ongoing, skilled or unskilled. They can be hands-on with beneficiaries or behind the scenes in support.

The challenge for charities is that investment in supporter research is under pressure; absolute budgets have reduced but also there is increasing public scrutiny of money spent (Exley, 2019). This hampers their ability to understand why a person might choose their organisation rather than another, and therefore who the charity should focus their resources on attracting and how. The purpose of this chapter is to contribute knowledge on this important issue, both to theory and practice. Of course, being successful at attracting volunteers is only part of the story – managing them well and retaining them (Faulkner & Romanuk, 2019; Kim et al., 2019) has a direct and immediate impact on how many new volunteers need to be recruited. However, even with the most effective volunteer management capability (primarily a HR and management issue rather than a marketing one), there will always be a natural churn in volunteers, as people

DOI: 10.4324/9781003134169-6

enter different life-stages such as starting a family, entering employment or becoming infirm (Hustinix, 2010).

Academic debate about nonprofit supporter choice is fraught with complexity. The language is traditionally one of values-based mission (Stride & Lee, 2007) and collaboration (Kylander & Stone, 2012). This is changing in the face of increased pressure on funding and growing service need. If volunteers have choice, and charities need to attract volunteers, then it can be described as a competitive situation.

> from a consumer behaviour perspective, volunteering can be considered as one of the outcomes of marketing communication from nonprofit firms.
>
> *(Wymer & Samu, 2002, p. 972)*

This chapter starts with the 'consumer', in this case the volunteer, to understand their needs: effectively the '**why**?' question. It then considers the decision-making process of the volunteer including they ways they build knowledge of a charity brand: the '**how**?' It concludes with a call for a new mindset, extending the concepts of business to consumer (B2C) and business to business (B2B) to business to volunteer (B2V) with a discussion of the implications for theory and practice. This is the '**so what**?' question.

Why? Understanding the drivers of volunteer choice of charity

Despite a vast body of work interrogating why people volunteer *generically*, there has been minimal insight into the choice of *specific* organisations by volunteers. Given the economic significance of the sector, prevalence of volunteering amongst the population and the pressing need to support the vulnerable, this oversight led to a new research stream, shared in this chapter. Volunteer choice of charity is driven by need, role, cause, availability/convenience and brand.

Charity choice driven by need

Volunteer research has focused on the 'need' level of decision-making, that is the personal values and goals the individual is motivated to fulfil in exchange for time given. Underpinned theoretically by social exchange theory, this assumes people act in their own self-interest: donating their time and rationally expecting benefits in return. Blau (1964) believes the social exchange is contingent on reaction by others:

> The tendency to help others is frequently motivated by the expectation that doing so will bring social rewards, the social approval of those whose opinions we value is of great significance to us.
>
> *(Blau, 1964, p. 17)*

This perspective is in contrast to altruism, defined as helping others selflessly (Piliavin & Hong-Wen, 1990). However, Wilson and Musick (1997) argue altruism underestimates the role of self-identity, for example someone who thinks of themselves as the type of person who helps others. Anchored in self-identity theory, the volunteer is saying something about themselves, their values and their personality through their choice of brand with whom they want to volunteer.

The Volunteer Function Inventory (VFI) acts as the theoretical bedrock for understanding how personal needs motivate the generic decision to volunteer (Clary et al., 1998). The VFI argues that people evaluate the benefits of volunteering against one or more of six needs: meeting personal values, understanding (of service users), career enhancement, social, protective and self-esteem. Recent research (Mitchell & Clark, 2020c) extends this generic motivation to understand the motivation for choosing one charity instead of another, the issue of primary concern for marketing an individual charity seeking to attract new volunteers. Through laddering interviews with service-delivery volunteers from a large sample, connections were revealed between the attributes that attracted the volunteer to a specific organisation, the perceived consequences of those attributes, and how they fulfil personal needs. Volunteers identified seven dominant needs as reasons for their choice of a particular charity. These were *self-respect,* [1] *social recognition, sense of accomplishment, sense of belonging, living my values, pleasure* and *excitement.* Meeting these needs was the ultimate reason for the choice of a specific organisation. Through conceptualising the decision as being driven by personal needs, the choice of volunteering as a way of meeting those needs can be seen in the context of other solutions. For example, the need for a sense of accomplishment could alternatively be met through career success, family or sport.

The results also show that previous constructs of volunteer motivation, such as within the VFI, are more often attributes or consequences than higher order needs and values. For example, the VFI category of social is defined as being with friends and also taking part in socially recognised activities (Clary et al., 1998). However, this research found that taking a role that has the attribute of being *social,* that is working with other people, meets that motivation but then as a consequence the volunteer feels *part of a team,* which ultimately enables them to achieve their personal goal of having a *sense of belonging* to a group. The desire to meet personal needs and values is the foundation from which other decisions flow, for instance choice of a specific brand, role and cause. This deeper understanding stems from the methodological choice of laddering interviews which enable the volunteer to go beyond top-of-mind reasons for volunteering (a risk for nonprofit surveys) to make connections through to personal needs and values that may be implicit or abstract and, therefore, not immediately obvious.

Research Insight #1: The decision to volunteer for one charity rather than another is anchored in meeting higher order needs and values.

Charity choice driven by role

Support for a charity can manifest itself in a variety of ways, such as becoming a donor, volunteer, advocate or customer. Understanding this decision-making process is at the heart of uncovering the nature of the social exchange; the needs met through frontline volunteering are quite different from those met through donating goods to a charity shop or taking part in a fundraising event. However, within each of these broad supporter roles there is also choice, a second-stage decision. In volunteering, for example, specific role choice includes service-delivery, retail or fundraising functions with different levels of time and emotional commitment and, as a consequence, different needs met.

From a charity marketing perspective, there is minimal research on role choice in the nonprofit context. What is known is the importance of role to the supporter's need for social identity. Ho and O'Donohoe (2014) examined how volunteers managed their social identities given the stereotypes associated with different volunteering roles. White et al. (2016) examined role identity in relation to three donation roles – giving money, time and blood. They found that the important driver of donation behaviour was the person's identity as a donor rather than having been seen as helpful or other general personality characteristics (van Ingen & Wilson, 2016). This particularly resonates with the role acquisition function within symbolic consumption theory (Hoyer et al., 2012) where role directly relates to personal identity, particularly in the absence of other productive roles (van Ingen & Wilson, 2016).

The extensive UK research study 'Pathways into Participation' (Brodie et al., 2011) examined three types of nonprofit support roles – individual (such as donating and buying Fairtrade), social (formal and informal volunteering) and public (voting and social action). Although it did not specifically examine motivations for one support role compared to another, the research did consider how participation changed:

> We found that people's involvement changes over their life course as they experience different life events and triggers... people follow a range of pathways to move between different types of activity, with one form of engagement often prompting or leading to another.
>
> *(Brodie et al., 2011, p. 69)*

Historically, what was not understood was the implication of role in the volunteer choice of charity: whether, for example, role is synonymous with cause, role choice leads to specific cause or brands, whether the relationship is with the brand and, subsequently, type of support roles considered such as fundraising, donating and advocacy.

Our recent research with service-delivery volunteers identifies that the type of volunteering role is a driver of volunteer choice of charity (Mitchell & Clark, 2020c). These volunteers selected roles that were a *challenge*, that were *hands-on* and that used their *existing skills and experience*. The consequence was volunteers wanting to *make a difference, feel useful, feel valued* and be *still learning*. Ultimately, the needs they were seeking to fulfil from such a hands-on and challenging role were a *sense of accomplishment, living my values*, and *self-respect* for themselves but also *social recognition* by others for taking on such a challenging support role. For the first time, the data identifies how the decision to become a volunteer enables the person to feel useful and valued, building their sense of self but also how they are perceived by the wider world, including within their own family. In particular, the consequences of *feeling useful* and *valued* led through to a *sense of accomplishment, self-respect* and *social recognition*. Other people support nonprofits through alternative ways that better fit their needs, such as becoming a donor, customer or advocate. This can be conceptualised as a broad competitive set within which supporter roles reside. There was little evidence in the data of the volunteer supporter group adopting multiple roles of support for an organisation. Volunteering was the best fit for their needs. However, it did not preclude lower level involvement support for other charities, such as making one-off donations or buying clothes from a charity shop.

The second stage of the decision is the specific role choice. Service-delivery volunteering is not a decision taken lightly; the regular time commitment made is considerable and if the volunteer fails to honour their commitment, the beneficiary is let down. Other volunteering roles meet different needs, for example enhancing education and career prospects through volunteering hours at the Children's Society, or building a sense of belonging to a local community, as seen with the popularity of the NHS Volunteer Responders scheme run by RVS[2] during the Covid pandemic. Therefore, an important driver of NPO choice is the perceived ability of the organisation to offer roles that meet the different needs that people have.

Research Insight #2: People select a role to support charities depending on which personal needs and values they want to meet.

Charity choice driven by cause

Henke and Fontenot (2009) argue cause selection is ultimately driven by personal need. They identify that for American donors the:

> warm glow that comes with giving is a significant predictor of giving to causes for children and the elderly, while a sense of civic duty is a significant predictor of giving to weatherize homes and provide medical assistance for the poor...
>
> *(Henke & Fontenot, 2009, p. 16)*

The relationship is between the personal need the supporter is seeking to fulfil and perceived characteristics of different causes. Sargeant et al. (2008), in their donor research, identified distinct personality traits for charities within three types of cause – labelled service, class and faith. For example, education and arts charities were seen as elite and upper-class, which appealed to some donors but were rejected by others. Randle et al. (2013), in their analysis of volunteer data from the World Values Survey, also explore choices at cause level, observing five clusters – church, political, professional associations, leisure and a fifth category labelled 'altruism'. They argue that switching from one organisation to another is more likely to occur within a competitive cluster than across clusters, for example from a labour union to a political party rather than supporting older people. The implication is that charities consider competition for volunteer recruitment at the cause cluster level, not just brand or individual cause level.

Our research identifies cause as an important driver of charity choice (Mitchell & Clark, 2020c), enabling volunteers to *make a difference*, bringing them a *sense of accomplishment* as well as enabling them to live according to their values. Through empathy to the cause specifically, and wanting to make a difference generally, they feel that they gain personally in what they achieve and how they live their lives. The research identifies that the choice of role drives the choice of cause. These supporters identified volunteering as the best fit to meet their needs and then made choices about cause and brand. None had considered donating instead, for example.

In addition, the research identifies two other new and interesting dimensions of cause as a decision driver. Firstly, the strength of the emotional language about the cause. Emotion has been found to stimulate action, particularly helping actions such as prosocial behaviour (Cialdini et al., 1987) and achievement of goals (Bagozzi & Pieters, 1998; Frijda, 1987). Interestingly emotion is also one of the few proven differentiators between charity brands (Michel & Rieunier, 2012). In this way, the emotion attached to cause choice not only drives the decision to volunteer but also the choice of specific organisation with whom to volunteer.

Secondly, the depth of relationship between the individual volunteer and the cause varied considerably. It can be conceptualised as a spectrum from interest in the cause, through empathy, then relevance and, finally, to a deep personal connection. The more empathetic a person feels towards cause, the more likely they are to support it. Where there is personal relevance, the motivation to select an organisation within that cause sector is stronger. Therefore, this research identifies cause as a key driver of specific NPO choice but also discovers that choice of cause follows choice of role.

Research Insight #3: The decision about choice of supporter role, such as volunteering, comes before choice of brand or cause.

Research Insight #4: Emotional engagement with a charity is most closely linked to cause.

Charity choice driven by availability and convenience

Within consumer behaviour literature, the relationship between brand choice and availability is well described (Shah et al., 2015). A lack of availability nearby can influence the consumer to select a brand that was not their first choice (Rundle-Thiele & Bennett, 2001). Geographical proximity in particular has been found to be particularly influential for consumers who are new to the category (Janakiraman & Niraj, 2011). Within nonprofit practitioner guides, nearness of location has been seen as a key driver of volunteer recruitment by charities (Whittich, 2000) and the 'Pathways to Participation' report (Brodie et al., 2011) identified local availability as a potential constraint on voluntary engagement.

Our research showed volunteers did identify the importance of needing something that *fits with my life* in a practical way, being convenient in terms of time and location. However, this did not lead through to meeting any higher order needs and so did not drive charity choice.

Research Insight #5: Local availability and convenience of volunteering roles acts as a constraint on, not a driver of, charity choice.

Charity choice driven by brand

Brand has been consistently identified as a driver of consumer behaviour, particularly through enabling differentiation within a category (Aaker, 2003), resulting in increased consumer preference (Erdem & Swait, 2004). Michel and Rieunier's (2012) research on charities showed that four dimensions of brand image (affect, efficiency, usefulness and dynamism) explained 24% of intentions to donate time and 31% of money (Michel & Rieunier, 2012). An evolved scale with six dimensions (including reliability and ethicality) has been shown to explain 54% of time and 51% of money (Michaelidou et al., 2015). Both studies recognise brand as a significant influence on the decision to support charities. However, they did not explain how brand affects choice between organisations.

Brand is a difficult concept within the charity sector, particularly given the wide variation in marketing activity by charities. The larger, donation-led organisations are usually, although not exclusively, at one end of the spectrum with investment in both understanding and communicating their brands. In the middle ground are charities applying day-to-day branding but often under different terminology. As Tapp (1996) explains.

> Charities do not describe much of what they do as branding. However, organisations have long been concerned with maintaining a consistent style and tone of voice… to ensure that a consistent personality is projected to important stakeholders.
>
> *(Tapp, 1996, p. 335)*

Finally, at the other end of the marketing spectrum are smaller and/or statutory funded charities, whose focus is frontline service provision and who operate with minimal central support functions including marketing. However, whatever their level of marketing capability, a primary objective for charities is inducing people to donate time and/or money to enable them to achieve their mission; as Andreasen (1994) explains, 'the bottom line of social marketing is behavioural change' (p. 110).

Our research identified that volunteers who choose a 'big name' charity do so because they feel it enables them to *make a difference* and *feel valued* by others, *feel useful* themselves or *help their career*. Ultimately, they believe volunteering for a well-known brand would bring a *sense of accomplishment, self-respect, social recognition* and enable them to *live their values*. What is interesting is the way the brand contributes to the choice of organisation through self-efficacy; they view the well-known brand as effective and, therefore, trust their time will not be wasted. In this way, a well-established brand enables the volunteer to feel worthwhile, enabling their personal value of *sense of accomplishment* to be met.

The research also identifies the relationship between brand and meeting personal needs of self-respect and social recognition (He et al., 2012). The choice of brand reflects the groups to which they want to belong. Volunteering can strengthen their identification with a particular social tribe, for example role in the congregation (e.g. Christian Aid[3]), role in the community or role as a parent (e.g. local PTA[4]). Both social- and self-identity motivations drive the choices about and between brands, reflecting what the person wants to say about themselves and the groups to which they wish to belong. Volunteering for a well-known brand has, for some volunteers, a real kudos with a direct link to self-esteem, social recognition and organisational identification (Ashforth et al., 2008). Therefore, the role of brand in charity choice is identified as twofold: enabling the volunteer to make a difference and meeting their needs for self and social identity.

Research Insight #6: People volunteer for well-known brands as they believe their time will be used effectively.

Research Insight #7: People volunteer for well-known brands due to the perceived impact on their self and social identity.

The relationships between these five drivers are illustrated in Figure 3.1. The decision-making sequence between cause and brand reveals two distinct pathways. For some volunteers, the brand is an automatic choice following the decision to volunteer and the cause was a consequence of the brand choice. The brand is synonymous with a particular cause. For others, the stronger relationship is with the cause, particularly in cases of personal relevance and empathy.

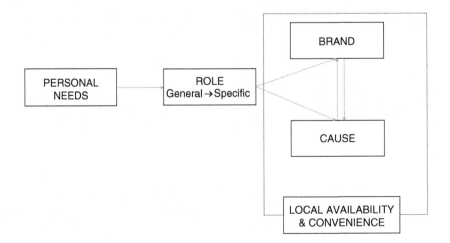

FIGURE 3.1 Conceptual framework of volunteer choice of specific charity

How? Understanding the volunteer decision-making process

In order to develop an effective charity marketing strategy for attracting new volunteers, we need to go beyond simply understanding *why* a volunteer chooses one brand over another. We also need to understand *how* volunteers find out about different charities and the decision-making process they go through in order to make a final choice.

Source of brand knowledge

Volunteers build knowledge over time from a wide range of touchpoints which, in turn, enables them to differentiate between organisations (Venable et al., 2005). Interestingly, it is not simply the frequency of interaction with these touchpoints that strengthens the relationship with the brand but also the positivity of that experience (Baxendale et al., 2015).

They recollect brand experiences such as visiting a charity shop, seeing local fundraisers, and/or hearing about the difference a charity made to a family member. These sources of information are described as macro, micro, and mego brand touchpoints (Mitchell & Clark, 2020a). Macro touchpoints include national advertising or fundraising campaigns: mass communication that tends not to be personalised. Micro touchpoints are within local communities: the places where people live and work. No evidence was found of a meso level, traditionally defined as between macro and micro. However, people learning about charities through the personal experience of being supported or a family member/close friend being helped is known as the mego level, illustrated in Figure 3.2 as a charity brand touchpoint map.

Brands with strong above-the-line budgets and professionally integrated marketing campaigns, such as Cancer Research UK,[5] obviously have a greatly enhanced ability to communicate at the macro level. Likewise, for charities with a significant retail

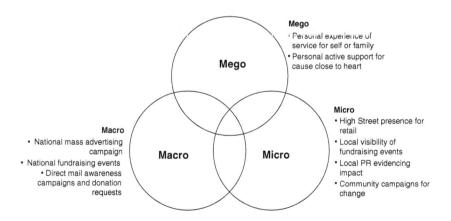

FIGURE 3.2 Charity brand touchpoint map

component, such as Oxfam[6] with their 650 physical stores, their visibility on the high street acts as a constant micro reminder. However, each potential volunteer will experience the brand differently, and over time their unique implicit knowledge is built from these sources (Merrilees, 2016).

Research Insight #8: People build implicit knowledge of charity brands over time and from a variety of brand touchpoints, including local and personal.

Level of brand engagement

A second consideration for charities seeking to attract volunteers is the *level* of knowledge people have about them. Our research showed three distinct levels (Mitchell & Clark, 2020a). At the point of decision-making, the volunteer either is unaware/minimally aware of the brand, has some knowledge of the brand, or is already well engaged with the brand. Table 3.1 describes these three levels of brand engagement as Brand Ignorant, Brand Aware and Brand Wise.

According to the familiarity heuristic, brands that are more familiar are chosen more quickly and easily even from a wide range of options. Our research found that people tend to be 'Brand Wise' about the charities they subsequently select to volunteer with (Mitchell & Clark, 2020a). They already have an understanding of the organisation beyond simple brand awareness. This familiarity eases their decision-making process rather than having to compare and contrast different options. In effect, the effort of processing information about the brand, the behavioural cost, has been reduced.

Process of brand discovery

The third consideration for charities seeking to attract volunteers is how the decision is made: the behavioural process of organisational choice, described as 'brand discovery'. This considers whether the volunteer proactively identifies a specific brand to support, whether someone at the charity asks the potential volunteer if they would be interested, if the choice is made in reaction to an external stimulus such as an advertisement, or if it emerged from a search shortlist. These categories of behaviour within the brand discovery theme are defined and described in Table 3.2 using the shorthand

TABLE 3.1 Brand Engagement Levels

Brand engagement	Definition	Label
Engagement Level 1	Potential volunteer has knowledge of charity beyond just the name, often from range of touchpoints.	Brand Wise
Engagement Level 2	Potential volunteer has heard of the specific charity and generally knows what it does.	Brand Aware
Engagement Level 3	Potential volunteer had not heard of the brand before volunteering there (but may use their services prior to volunteering).	Brand Ignorant

TABLE 3.2 Description of Brand Discovery Behaviour Types

Discovery	Definition	Label
Behaviour 1	The volunteer seeks out a specific charity brand to find out how to volunteer with them.	Seek
Behaviour 2	The volunteer is asked by someone within the charity if they would be interested in volunteering for them.	Sought
Behaviour 3	Volunteer learns about the specific charity through seeing some marketing material (passive) or hearing through word of mouth (active).	See (and hear)
Behaviour 4	Charity search is self-generated, proactive, and wide ranging. It is often online either through search engine or volunteering portals such as 'Do It'.	Search

labels of Seek, Sought, See (and hear) and Search. For clarity, the 'See' discovery behaviour is sub-divided into passive, such as seeing promotional material, for example an advert on Facebook, or active, such as being recommended by a friend.

For charities seeking to attract volunteers, understanding the interaction between the existing level of brand knowledge and the process of volunteer decision-making is key, as shown in Figure 3.3.

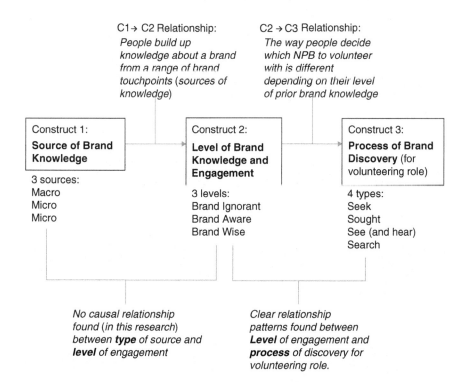

FIGURE 3.3 Construct relationships underpinning volunteer choice of charity

People who do know about charities (Brand Wise and Brand Aware) have accumulated implicit brand knowledge over time and from different sources (level of brand engagement). In addition, it could be anticipated that the commitment to volunteer would follow the pattern of a high-involvement decision, particularly given the significant time involved. High involvement implies both the presence of alternatives, a competitive set from which to evaluate best fit, and also a measured decision-making process (process of brand discovery). For volunteers who 'Search', the alternatives either emerged from specific volunteering websites (such as www. doit.org.uk), or a proactive internet search of charities of interest. 'Search' involves a more considered and time-consuming process. Two types of volunteers follow this pattern: *novices*, with minimal previous exposure to the category, who therefore need to actively seek out information, and *role seeking* volunteers needing to fulfil volunteer hours required for a college course, volunteering award or to enhance their career through work experience. For example, to achieve the Duke of Edinburgh Award[7] requires three (Bronze), six (Silver) or twelve (Gold) months volunteering commitment from the young people participating. Novice and role-seeing volunteers may not be able to make an automatic choice of organisation as they know little about them. Instead, both groups used a more explicit and rational decision-making process developing a conscious competitive choice set, potentially driven by cause, and moderated by local availability and awareness.

However, what is more interesting is the greater number of volunteers whose decision-making behaviour is one of *automatic choice*. For volunteers exhibiting the three behaviours labelled 'Seek', 'Sought' and 'See' there was *no* evidence of a competitive set at the point of decision-making. Despite the significant time commitment involved in regular service-delivery volunteering, the process of choice for these three behaviours was surprisingly quick and easy. There are two potential explanations for this behaviour: typicality and connectivity. Strong charity brands leading their sector become an automatic choice, underpinned by first choice brand effect theory (Hubert & Kenning, 2008). For these brands, awareness and understanding has built up over time generating credibility and embodiment of the generic category goal, for example supporting underprivileged people overseas or protecting wildlife from extinction. Michel and Rieunier (2012) refer to this as typicality, where an organisation is perceived as representative of the sector. The more representative the perception, the higher the intention to donate time or money (Mitchell & Clark, 2020b). For charities synonymous with a particular type of work, the implied effect is one of automatic choice (Le Roux et al., 2016). Thought-provoking support for this thesis comes from a different field; Barwise and Meehan (2004) argue brands win consumers through being 'simply better' at delivering the generic category benefits. This effect is further strengthened through the positive reputational benefits of high awareness. The more the volunteer has heard of the charity, the more important they perceive it to be (McQuail, 1985; Zajonc, 1968). The volunteers are, in effect, 'leader-lovers'. Therefore, despite the personal cost in terms of time commitment, for some decision-makers the choice of brand is automatic. Given the importance of brand saliency in consumer choice, there is a significant prize for being category leader: being top-of-mind when the category is being considered, enabling an automatic choice rather than a considered choice amongst alternatives.

Secondly, for brands framed by a specific cause, the brand and/or cause may exhibit close personal connectivity to the decision-maker (Mogilner & Aaker, 2009). Volunteer time is freely given in return for help received in the past, either directly to themselves or their wider family and friendship group, or as a 'down-payment' for help anticipated in the future. In this case the decision-making behaviour is also automatic, made without consideration amongst a competitive set, and is prevalent amongst supporters of specific health charities such as Parkinsons UK[8] or Rett UK.[9]

Therefore, two patterns of decision-making have been identified through this research – the *automatic choice* of cause leaders and personally relevant brands as well as the *explicit search* by skill acquisition seekers and novices. In addition, within the nonprofit sector there are a plethora of charity brands that fall outside these two cases and are *considered choices*, based on personal exposure and experience of the brand across a combination of touchpoints. The type of *considered choice* these volunteers make will depend on whether they are maximisers or satisfiers (Iyengar & Lepper, 2000), particularly to avoid the negative effects of having too much choice. For example, Carroll (2014) found evidence for the 'too much choice effect' – the greater the number of options looked at on a volunteering website, such as Volunteering England, the more likely the decision was deferred. Extensive search was found to be problematic as people did not to go back to deferred decisions so the opportunity for attracting a volunteer was lost (Carroll, 2014).

Building on the three volunteer behavioural segments (automatic, explicit search and considered) identified through this research, and drawing on decision-making theory (Iyengar & Lepper, 2000; Mogilner et al., 2008), six volunteer typologies can be developed, shown in Table 3.3. Volunteers who choose the sector leader (leader-lover) or have a personal connection will make an automatic choice.

TABLE 3.3 Re-categorising Nonprofit Brands Through Volunteer Decision-making Process

Volunteer decision-making process	Description	Volunteer typologies
Automatic choice	Despite the significant investment of time required for regular volunteering, the choice of organisation is made quickly and easily based on prior knowledge or personal connection.	Leader-lover Personally connected
Explicit search	Conscious search of NPB options available due to lack of prior knowledge.	Novice Role-seeker
Considered choice	Implicit knowledge of brand and alternatives is evoked at the point of decision-making and compared to personal need and local availability.	Maximiser Satisficer

Volunteers who are novices to the nonprofit context or looking for a particular role/number of volunteering hours make a choice after an explicit search of options. The remaining volunteers make a considered choice from a competitive set list, the length of which varies depending on whether they are maximisers or satisficers in their decision-making style.

The ultimate goal for charities is for potential new volunteers to select their brand automatically. Strengthening the pathways, including through demonstrating typicality and category leadership or framing through personal connections, will enable that automatic choice. Therefore, this chapter extends beyond traditional theories of rational choice, based on evaluation within a competitive set, to contribute six typologies of volunteers categorised by decision-making behaviour.

So what? Implications for practice

Concepts of marketing, brand and competition sit uneasily in charity practice, jarring with discussion of mission, collaboration and altruism. However, the tightening of charity funding, increasing calls on potential volunteers' time and relentless proliferation of charity organisations are now the reality of this sector. Given the natural churn in volunteering, strengthening the efficacy of volunteer recruitment is fundamental to mission sustainability. There are direct and significant consequences for growth and profitability if service-delivery resources are not attracted to their specific organisation.

The challenge is not to understand why people volunteer but why they would choose their brand instead of another. This has important implications for charity marketing strategy. In particular, it requires a redefinition of competitiveness set from the volunteer perspective to understand the alternatives considered prior to selection of one organisation. Potentially, this includes charities with similar missions, those that are better known or informal local community opportunities. The implication for charity practice is a need to recalibrate the brand positioning to ensure it resonates effectively with volunteer motivators for choice. Understanding the relationship between their personal needs, the type of volunteering role and the importance of cause vs brand will strengthen the effective use of scarce marketing resources.

Therefore, this chapter calls for practitioner focus to move away from application of the for-profit models of B2B and B2C towards a context-relevant B2V approach: to understand how and why volunteers make choices *between* nonprofit businesses. Through adopting a B2V mindset internally, the charity not only recognises the importance of volunteers as a fundamental enabler to achieving the mission, but also considers the distinct characteristics of the nonprofit sector within which they operate. This involves mapping how volunteers find out about the organisation, what level of knowledge they have, and how they made the decision.

Four dominant patterns of behaviour for volunteer choice of charity were identified through research. Only one involved search and choice from amongst a competitive set. Knowledge of charities has been found to build over time to enable instinctive and automatic decision-making behaviour at the moment of volunteer choice. Automatic decision-making in response to a charity-specific trigger is exhibited where there is strong brand knowledge and/or emotional connection to the cause or brand. For a sector where discussion about brand still sits uneasily for some, the chapter also contributes to theory though identifying the role of brand in volunteer choice. The brand acts as shorthand for the bundle of tangible and intangible attributes, enabling cut through at the point of decision-making.

The data identified that the decision-makers had gathered brand knowledge from a variety of touchpoints over time. At the moment of choice, the volunteer either sought out the charity with strong personal meaning for them or responded to a charity-specific trigger such as seeing a poster or hearing about them. The final behaviour type identified was decision-making based on simply being asked. The novices and role seekers lack knowledge about the brand so have to explicitly search for it. For the others, despite the significant commitment being made, a rapid decision can be made as it accesses the body of brand knowledge already stored in their subconscious. At the point of decision-making about the charity with which to volunteer, that knowledge becomes relevant. The brand behaviour segments (Table 3.2), and volunteer typologies (Table 3.3) present an alternative to the life-stage approach to recruitment. They enable charities to consider their current brand strength against their volunteer recruitment needs. In particular, the research demonstrates the importance of building brand awareness over time through a variety of touchpoints.

Considering the B2V approach and framing the marketing challenge of recruitment through the lens of the individual volunteer carries significant implications for the communication frame around the brand. For each charity, understanding the relationship between the needs met through volunteering with them, level of prior brand engagement and the behaviour involved in making the volunteering choice can be used directly to understand current and potential volunteer behaviour, identifying where future opportunities lie. For example, if current volunteers talk about the moment of serendipity, commonly found in the recent research, then low-cost communication techniques such as local posters and leaflets can be just the trigger that the potential volunteer is looking for. Likewise, understanding the different ways that people found out about the charity brand, over time, and then plotting the information onto the charity brand touchpoint map will support charities in identifying where their marketing budgets are visible and effective.

Chapter discussion questions

1. How has Parkrun[10] created an unwritten expectation of volunteering one in ten times you run in whatever role is needed?
2. In a post-lockdown world, what is the future for online volunteering such as through UNV[11] or Catchafire?[12]
3. What will be the lasting legacy of the local support groups[13] that emerged rapidly to support the vulnerable during the Covid pandemic?

Notes

1 Use of italics indicates a theme identified in the research.
2 www.royalvoluntaryservice.org.uk
3 www.christianaid.org.uk
4 Parents teachers association, attached to a school to raise funds.
5 www.cruk.org
6 www.oxfam.org
7 www.dofe.org
8 www.parkinsons.org.uk
9 www.rettuk.org
10 www.parkrun.org.uk
11 www.onlinevolunteering.org
12 www.catchafire.org
13 e.g. www.covidmutualaid.org

References

Aaker, D.A. (2003). The power of the branded differentiator. *MIT Sloan Management Review*, 45, 83–87.

Andreasen, A. (1994). Social marketing: Its definition and domain. *Journal of Public Policy & Marketing*, 13(1), 108–114.

Ashforth, B.E., Harrison, S.H. & Corley, K.G. (2008). Identification in organizations: An examination of four fundamental questions. *Journal of Management*, 34, 325–374.

Bagozzi, R.P. & Pieters, R. (1998). Goal-directed emotions. *Cognition & Emotion*, 12, 1–26.

Barwise, P. & Meehan, S. (2004). Don't be unique, be better. *MIT Sloan Management Review*, 45, 23–26.

Baxendale, S., Macdonald, E.K. & Wilson, H.N. (2015). The impact of different touchpoints on brand consideration. *Journal of Retailing*, 91, 235–253.

Blau, P.M. (1964). *Exchange and Power in Social Life*. Transaction Publishers.

Brodie, E., Hughes, T., Jochum, V., Miller, S., Ockenden, N. & Warburton, D. (2011). *Pathways through Participation: What Creates and Sustains Active Citizenship*. Institute of Volunteering Research/NCVO.

Carroll, L. (2014). *The Effect of Choice Set Size and Other Choice Architectures on Decisions to Volunteer*. PhD thesis, Plymouth University.

Cialdini, R.B., Schaller, M., Houlihan, D., Arps, K., Fultz, J. & Beaman, A.L. (1987). Empathy-based helping: Is it selflessly or selfishly motivated? *Journal of Personality and Social Psychology*, 52, 749.

Clark, D. (2021). Charities with the most volunteers in England And Wales 2021. Available at www.statista.com/statistics/283446/united-kingdom-uk-charities-with-most-volunteers/ (accessed 18 August 2021).

Clary, E.G., Ridge, R.D., Stukas, A.A., Snyder, M., Copeland, J., Haugen, J. & Miene, P. (1998). Understanding and assessing the motivations of volunteers: A functional approach. *Journal of Personality & Social Psychology*, 74, 1516–1530.

Clifford, D. (2017). Charitable organisations, the Great Recession and the age of austerity: Longitudinal evidence for England and Wales. *Journal of Social Policy*, 46, 1–30.

Erdem, T. & Swait, J. (2004). Brand credibility, brand consideration, and choice. *Journal of Consumer Research*, 31, 191–198.

Exley, C.L. (2019). Using charity performance metrics as an excuse not to give. *Management Science*, 66(2). doi:10.1287/mnsc.2018.3268.

Faulkner, M. & Romanuk, J. (2019). Supporters' perceptions of benefits delivered by different charity activities. *Journal of Nonprofit & Public Sector Marketing*, 31, 20–41.

Frijda, N.H. (1987). Emotion, cognitive structure, and action tendency. *Cognition and Emotion*, 1, 115–143.

He, H., Li, Y. & Harris, L. (2012). Social identity perspective on brand loyalty. *Journal of Business Research*, 65, 648–657.

Henke, L. & Fontenot, G. (2009). Why give to charity? How motivations for giving predict type of causes supported. *Allied Academies International Conference: Proceedings of the Academy of Marketing Studies (AMS)*, 14, 16.

Ho, M. & O'Donohoe, S. (2014). Volunteer stereotypes, stigma, and relational identity projects. *European Journal of Marketing*, 48, 854–877.

Hoyer, W.D., Macinnis, D.J. & Pieters, R. (2012). *Consumer Behaviour*. South-Western Cengage Learning.

Hubert, M. & Kenning, P. (2008). A current overview of consumer neuroscience. *Journal of Consumer Behaviour*, 7, 272–292.

Hustinix, L. (2010). I quit, therefore I am? Volunteer turnover and the politics of self-actualization. *Nonprofit and Voluntary Sector Quarterly*, 39, 236–255.

Iyengar, S.S. & Lepper, M.R. (2000). When choice is demotivating: Can one desire too much of a good thing? *Journal of Personality and Social Psychology*, 79, 995.

Janakiraman, R. & Niraj, R. (2011). The impact of geographic proximity on what to buy, how to buy, and where to buy: Evidence from high-tech durable goods market. *Decision Sciences*, 42, 889–919.

Kim, B.J., Kim, M.H. & Lee, J. (2019). Congruence matters: Volunteer motivation, value internalization, and retention. *Journal of Organizational Psychology*. doi:10.5465/AMBPP.2019.11234abstract.

Kylander, N. & Stone, C. (2012). The role of brand in the nonprofit sector. *Stanford Social Innovation Review*, 10, 35–41.

Le Roux, A., Thébault, M., Roy, Y. & Bobrie, F. (2016). Brand typicality impact on brand imitations evaluation and categorization. *Journal of Product & Brand Management*, 25, 600–612.

McQuail, D. (1985). Sociology of mass communication. *Annual Review of Sociology*, 11, 93–111.

Merrilees, B. (2016). Interactive brand experience pathways to customer-brand engagement and value co-creation. *Journal of Product & Brand Management*, 25, 402–408.

Michaelidou, N., Micevski, M. & Cadogan, J.W. (2015). An evaluation of nonprofit brand image: Towards a better conceptualization and measurement. *Journal of Business Research*, 68, 1657–1666.

Michel, G. & Rieunier, S. (2012). Nonprofit brand image and typicality influences on charitable giving. *Journal of Business Research*, 65, 701–707.

Mitchell, S.-L. & Clark, M. (2020a). Rethinking non-profit brands through a volunteer lens: Time for B2V. *Journal of Marketing Management*, 37(5–6), 464–487.

Mitchell, S.-L. & Clark, M. (2020b). Telling a different story: How nonprofit organizations reveal strategic purpose through storytelling. *Psychology and Marketing*, 38, 142–158.

Mitchell, S.-L. & Clark, M. (2020c). Volunteer choice of nonprofit organisation: An integrated framework. *European Journal of Marketing* 55, 63–94.

Mogilner, C. & Aaker, J. (2009). 'The time vs. money effect': Shifting product attitudes and decisions through personal connection. *Journal of Consumer Research*, 36, 277–291.

Mogilner, C., Rudnick, T. & Iyengar, S.S. (2008). The mere categorization effect: How the presence of categories increases choosers' perceptions of assortment variety and outcome satisfaction. *Journal of Consumer Research*, 35, 202–215.

Piliavin, J.A. & Hong-Wen, C. (1990). Altruism: A review of recent theory and research. *Annual Review of Sociology*, 16, 27–65.

Randle, M., Leisch, F. & Dolnicar, S. (2013). Competition or collaboration and quest: The effect of non-profit brand image on volunteer recruitment strategy. *Journal of Brand Management*, 20, 689–704.

Rundle-Thiele, S. & Bennett, R. (2001). A brand for all seasons? A discussion of brand loyalty approaches and their applicability for different markets. *Journal of Product & Brand Management*, 10(1), 25–37.

Sargeant, A., Hudson, J. & West, D.C. (2008). Conceptualizing brand values in the charity sector: The relationship between sector, cause and organization. *Service Industries Journal*, 28, 615–632.

Shah, D., Kumar, V. & Zhao, Y. (2015). Diagnosing brand performance: Accounting for the dynamic impact of product availability with aggregate data. *Journal of Marketing Research*, 52, 147–165.

Stride, H. & Lee, S. (2007). No logo? No way. Branding in the non-profit sector. *Journal of Marketing Management*, 23, 107–122.

Tapp, A. (1996). Charity brands: A qualitative study of current practice. *International Journal of Nonprofit and Voluntary Sector Marketing*, 1, 327–336.

Van Ingen, E. & Wilson, J. (2016). I volunteer, therefore I am? Factors affecting volunteer role identity. *Nonprofit and Voluntary Sector Quarterly*, 46, 29–46.

Venable, B.T., Rose, G.M., Bush, V.D. & Gilbert, F.W. (2005). The role of brand personality in charitable giving: An assessment and validation. *Journal of the Academy of Marketing Science*, 33, 295–312.

White, K.M., Poulsen, B.E. & Hyde, M.K. (2016). Identity and personality influences on donating money, time, and blood. *Nonprofit and Voluntary Sector Quarterly*, 46, 372–394.

Whittich, B. (2000). *The Care and Feeding of Volunteers*. Knowledge Transfer Publishing.

Wilson, J. & Musick, M. (1997). Who cares? Toward an integrated theory of volunteer work. *American Sociological Review*, 62, 694–713.

Wymer Jr, W.W. & Samu, S. (2002). Volunteer service as symbolic consumption: Gender and occupational differences in volunteering. *Journal of Marketing Management*, 18, 971–989.

Zajonc, R.B. (1968). Attitudinal effects of mere exposure. *Journal of Personality and Social Psychology*, 9, 1–27.

4

DON'T ASK, DON'T GET

The ethics of fundraising

Ian MacQuillin

The gap between applied and normative ethics in fundraising

Some years ago, a fundraiser was offered a donation from an unusual source – a local swingers club, which wanted to donate the proceeds of their next 'event' to her charity, a small, local organisation for children with a learning disability.[1]

Should she accept this offer? What factors should she consider in deciding whether to accept or refuse this gift? What current ethical theory is available that would guide her ethical decision making?

The answer to this last question is 'very little'.

Whereas marketing has a sizeable literature on ethics – one five-volume set (Smith & Murphy, 2012) contains reprints of 90 papers published in academic journals – fundraising by contrast has an 'ethics gap', having just a handful of academic papers that address fundraising ethics (MacQuillin, 2016a, p. 8). There are only two single author books dedicated to the topic, both now 20-plus years old (Anderson, 1996; Fischer, 2000), and two books of essays about fundraising ethics (Elliot, 1995; Pettey, 2008, 2013).

Both Anderson's and Fischer's are books on applied ethics. But the profession has very little in the way of normative ethics that underpins the attempt to apply ethics in practice, which is a further facet of fundraising's ethics gap.

It's fair to say that the fundraising profession's academic branch has never really made a concerted effort to develop a bespoke normative theory of fundraising ethics.

When the fundraising profession itself comes to tackle fundraising ethics – through official guidance from the likes of the Association of Fundraising Professionals in the USA or the Chartered Institute of Fundraising in the UK, or book chapters, collected essays, blogs or magazine articles – this is almost always in the realm of applied ethics, but with very little recourse to normative theory. For example, the first edition of *Ethical Fundraising: A Guide for Nonprofit Board and*

DOI: 10.4324/9781003134169-7

Fundraisers [2] (Pettey, 2008) considers ethical questions such as 'the appearance of impropriety', 'rights of donors', 'tainted money' (of course) and 'ethical relationships between grantees and funders'. It is described as providing 'practical and helpful guidance for all fundraising and nonprofit professionals' (ibid., p. xvi). But the words 'consequentialism' and 'deontology' do not feature once throughout the book's 330 pages, indicating that little of this practical and helpful guidance is grounded in normative theory.

The range of ethical issues explored by practitioners can also be relatively narrow, with two issues in particular commanding attention.

The first of these is commission-based payment – accepting a percentage of money raised as remuneration (e.g. Anderson, 1996, pp. 65–68; Boris & Odendahl, 1990, p. 1999) – which is actually prohibited by most codes of practice (Association of Fundraising Professionals, 1992/2016); while Fischer (2000, pp. 20–29) uses this issue as the basis for an ethical decision-making model.

The second favoured topic is 'tainted money' – donations from an ethically dubious source or a source that conflicts with a charity's mission (e.g. Harrison, 2001; Payton, 1987; Tempel, 2008; and professional guidance, such as the Chartered Institute of Fundraising, 2018).[3]

So what we mainly have in the domain of fundraising ethics is guidance on tackling ethical dilemmas – applied ethics. Much of that is found in the various codes of conduct and practice that have been developed by many national fundraising associations.

There is a lot of cross over and a lot of shared ideas between these codes (Rosen, 2005, p. 177), particularly in English-speaking countries. Here are a few examples of ideas that are common to many:

- Don't engage in activities that bring the profession into disrepute.
- Fundraisers will tell the truth and not exaggerate.
- Donations will be used in accordance with donors' intentions.
- Ensure all solicitation and communication materials are accurate and reflect the organisation's mission and use of solicited funds.
- Give donors the opportunity to remove their names from marketing lists.

Codes of practice and standards create the skeleton of fundraising's professional ethics. If the code prohibits a particular action, then to perform that action would be unethical. But not all professional ethics can be found in, nor reduced to, a code or practice. Whereas professional standards set strict liability offences, codes of ethics are seen as a set of aspirational codes of principles that signatories strive to achieve (Lloyd & de las Casas, 2006).

Professional ethics is therefore more concerned with the values that ought to guide professional practice, and be used to interpret the grey areas of the code, or areas that are not explicitly covered by the code (MacQuillin et al., 2019, p. 11).

For example, the UK code of practice stipulates that fundraisers must not subject people to 'undue' pressure to make a donation (Fundraising Regulator, n.d., s1.2.1).

The code, however, does not define 'undue pressure', nor in what contexts and situations it would apply – are the conditions for undue pressure the same for a pensioner receiving a telephone call asking her to increase her direct debit as for a wealthy philanthropist who has made his millions in a competitive field of business?

If 'undue' pressure is not permitted, this strongly implies that some pressure is 'due', or permissible. And to complicate matters, the Fundraising Regulator's code of practice further prohibits fundraisers from making 'unreasonable intrusions' into a person's privacy or engaging in fundraising that is 'unreasonably persistent' (s1.2.1). This implies that some intrusion into a person's privacy is 'reasonable', as is some level of persistence. What level of pressure, persistence and intrusion by fundraisers is permissible and in what contexts is something that only ethics can settle; it cannot be proscribed or prescribed by a code of practice/standards.

The Fundraising Regulator's code also contains further stipulations that also become ethical requirements, i.e. it is unethical to:

- Take advantage of mistakes made by the donor (s1.3.3).
- Exaggerate facts about beneficiaries (s1.3.1).
- Try to get someone to switch a donation from another charity (s1.1.4).
- Not act in the best interest of the charity when deciding to refuse a gift (s2.1.3).
- Include a gift in DM that is aimed at generating a donation based on 'financial guilt'[4] (s9.3.3).

These are statements about applied ethics. But what the code cannot tell us is why it is, or should be, unethical to try to get someone to switch their donation to a different charity (perhaps the charity you are trying to get them to switch to is both more effective and more efficient), or why it should be unethical to enter into a corporate partnership where there are conflicts of interest (perhaps working with a corporate partner is the best way to resolve the conflict). Answering these questions is the scope of normative ethics.

Here are a few further potentially grey areas of applied fundraising ethics that are unanswered or ambiguously answered in the codes:

- Is it acceptable for people to feel guilty (not just financial guilt) – either as an intentional tactic of the fundraiser or simply as a result of having been asked? Why shouldn't it be ethically acceptable to use guilt as an emotion when fundraisers regularly use other emotions such as empathy, anger, joy and pity?
- Is it acceptable to spend donors' money on fundraising, and if so, how much?
- Are donors allowed to derive benefits from their giving or should all charitable giving be purely 'altruistic', and if so, should fundraisers offer such 'benefits'?
- Do fundraisers have a right or a duty to approach people for a donation?
- Do the public have a right not to be asked for donations?
- How transparent about the costs and mechanisms of fundraising should charities be?
- Do people have a 'duty' to give to charity and if so, how can fundraisers help people discharge that duty?

How do we attempt to answer these questions and navigate grey areas?

There are some ethical decision-making frameworks provided in the practitioner and pracademic literature (Anderson, 1996, pp. 73–81; Fischer, 2000, pp. 20–29; Levy, 2008, pp. 174–176; Marion, 1994). These are informed to a large extent by the virtues an ethical fundraiser ought to have, such as integrity, trustworthiness, honesty. This undoubtedly provides some helpful guidance. But how precisely does being honest, trustworthy and having integrity help a fundraiser navigate an ethical dilemma such as deciding how much persistence in asking is 'reasonable' or whether to accept money from a sex club?

To better help with those dilemmas, we need a theory (or theories) of normative fundraising ethics that is specifically tailored to help us navigate such questions.

As we have already seen, one book on applied fundraising ethics (Pettey, 2008) doesn't contain a single mention of two major strands of normative ethics – consequentialism and deontology – though it is informed by virtue ethics.

This lack of normative ethical theory underpinning fundraising ethics is exhibited in the CIoF guidance on acceptance and refusal of donations (Chartered Institute of Fundraising, 2018). This states that while an organisation's 'ethics and values will be important in reaching the decision [whether to refuse a gift from a tainted source], these cannot be a decisive factor'. It then goes on to say that the charity would need to show that had they accepted the gift, this would have been detrimental to achieving its purposes, for example, by leading other funders to withdraw their support (ibid., p. 10).

But the use of the word 'ethics' in the same breath as 'values' suggests a deontological conception of fundraising ethics, ignoring the fact that whether accepting the donation leads to bad outcomes is as much a matter of ethics (consequentialist ethics) as whether accepting it conflicts with the charity's values.

Are such theories – theories that would help the fundraiser we encountered at the start of this chapter decide whether to accept a donation from a sex club – to be found?

Normative fundraising ethics

Before we look for normative theories of fundraising ethics in the literature, it serves us to take a whistle-stop introduction to the field of ethics for those who may be unfamiliar with some of its key concepts.

Normative ethics is concerned with the content of moral judgements, and the criteria for what is right or wrong. Normative ethical theories attempt to provide a general theory of how we ought to live. There are three major approaches to normative ethics: consequentialism, deontology and virtue ethics, though for space reasons, we're only considering the first two in relation to fundraising ethics.

Consequentialism (sometimes called teleology) dictates that we are morally obliged to act in a way that produces the best consequences (hence the name). Perhaps the best-known consequentialist theory is utilitarianism.

In contrast to consequentialism is deontology – or 'duty-based ethics'. Deontological ethics requires us to carry out an act because it is the 'right thing to do' because it conforms to a moral norm, irrespective of the consequences: what is right takes precedence over what is good (Alexander & Moore, 2012).

Applied ethics is the application of our preferred normative theory (or theories) to specific issues, such as racial equality or animal rights, telling us the right things we should do, and the wrong things we should refrain from doing.

In a nutshell, applied ethics, particularly in the context of a code of standards or conduct, tells you *what* you ought (or ought not) do; normative ethics helps you understand *why* you ought (or ought not) do it, thus informing the kinds of factors that should be covered by the applied ethics.

And of course, one of the specific issues that normative ethics can be applied to is fundraising. So, has it been?

The answer is not really. There has been little scholarship of this matter within academy, while practitioner literature has focused on applied ethics in relation to specific ethical challenges such as commission-based payment and 'tainted money'. Few people have set out to construct a bespoke theory of professional ethics specially designed to help navigate the types of ethical dilemmas encountered by fundraising practitioners. But it is possible to infer and draw out some normative ideas from the literature, three of which are presented here:[5]

- Protection of public trust – Trustism.
- Servicing the donor's needs, wants and aspirations – Donorcentrism.
- Servicing Philanthropy.

Trustism

Building and maintaining trust has been a core theme in normative fundraising ethics, particularly trust between donors and fundraisers and the institutions they represent (e.g. Elliot & Gert, 1995); Anderson (1996, p. 75), says that building trust is a 'fundamental principle [that] underscores the centrality of ethical relationships to fundraising'.

Writing in 1994, fundraising consultant and board member of the AFP Marianne Briscoe argued that the first stakeholder of any ethical dilemma in fundraising should be the 'endeavour of philanthropy', which is contingent on public trust (Briscoe, 1994, p. 110).

And fundraising pracademic Michael Rosen argues that the purpose of the codes is to protect public trust in fundraising: 'One way in which organizations can enhance the public trust is to maintain the highest ethical standards and to communicate this commitment to donors and prospective donors' (Rosen, 2005, p. 177).

As a normative theory of fundraising ethics, 'Trustism' states:

> Fundraising is ethical when it promotes, sustains, protects or maintains public/donor trust in fundraising, and unethical when it damages these things.

This makes Trustism a consequentialist theory since ethical actions are based on consequences to public trust.

Many of the provisions contained in various codes of practice are likely included to protect and maintain public trust in fundraising.

The reason maintaining trust is so important – from a consequentialist perspective – is that trust in the nonprofit sector is a determinant of whether people will give to charity: people lacking trust in the sector are significantly less likely to be donors (Sargeant & Lee, 2002a), and trust is a main driver of donor commitment (Sargeant & Lee, 2002b), which in turn is a major predictor of donor lifetime value (Sargeant & Lee, 2004).

Donorcentrism

Donorcentrism is a collection of ideas that share the theme of putting the donor at the 'heart' of charity communications (e.g. Orland, 2011; Pegram, 2016) or at the 'centre of fundraising strategies' (Etherington et al., 2015, p. 63), As one fundraiser puts it (MacQuillin, 2016b, p. 15):

> Essentially, this is about placing the donor, or prospective supporter, at the heart of all your activities; planning and executing your fundraising according to what is most likely to strengthen your relationship with them, according to their preferences, rather than what you, the fundraiser, may simply assume will be most beneficial for your charity.

Donorcentrism has largely grown out of professional practice – although the term 'donor-centred' had been used previously (e.g. Pitman, 2002; Savage, 2000) it was popularised by American consultant Penelope Burk in her book in 2003) – but had never been fully articulated into an ethical theory. However it is a candidate for a normative ethical theory, which has its intellectual roots in the burst of interest in ethics in the United States in the early- to mid-1990s – for example, 'an ethical belief in the importance of the donor' that 'recognis[es] that the donor comes first... always putting the donor first in regard to when to ask, how to ask and what to ask for' (Geever, 1994, p. 70). In the US in the 1990s, the standards of the National Committee on Planned Giving placed the welfare of the donor above every other interest (Anderson, 1996, p. 59).

British fundraising thought leader Ken Burnett developed the closely-related idea of 'relationship fundraising' in the early 1990s, which he defines as (2002, p. 38):

> An approach to the marketing of a cause that centres on the unique and special relationship between a nonprofit and each supporter. Its overriding consideration is to care for and develop that bond and to do nothing that might damage or jeopardize it. Every activity is therefore geared toward making sure donors know they are important, valued, and considered, which has the effect of maximizing funds per donor in the long term.

It is not totally apparent whether Donorcentrism is a consequentialist or deontological theory. Burnett's conceptualisation would suggest that – as it relates to relationship fundraising – it is a consequentialist best practice doctrine: understanding the needs and motives of their donors and providing them great customer service that makes them feel great about their giving will result in those donors being more committed to, and continuing to give – and give more – to your cause.

However, there is a tension in both the philosophy and practice of donor-centred ideas. Donorcentrist ethics begin as a consequentialist idea that being donor-centred will lead to better and more sustainable relationships with donors, but shades into deontology – that you ought to put the donor at the heart of what you do because that is right in and of itself. Burnett says fundraisers must do 'nothing to damage the bond'. That creates an ethical imperative, but is it an ethical imperative to protect income or to do right by the donor?

And recall that Geever talks about the 'ethical belief' in the importance of the donor, whose interests must 'always' come first. And in 2016, the UK's Direct Marketing Association claimed that donors are the 'most important people in the entire charity process'[6] (Direct Marketing Association, 2016).

There are, therefore, two possible alternatives for Donorcentric ethics, one consequentialist and the other deontological.

Under a consequentialist Donorcentric approach to fundraising ethics, fundraising is ethical when it:

> Gives priority to the donor's wants, needs, desires and wishes provided that this maximises sustainable income for the nonprofit.

Under a deontological Donorcentric approach to fundraising ethics, fundraising is ethical if it:

> Gives priority to the donor's wants, needs, desires and wishes.

Many provisions in codes of practice appear to be grounded in Donorcentrist ethics.

Service of Philanthropy

Philanthropy has been described as a 'social relationship between donors and recipient [organisation]' (Ostrander, 2007, p. 356; Ostrander & Schervish, 1990, p. 74), in which giving is a voluntary act. Fundraising is 'in service to that relationship and act' (Elliot & Gert, 1995, p. 35). Another way of saying this is that fundraising is the 'servant of philanthropy'. This is the term popularised by acknowledged US fundraising 'guru' Hank Rosso, who in 1991 wrote that: 'Fundraising is justified when it is used as a responsible invitation guiding contributors to make the kind of gift that will meet their own special needs and add greater meaning to their lives' (Tempel, 2003, p. 4).

This is a clear normative statement about how fundraising ought to be practised and is consequentialist because it specifies that the right course of action for a fundraiser is the one that results in consequences that meet the donors' needs and bring meaning to them. If fundraising is justified when it does this, then it follows that it is not justified if it does not do this. And although Rosso's statement doesn't explicitly create an ethical requirement to bring meaning to donors' philanthropy, it very strongly implies one.

Under Service of Philanthropy ethics:

> Fundraising is ethical when it brings meaning to a donor's philanthropy.

It is a moot point if fundraising is unethical when it does not bring meaning to a donor's philanthropy. But it implies it is. For example, it is argued that a fundraiser should refuse a gift if they feel that accepting it would not give the donor sufficient meaning, and then direct the donor to a charity they think would (Gunderman, 2010, pp. 591–592). Accepting the gift would therefore be unethical.

Rosso's notion that fundraising is the servant of philanthropy has widespread buy-in among practitioners and thought-leaders in fundraising (e.g. Harris, 2020; Sargeant, 2014) and is regularly cited by fundraising practitioners (e.g. Worth, 2016, pp. 25, 27).

Rights-Balancing Fundraising Ethics

It's notable that charity beneficiaries are largely absent from the thinking and theorising in the literature on fundraising ethics. Once you are aware of their absence, it's quite striking and not a little shocking.

In overlooking or ignoring the interests of beneficiaries, ethical theorising has failed to formally state that fundraisers have any ethical duties to beneficiaries – specifically to ensure the organisation they work for has sufficient funds to provide services for beneficiaries. Elliott and Gert (1995) state that the primary responsibility of fundraisers is to raise money, and failing to do this may be a moral/ethical failure (ibid.) – it is certainly a professional failure. But Elliot and Gert assign this moral responsibility to the organisations that fundraisers work for (ibid., p. 34). Yet the key metric of net income is the only one that never seems to improve, and recall that failing in this task – raising money – may be a moral and ethical failure (Elliot & Gert, 1995, pp. 33–34).

Rights-Balancing Fundraising Ethics (MacQuillin, 2016a; MacQuillin & Sargeant, 2019) aims to rectify that by arguing that fundraisers have duties to the donors and their beneficiaries (their principal duty being to ensure an organisation has sufficient voluntary income to provide services the beneficiaries need) and fundraising is ethical when these duties are in balance.

So under Rights-Balancing Fundraising Ethics:

> Fundraising is ethical when it balances the duty of fundraisers to ask for support (on behalf of their beneficiaries), with the relevant rights of donors, such that a mutually beneficial outcome is achieved and neither stakeholder is significantly harmed.

One of the rights of donors is not to be subject to undue pressure (a codified right in the UK and arguably an ethical requirement in countries where it is not specifically proscribed). Trustist and Donorcentrist might consider what is undue pressure entirely from the perspective of the donor (which is what the Fundraising Regulator tried to do in defining 'undue pressure' – see Caffery, 2017; MacQuillin & Sargeant, 2019, pp. 243–245), because the beneficiary is not a stakeholder to these ethical theories.

However, Rights-Balancing Fundraising Ethics weighs the harm done to donors by using 'pressure' (or guilt, or 'unreasonable persistence') against the potential harm done to beneficiaries if the ask is not made, and aims to strike a balance. For example, the harm done to donors by being slightly more persistent might be considerably outweighed by the good done to beneficiaries as a result of that persistence. What is 'reasonable' therefore becomes contingent on the outcome this has on beneficiaries, not just on how it makes donors feel.

Elliott and Gert (1995, p. 34) say that fundraisers are morally required to raise money, 'but not at any costs'. However, they may be permitted to do so at 'some' cost; and Rights-Balancing Fundraising Ethics seeks to balance that cost against the good it can achieve.

Applying the normative theories

The whole point of developing normative theories is to make it easier to make better and more consistent ethical decisions in professional practice.

So let's take a look at a general hypothetical situation and examine the question 'Is it ethical to make people feel guilty in trying to solicit a donation from them?' through each of the normative lenses.

Trustism – No. Arguably making donors feel guilty would undermine public trust and jeopardise long-term income. Any practice – such as mail pack enclosures that elicit financial guilt or images designed to make people feel guilty at not responding – would be prohibited by the codes.

Donorcentrism (consequentialist) – No. Because it makes them feel bad, making people feel guilty, even unintentionally, is likely to lead to them giving less in the future or not giving at all. As with the Trustist lens, codes would include provisions to prevent this outcome.

Donorcentrism (deontological) – No. It is in donors' interests to feel great about their giving, not bad because they didn't give. It is simply wrong – on a point of moral principle – to try to make people feel guilty in search of a donation.

Service of Philanthropy – No! You can't guilt trip donors into a 'meaningful' donation.

Rights-Balancing – Possibly. All the previous lenses lead to a general rule that using guilt to fundraise would be unethical, either as a point of moral principle or because of harmful consequences (to public trust or the donor; harmful consequences to the beneficiary are not considered). But Rights-Balancing Fundraising Ethics would consider each case in context, weigh up potential harm to donors of using guilt against potential good to beneficiaries, while also balancing that against longer-term interests of public trust. For example, an appeal for an ongoing emergency that required urgent funds might use images and language that fundraisers might reasonably expect would make some people feel guilty if they did not give. But that temporary harm to some individual donors could be outweighed by raising the money to help people in urgent need.

Guilt can be conceived of as a form of pressure, and it is therefore the role of fundraising ethics to consider when application of this pressure is due (and thus ethical) or undue (and thus unethical). It seems very likely that, for the kinds of ethical dilemmas fundraisers would face in day-to-day practice, this is the kind of balancing act that is required.

But it would almost certainly be impractical to go back to the first principles of ethical theory and go through such a balancing act every time they encounter a professional ethical dilemma, which would be time-consuming and intellectually intensive. Might there be easier and quicker heuristics that lead us to an appropriately ethical solution?

In most practical ethical dilemmas in fundraising, the rule of thumb will probably be for fundraisers to do what they think the donor would want. This is the 'Donorcentric Rule of Thumb' (MacQuillin, 2019). Deploying this rule will prevent harm to the donor (such as feelings of guilt and other negative emotions), protect sustainable income (as Trustism and consequentialist Donorcentrism require) and maintain public trust (the person asked is not likely to complain on social media about being subjected to undue pressure). But potential harm to beneficiaries as a result of not asking for a donation from any particular individual is likely to be minimal, assuming there is any harm at all – it is, after all, just a single donation that has been forgone.

However, while rules of thumb may help fundraisers resolve ethical dilemmas on the ground in real time, they can only take us so far, and even though following this rule may solve a single instantiation of a particular ethical dilemma, this does not mean that each of these can be aggregated to devise ethical policy that can then be codified into a set of standards. We've already considered the hypothetical case of an emergency appeal, where harm to individuals, by being made to feel guilty, even though discouraged by the Donorcentric Rule of Thumb in each individual case, nonetheless goes ahead because the cumulative harm to all donors is perceived to be outweighed by the cumulative good to all beneficiaries. The actual harm that can be caused by taking Donorcentrist ethics into ethical and regulatory policy-making is explored in the section on the ethics of donor consent below.

A more sophisticated approach to shortcutting back-to-theory, first principles ethical decision-making is to consider the overarching types of ethical questions that might arise from problematic situations, and think about how to respond to categories of questions in advance, rather than waiting for specific ethical issues to blow up. This approach has been taken for legacy fundraising during the Coronavirus/Covid-19 pandemic (Routley et al., 2020) and will be expanded for more general ethical challenges in fundraising (Routley & Koshy, forthcoming).

The ultimate aim is to turn normative theories into applied ethical decision-making frameworks, and one such framework is used to help us resolve the dilemma with which we began this chapter – should a children's charity accept money from a sex club?

The children's charity and the swingers' club

The framework we will use is the one devised by the fundraising think tank Rogare. The first stage of this is to consider whether something is against the law or the code of practice. Consensual sex between multiple adults is not illegal and accepting a donation for this source is not prohibited by the code of practice. So the fundraiser could have accepted the donation there and then.

However, there were other matters to consider about which the code had nothing to say, and that is potential reputational harm to the charity. The ethical dilemma this charity therefore faced was: Should this donation be accepted if it leads to potential reputational issues for the charity?

The next stage of the framework is to decide on the normative ethical theory in which decision-making is to be grounded. This author believes it is always best to adopt the Rights–Balancing approach as this forces the decision-making process to consider multiple stakeholders, in particular the beneficiary. But some fundraisers may prefer only to consider the effects on public trust, or how it makes donors feel.

In this case, from a Trustist perspective, there was a serious potential risk of reputational damage from media articles that could associate 'deviant' (as the media would likely see it) sexual activity with the care of children with learning disabilities. From a Rights–Balancing perspective, would the good to beneficiaries outweigh any harm done by accepting a small donation to a small charity? Possibly – in fact, probably – not.

Following on from these deliberations at stages three and four of the framework, the decision the fundraiser at this charity took was to reject the donation (stage five) and go straight to implementation (stage eight). Bigger charities with more resources could do more theorising and testing of the decision (stage six) before revision (stage seven) or implementation (stage eight).

But what if, for the sake of argument, the donation had been £500,000? Does this change the ethical decision-making? It should definitely change the decision-making process, since one of the material factors used to make the decision at stage four has changed – the amount of money involved, and for a small charity, £500,000 could be transformative.

A possible solution in this case would be to accept the donation after a conducting a risk assessment, assuming this showed the charity could weather any reputational risks.

But how can something that was 'unethical' suddenly become more ethical just because more money is involved? Because the amount of money raised – which is the whole raison d'être of the fundraising profession – is always a material consideration in applied fundraising ethics: it is always relevant to ask whether the fundraiser has successfully discharged their duty to ask for support on behalf of their beneficiaries. Failure to raise sufficient money to help their beneficiaries is a practical and professional failure; and as stated above, it may also be a moral and ethical failure (Elliot & Gert, 1995, pp. 33–34).

Contemporary issues in fundraising ethics

Ethics of donor consent

Either side of the 2017 New Year, the Information Commissioner's Office – the UK's data protection regulator – announced a slew of interventions against charities over how they processed donors' data to assess how much they could give (MacQuillin et al., 2019, p. 48). The ICO interventions fed the febrile atmosphere created by the so-called 'fundraising crisis' of 2015 – when the media erroneously blamed the death of a pensioner on the amount of direct marketing fundraising she had received (ibid., pp. 55–57).

Combined with ignorance and fear of the forthcoming (in May 2018) EU General Data Protection Regulations (GDPR), this led many charities to make a policy decision that they would only contact their donors by mail if they had their consent to do so. However, such consent was not required by either GDPR or the then current legislation, the Data Protection Act, because both permit processing of data using so-called 'legitimate interest'.

But in asking for donors' consent, many charities lost contact with huge numbers of donors (who, having failed to respond to the request for consent, were deemed to have withheld it). This meant charities could no longer ask those donors for money. Anecdotal evidence suggests some smaller charities lost 90% of their donor bases, while bigger charities lost tens of millions of pounds, and some have since reversed their consent-only rule (Cooney, 2019).

One justification for taking the consent-only route was that this was the right thing to do for donors, because contacting them without their consent was just 'not right' (even though the law permitted charities to do so) (Radojev, 2016; RNLI, 2016). This is deontological Donorcentrism. This is saying that as a moral rule or principle, you should not ask a donor for money unless you have their prior consent to do so.

A different – consequentialist – justification is that going for consent delivers better outcomes for the charity. It builds better relationships, gives donors a better experience, and improves metrics such as return on investment, response rate, etc. (Stern, 2016). But the key metric of net income it seems is the only one that never improved, and recall that failing in this task may be a moral and ethical failure (Elliot & Gert, 1995, pp. 33–34).

In fact, some charities switched between both consequentialist and deontological justifications, depending on which audience they were addressing. One charity in particular would use the 'it's the right thing for our donors' moral principle when talking to the national media, but the 'it gets us better results' consequentialist justification when addressing the charity sector media.

This has so far considered individual charities that chose the consent route, leaving them open to criticism from a Rights-Balancing Fundraising Ethics perspective that it has got the ethical balance wrong – that the prevention of potential harm to donors does not outweigh the potential harm to beneficiaries of lost income.

However, self-regulation of the fundraising sector also took steps (which were never realised) to make donor consent a requirement for all charities (MacQuillin et al., 2019, p. 57).

This is a demonstration of the Donorcentric Rule of Thumb taken too far, from interactions with individual donors, to charity procedures, to regulatory requirements. Had this come to pass, the execution of fundraisers' duties in respect of certain donor privacy rights would not have been correctly balanced with their duty to ask for donations on behalf of their beneficiaries. It would not have been a mutually optimal outcome, and one group would have been potentially significantly harmed.

Donor dominance

Even though it was noted more than 30 years ago that the social relationship of philanthropy grants more power to donors than to the organisations they give to, a situation that results in philanthropy being 'donor-led' (Ostrander & Schervish, 1990, pp. 74–75), and that donor-led philanthropy can lead to donor-controlled philanthropy (Ostrander, 2007), the abuse that can come with such power has become an increasingly important issue in recent years.

The abuse of power by donors in their relationships with charities is called 'donor dominance' (Clohesy, 2003, p. 134). Donors can influence relationships with charities in inappropriate ways, from demanding benefits to which they are not entitled (Hill & MacQuillin, 2019), to trying to direct a nonprofit's mission in a direction that is of more importance or relevance to the donor (mission creep) (Clohesy, 2003), through to sexual harassment of fundraisers (Appleby, 2019; Bayley-Pratt, 2019; Hill & MacQuillin, 2019; LeClair, 2019a, 2019b; Upton, 2017). A survey by the *Chronicle of Philanthropy* and the AFP in the USA found that 25% of female fundraisers had experienced sexual harassment, often perpetrated by donors (Sandoval, 2018).

The potential for such abuse is even acknowledged by donors themselves (Greer & Kostoff, 2020, p. 149). Yet donors can desire types of relationships with fundraisers – for example, friendship rather than a purely professional connection – that create new ethical dilemmas for fundraisers (ibid., p. 121; MacQuillin, 2020b).

Ethically rebalancing donor–fundraiser relationships to remove not just abuses of donor dominance but the temptation for such abuse is a major challenge for Trustism, Donorcentrism and Rights-Balancing Fundraising Ethics. But scandals such as the Presidents Club in the UK (MacQuillin, 2018) and the case of Jeffrey Epstein's donations to MIT Labs in the USA (Hill, 2019) illustrate how fundraisers can allow the demands of donors to distort, subvert and bastardise their professional ethics (Hill, 2019; MacQuillin, 2018).

Power, privilege and the donorcentred narrative

The emergence of movements such as BLM and #MeToo have confronted the power and privilege that many people hold in many walks of society. In 2020, a new movement emerged in the USA – called community-centric fundraising (CCF) – that aims to do precisely this for philanthropy and fundraising.

Building on the concept of decolonising wealth (Villaneuva, 2018), CCF – which emerged from the writings of American nonprofit thought leader Vu Le in a series of blogs starting in 2015 (e.g. Le, 2017/2020) – believes fundraising and philanthropy need to be rebuilt according to ten principles that will ground both practices in racial and economic justice (Community-Centric Fundraising, 2020).

CCF argues that standard fundraising practice, by focusing on the needs and wants of donors, as both Donorcentrism and Service of Philanthropy require, panders to people who already hold too much power and reinforces attitudes of white saviourism, white ideology and donor dominance.

Rather than foregrounding the needs of the donor as an ethical stakeholder, CCF prioritises the needs of 'the community', as an entity, above the needs of donors and even individual charity missions. A formulation of CCF ethics would therefore be (MacQuillin, 2020a, p. 14):

> Fundraising is ethical when it prioritises and/or serves the needs of the community, and unethical when it does not.

CCF therefore represents a direct challenge to many of the core tenets of donor-centred fundraising. But it raises many ethical questions of its own (ibid., pp. 14–16). CCF has said fundraisers ought to decline donations if they feel those donations would better help a different part of the community. How a fundraiser should navigate such an ethical minefield – deciding which parts of the community deserve more support – has not yet been articulated.

Fundraising during the Coronavirus pandemic

The moral purpose of fundraising is to ask for money to fund services for beneficiaries (Elliott & Gert, 1995, pp. 33–34). During the Coronavirus/Covid-19 pandemic, which began in 2020, many people in charities (though not usually fundraisers) started to argue that continuing to fundraise during the pandemic would be unethical, distasteful or inappropriate (Smith et al., 2020). Two reasons commonly advanced to support such arguments were that while people were struggling financially, it would not be right to ask them to make voluntary donations to help others, and that only charities engaged in directly responding to the health emergency ought to continue fundraising (ibid.).

As we saw in the section on applying normative theories, Routley et al. (2020) considered the types of ethical objections to legacy fundraising during the pandemic – grouped into the categories of 'offence' and 'urgency' – and then considered how to respond with an ethical justification through the lenses of Trustism, Donorcentrism and Rights-Balancing. For example, using the Donorcentrism lens, they argue that continued fundraising could meet potential donors' psychological needs (ibid., pp. 11–12).

The argument that only Covid-fighting charities should carry on fundraising presupposes that all voluntary sector activity ought to be directed to combatting the pandemic. As the only activity that needs to be conducted by charities, this is the only activity that needs – and indeed, ought – to be funded. It is unethical for charities to expend resources on anything else. It is therefore unethical to ask for funding for anything else.

If, however, we accept that other causes need to carry on delivering – universities and arts institutions need to keep functioning (even if they are closed during the pandemic) and animals and the environment (built and natural) need to be protected – then charities need the resources to continue to do those things; they need a continued supply of money to do so and so fundraising has to continue. We therefore have to conclude that continuing to fundraise is ethical.

And that perhaps is the lesson to draw from this exploration of fundraising ethics. Research shows that most people don't give unless they are asked to do so by a fundraiser (usually a paid one) (Bekkers & Weipking, 2010, pp. 931–932). If you don't ask, you don't get, and asking is inherently ethical.

Chapter discussion questions

1. A key component of this chapter has been to stress that there has been very little consideration/development of normative fundraising ethics as a foundation for applied practical ethics; applied ethics is often based upon what the practitioner 'feels' is right, while few scholars devote resources to developing the field. What can be done to promote interest in the study and development of fundraising ethics within the academy, and how can fundraising practitioners be encouraged to engage with this process? At the same time, ethics often feels like an adjunct to fundraising textbooks and training courses. What needs to change to make ethics a central focus of fundraising training and education?
2. How can various normative theories or lenses of fundraising ethics be operationalised into ethical decision-making frameworks?
3. The issues of power and privilege and the decolonisation of fundraising represent an existential critique of the standard donor-centred narrative. How can donor-centred fundraising change to accommodate this critique, and is an accommodation even desirable from the community-centric fundraising perspective?

Notes

1 This is a genuine situation faced by a fundraiser. And if you don't know what swingers are, there's always Google.

2   The second edition of this book in 2013 changed the title to *Nonprofit Fundraising Strategy*, with a tag line of 'A guide to ethical decision making and regulation for nonprofit organizations', thus rather downplaying the ethics focus of the book in favour of strategy development.
3   Despite this focus on the ethics of 'tainted money', the case of fundraisers keeping quiet about sex-abuser Jeffrey Epstein's donations has revealed a 'crisis of ethics' at American charities (Hill, 2019).
4   In the context of the code, 'financial guilt' means that the value of the gift – such as an umbrella or pair of gardening gloves – makes the donor feel obligated to make a return gift of similar or greater financial value.
5   For the others, see MacQuillin (2016a).
6   More important than charity beneficiaries?

References

Alexander, L. & Moore, M. (2012). Deontological ethics. In *Stanford Encyclopedia of Philosophy*. Available at http://plato.stanford.edu/entries/ethics-deontological/ (accessed 22 May 2016).

Anderson, A. (1996). *Ethics for Fundraisers*. Indiana University Press.

Appleby, C. (2019). Gender issues in fundraising: Sexual harassment and violence. *Critical Fundraising*, 23 April. Available at https://criticalfundraising.com/2019/04/23/knowledge-gender-issues-in-fundraising-sexual-harassment-and-violence/ (accessed 25 January 2021).

Association of Fundraising Professionals. (1992/2016). Professional compensation: A position paper. Available at https://afpglobal.org/sites/default/files/attachments/2018-10/2016ProfCompensationPositionPaper.pdf (accessed 19 January 2021).

Bayley-Pratt, R. (2019). It's time to face up to sexual harassment in fundraising. *Civil Society Fundraising*, 11 March. Available at www.civilsociety.co.uk/fundraising/ruby-bayley-pratt-agent-provocateur.html (accessed 25 January 2021).

Bekkers, R. & Weipking, P. (2010). A literature review of empirical studies of philanthropy: Eight mechanisms that drive charitable giving. *Nonprofit and Voluntary Sector Quarterly*, 40 (5), 924–973.

Boris, E.T. & Odendahl, T.J. (1990). Ethical issues in fund raising and philanthropy. In J. van Til (ed.), *Critical Issues in American Philanthropy: Strengthening Theory and Practice*. Jossey Bass.

Briscoe, M.G. (1994). Ethics and fundraising management. *New Directions for Philanthropic Fundraising*, 1994(6), 105–120.

Burk, P. (2003). *Donor Centred Fundraising*. Cygnus Applied Research Inc / Burk and Associates Ltd.

Burnett, K. (2002). *Relationship Fundraising: A Donor-Based Approach to the Business of Raising Money* (2nd edn), Jossey Bass.

Caffery, N. (2017). *Code of Fundraising Practice: Report from the Public Conducted by Light and Shade Research*. Fundraising Regulator.

Chartered Institute of Fundraising. (2018). Acceptance, refusal and return. A practical guide to dealing with donations. Available at https://ciof.org.uk/events-and-training/resources/acceptance,-refusal-and-return-a-practical-guide-t (accessed 26 January 2021).

Clohesy, W.W. (2003). Fund-raising and the articulation of common goods. *Nonprofit and Voluntary Sector Quarterly*, 32(1), 128–140.

Community-Centric Fundraising. (2020). CCF's 10 principles. Available at https://communitycentricfundraising.org/ccf-principles/ (accessed 26 January 2021).

Cooney, R. (2019). RNLI to drop opt in-only consent policy this week. *Third Sector*, 1 October. Available at www.thirdsector.co.uk/rnli-drop-opt-in-only-communications-policy-week/fundraising/article/1661115 (accessed 30 January 2019).

Direct Marketing Association. (2016). An ideal future for one-to-one fundraising. Available at https://dma.org.uk/article/an-ideal-future-for-one-to-one-fundraising (accessed 22 January 2021).

Elliott, D. (ed.) (1995). *The Ethics of Asking: Dilemmas in Higher Education Fund Raising*. John Hopkins University Press.

Elliott, D. & Gert, B. (1995). The moral context of fund raising. In D. Elliott (ed.), *The Ethics of Asking: Dilemmas in Higher Education Fund Raising*. John Hopkins University Press.

Etherington, SirStuart, LordLeigh of Hurley, BaronessPitkeathley, LordWallace of Saltaire (2015). *Regulating Fundraising for the Future – Trust in Charities, Confidence in Fundraising Regulation*. National Council for Voluntary Organisations.

Fischer, M. (2000). *Ethical Decision Making in Fund Raising*. John Wiley.

Fundraising Regulator. (n.d.). Fundraising code of practice. www.fundraisingregulator.org.uk/code (accessed 25 January 2021).

Geever, J.C. (1994). Ethics and the nonprofit board of directors. *New Directions for Philanthropic Fundraising*, 1994(6), 63–74.

Gunderman, R. (2010). The social role of fundraising. In A. Sargeant & J. Shang. (eds), *Fundraising Principles and Practice*. Jossey Bass.

Greer, L. & Kostoff, L. (2020). *Philanthropy Revolution: How to Inspire Donors, Build Relationships and Make a Difference*. Harper Collins.

Harris, N. (2020). For love or money? Giving Architects blog, 7 October. Available at www.givingarchitects.com/for-love-or-money/ (accessed 21 January 2021).

Harrison, W.J. (2001). Tainted money. *Fund Raising Management*, 32, 34–37.

Hill, H.R. (2019). MIT scandal exposes a crisis of ethics at all nonprofits. *Chronicle of Philanthropy*, 12 September. Available at www.philanthropy.com/article/mit-scandal-exposes-a-crisis-of-ethics-at-all-nonprofits/ (accessed 25 January 2021).

Hill, H.R. & MacQuillin, I.R. (2019). Initial results from Donor Dominance survey. Rogare – The Fundraising Think Tank. Available at www.rogare.net/donor-dominance (accessed 25 January 2021).

Le, V. (2017/2020). How donor-centrism perpetuates inequity, and why we must move toward community-centric fundraising. *NonprofitAF*, 15 May 2017, updated 8 August 2020. Available at https://nonprofitaf.com/2017/05/how-donor-centrism-perpetuates-inequity-and-why-we-must-move-toward-community-centric-fundraising/ (accessed 25 January 2021).

LeClair, L. (2019a). Sexual harassment runs rampant in non-profits and its time of our #MeToo moment. *Canadian Broadcasting Corporation*, 2 January. Available at www.cbc.ca/news/canada/nova-scotia/metoo-sexual-violence-harassment-fundraising-1.4945951 (accessed 25 January 2021).

LeClair, L. (2019b). Beyond fundraising: What I've learned as a survivor of sexual harassment. *Advancing Philanthropy*. 1 October. Available at https://afpglobal.org/news/beyond-fundraising-what-ive-learned-survivor-sexual-harassment (accessed 25 January 2021).

Levy, B. (2008). Choosing a leadership role. In J.G. Pettey (ed.), *Ethical Fundraising: A Guide for Nonprofit Board and Fundraisers*. John Wiley and Sons.

Lloyd, R. & de las Casas, L. (2006). *NGO Self-Regulation: Enforcing and Balancing Accountability*. One World Trust.

MacQuillin, I.R. (2016a). *Rights Stuff: Fundraising's Ethics Gap and a New Theory of Normative Fundraising Ethics*. Rogare – The Fundraising Think Tank.

MacQuillin, I.R. (2016b). *Relationship Fundraising: Where Do We Go from Here?* Vol. 3: *Trends and Challenges Identified by Practitioners*. Rogare – The Fundraising Think Tank.

MacQuillin, I.R. (2018). What do we need to learn from the Presidents Club debacle? *Critical Fundraising*, 25 January. Available at https://criticalfundraising.com/2018/01/25/

opinion-what-do-we-need-to-learn-from-the-presidents-club-debacle/ (accessed 25 January 2021).

MacQuillin, I.R. (2019). Fundraising ethics – raise more money while keeping your donors happy. What could be simpler? Part 2: SOFII. Available at https://sofii.org/article/fundraisin g-ethics-raise-more-money-while-keeping-your-donors-happy (accessed 25 January 2021).

MacQuillin, I.R. (2020a). The donor-centred baby and the community-centric bathwater: Is an accord between the two philosophies possible? Available at www.rogare.net/comm unity-centric-fr (accessed 25 January 2021).

MacQuillin, I.R. (2020b). You say you want a revolution. *Critical Fundraising*, 19 October. Available at https://criticalfundraising.com/2020/10/19/book-review-you-say-you-wa nt-a-revolution/ (accessed 25 January 2021).

MacQuillin, I.R. & Sargeant, A. (2019). Fundraising ethics: A rights-balancing approach. *Journal of Business Ethics*, 160(1), 239–250.

MacQuillin, I.R., Sargeant, A. & Day, H. (2019). Fundraising self-regulation: An analysis and review. European Center for Not-for-Profit Law. Available at www.rogare.net/self-regulation (accessed 26 January 2021).

Marion, B.H. (1994). Decision making in ethics. *New Directions for Philanthropic Fundraising*, 1994(6), 49–62.

Orland, L. (2011). Donor centred fundraising: Putting the donor at the heart of the organisation. Available at www.totalfundraising.com.au/wp-content/uploads/2017/11/Donor-Centered-Fundraising.pdf (accessed 26 January 2021).

Ostrander, S.A. (2007). The growth of donor control: Revisiting the social relations of philanthropy. *Nonprofit and Voluntary Sector Quarterly*, 36(2), 356–372.

Ostrander, S.A. & Schervish, P.G. (1990). Giving and getting: Philanthropy as a social relation. In J. van Til (ed.), *Critical Issues in American Philanthropy: Strengthening Theory and Practice*. Jossey-Bass.

Payton, R.L. (1987). Tainted money: The ethics of rhetoric and divestment. *Change*, May–June, pp. 55–60.

Pegram, G. (2016). A brief history of fundraising. Available at http://101fundraising.org/2016/05/brief-history-fundraising/ (accessed 22 January 2021).

Pettey, J.G. (ed.) (2008). *Ethical Fundraising: A Guide for Nonprofit Board and Fundraisers*. John Wiley and Sons.

Pettey, J.G. (ed.) (2013). *Nonprofit Fundraising Strategy: A Guide To Ethical Decision Making and Regulation for Nonprofit Organizations*. John Wiley and Sons.

Pitman, M. (2002). Review of *The Seven Faces of Philanthropy: A New Approach to Cultivating Major Donors*. Available at https://fundraisingcoach.com/articles/sevenfaces.htm (accessed 30 January 2021).

Radojev, H. (2016). Ed Aspel: 'I don't really understand resisting the FPS. I do understand making sure it works in the right way'. *Civil Society Fundraising*, 8 May. Available at www.civilsociety.co.uk/fundraising/ed-aspel—i-don-t-really-understand-resisting-the-fps–i-do-un derstand-making-sure-it-works-in-the-right-way-.html (accessed 30 January 2021).

RNLI (Royal National Lifeboat Institution). (2016). It's the final countdown for opting in. Available at https://rnli.org/support-us/volunteer/volunteer-zone/volunteer-news/its-the-final-countdown-for-opting-in (accessed 30 January 2021).

Rosen, M.J. (2005). Doing well by doing right: A fundraiser's guide to ethical decision-making. *International Journal of Nonprofit and Voluntary Sector Marketing*, 10(3), 175–181.

Routley, C. & Koshy, K. (forthcoming). Identifying and addressing fundraising's overarching ethical questions. *Journal of Philanthropy and Marketing* (special issue on fundraising ethics).

Routley, C., Koshy, K., Lowthian, L., Niles, M., Wishart, R., Rosen, M.J., Hill, H.R, Pena, L. & Watt, A. (2020). *The Ethics of Legacy Fundraising During Emergencies*. Rogare – The Fundraising Think Tank.

Sandoval, T. (2018). Sexual harassment is widespread problem for fundraisers, survey says. *Chronicle of Philanthropy*, 5 April. Available at www.philanthropy.com/interactives/fundra iser-poll (accessed 25 January 2021).

Sargeant, A. (2014). Servants' exit: Why are some people trying to sever the connection between fundraising and philanthropy? *Critical Fundraising*, 27 November. Available at https://criticalfundraising.com/2014/11/27/opinion-servants-exit-why-are-some-peop le-trying-to-sever-the-connection-between-fundraising-and-philanthropy/ (accessed 22 January 2021).

Sargeant, A. & Lee, S. (2002a). Improving public trust in the voluntary sector: An empirical analysis. *International Journal of Nonprofit and Voluntary Sector Marketing*, 7(1), 68–83.

Sargeant, A. & Lee, S. (2002b). Individual and contextual antecedents of donor trust in the voluntary sector. *Journal of Marketing Management*, 18(7–8), 779–802.

Sargeant, A. & Lee, S. (2004). Donor trust and relationship commitment in the UK charity sector: the impact of behaviour. *Nonprofit and Voluntary Sector Quarterly*, 33(2), 185–202.

Savage, T. (2000). Donor relations: Achieving effective donor-centered stewardship. In P.M. Buchanan (vol. ed.) & M.J. Worth (section ed.), *Handbook of Institutional Advancement*. Jossey-Bass.

Smith, N.C. & Murphy, P.E. (2012). *Marketing Ethics*. London: Sage.

Smith, V., Gallaiford, N. & Locilento, J. (2020). *Advocating for Fundraising During Emergencies: How to Respond to Arguments that Fundraising is 'Inappropriate' During the Coronavirus Pandemic*. Rogare – The Fundraising Think Tank.

Stern, M. (2016). Come on board: The RNLI's journey to permission-led fundraising. *Civil Society Fundraising*, 18 March. Available at www.civilsociety.co.uk/governance/come-on-boa rd-the-rnli-s-journey-to-permission-led-fundraising.html (accessed 30 January 2021).

Tempel, E.R. (2003). A philosophy of fundraising. In E.R. Tempel (ed.), *Hank Rosso's Achieving Excellence in Fundraising*. John Wiley and Sons.

Tempel, E.R. (2008). Tainted money. In J.G. Pettey (ed.). *Ethical Fundraising: A Guide for Nonprofit Board and Fundraisers*. John Wiley and Sons.

Upton, B. (2017). My experience of being a woman in the charity sector. *UK Fundraising*, July 14. Available at https://fundraising.co.uk/2017/07/14/experience-woman-charity-sector/#.WoMLb5OFjDZ (accessed 25 January 2021).

Villanueva, E. (2018). *Decolonizing Wealth: Indigenous Wisdom to Heal Divides and Restore Balance*. Berrett-Koehler Publishers.

Worth, M.J. (2016). *Fundraising Principles and Practice*. Sage Publications.

5

SPOILT FOR CHOICE?

Understanding how donors choose which charities to support

David J. Hart and Andrew J. Robson

Introduction

Perhaps the most comprehensively answered question in third sector marketing is 'why do people give to charity?' Best surmised by Bekkers and Wiepking in 2011, an exhaustive range of empirical work on what drives charitable giving was consolidated into eight mechanisms. These drivers range from anticipating certain material or immaterial benefits (invites to exclusive events or impact on donor image, for example Lacetera & Macis, 2010) to what has been labelled the pure concept of altruism (Andreoni et al., 2017). Other drivers are more practical in nature. Before donors will consider acting they must have an awareness of need for donations, and after that a crucial mechanism is solicitation (the act of asking for a donation; Fajardo et al., 2018). Donation behaviour is also influenced by the prosocial values of the donor, the extent to which they believe their donation will make a difference (efficacy) and a broader cost-benefit analysis that in many ways replicates more standard consumer decision-making (Bekkers & Wiepking, 2011).

However, far less is known in response to the question 'How do donors choose which charities to support?' This knowledge gap has been previously identified as a cause for concern by Bennett (2003), Andorfer and Otte (2013) and Breeze (2013). Thankfully for academia and practitioners alike, in recent years there has been an uplift in work attempting to answer this question. Before we explore this work, however, it is critical to appreciate two environmental factors, competition and disposable income, which have combined to create an intensely competitive marketplace.

The sheer volume of registered charities offers potential donors a significant (and perhaps overwhelming) range of charitable alternatives. Within the UK, there are approximately 168,000 active organisations (Charity Commission, 2018a), with the US

DOI: 10.4324/9781003134169-8

being home to 1.5 million charities (National Center for Charitable Statistics, 2019). The range of alternatives in this global arena can be grouped into 12 categories defined by the International Classification of Nonprofit Organizations (Table 5.1), which has built on the long-established research from Salamon and Anheier (1996) within The Johns Hopkins Institute for Policy Studies. Whereas religious charities enjoy relative dominance in the US, health charities lead the way in the UK, the latter boosted in recent years through greater legacy giving (Legacy Fundraising Market, 2019).

To understand the significance of the voluntary sector in the UK and its economic contribution, it is worth considering data provided by the National Council for Voluntary Organisations (NCVO). As part of the UK Civil Society Almanac 2020, NCVO (2020) provide a powerful overview of the size and scope of the sector. The bottom-line contribution was £18.2 billion, or 0.9% of GDP, in 2017/2018. As a recognisable part of this, the international and social services sub-sectors provide the most visible contribution, upwards of £3.3 billion each. Around 910,000 people are employed across the sector, representing 3% of the UK workforce and a 17% growth in the last decade. The economic value of formal volunteering was estimated at £23.9 billion in 2016.

In addition to levels of competition, charities also face a very different economic environment as a consequence of the Covid-19 pandemic. In the UK for example, the global pandemic shrunk the economy around 8% (ONS, 2020a), increased unemployment by 1% (ONS, 2020b) and, as of December 2020, almost 10 million jobs have been furloughed (ONS, 2020c). Whilst the pandemic has seen more people report wider prosocial behaviours towards others, such trends have put a squeeze on what was already a competitive sector (Wall Street Journal, 2020) and led to two-thirds of charities reducing their service offering at a time when many

TABLE 5.1 International classification of nonprofit organisations (Source: Adapted from Salamon & Anheier, 1996)

Group	Charity classification
1	Culture and Recreation (e.g. arts, sports)
2	Education and Research (e.g. education institutions and research bodies)
3	Health (e.g. hospitals, nursing and mental health)
4	Social Services (e.g. income support, emergency assistance)
5	Environment (e.g. planet and animal protection)
6	Development and Housing (e.g. community development and training)
7	Law, Advocacy and Politics (e.g. political organisations, legal services)
8	Philanthropic Intermediaries (e.g. grant-making foundations)
9	International Causes (e.g. development work, emergency aid)
10	Religion (e.g. places of worship)
11	Business and Professional Services (e.g. trade unions)
12	Not elsewhere classified

are most needed (Charities Aid Foundation, 2020). This further squeezes a sector which already saw the largest charities dominate in the race for private donations, leaving the majority of smaller causes to fight for relative scraps.

What is clear is that support for the most vulnerable is more critical than ever (Sharfuddin, 2020). Whilst governments and international bodies have responded to some calls for greater investment in services often provided by charities, Fuentenebro (2020) questions whether such interventions can deliver across-the-board solutions. Nonprofits are thus charged with responding to the crisis with greater innovation whilst experiencing reduced funding and experimenting with previously untested fundraising channels (Maher et al., 2020).

The aim of this chapter is to provide a review of the drivers which may lead to support being made to either a specific type of charitable cause or indeed a specific individual charity. We do at this point acknowledge that 'support' can take many forms. Peloza and Hassay (2007) developed a typology that distinguished between low and high involvement support behaviours. Whilst lower involvement activities may include donating old items and engaging with charity events, more engaged donors may demonstrate their commitment through more significant financial donations and volunteering. The majority of work cited here refers to financial contributions (which reflects the emphasis of much third sector literature), however it is important to appreciate that not all donations are financial: donors will also provide their time, expertise and personal properties such as their blood (Piersma et al., 2019). Indeed, it has been suggested that the drivers of donors volunteering their time may be distinct from those for financial contributions (Lee & Chang, 2007). However, for simplicity we will consider all forms of support collectively in the subsequent discussion.

Donor choice

We define donor choice as an individual's decision of what type of charitable cause to support and/or which specific charity to which they eventually donate. Donor choice decisions may occur separately to the initial decision to donate 'somewhere', or indeed the two may be intertwined (for example, should an individual be directly approached for a donation by a specific cause). This convergence of decisions is important given previous work which highlighted that charitable giving is in many cases a 'limited problem-solving' decision, characterised by donors spending relatively little time searching for alternatives and reaching a decision (Breeze, 2013; Hibbert & Home, 1997). It is widely accepted that donors are not 'equal' in their generosity (Strombach et al., 2014), which inevitably leads to the notion of some charitable causes being more popular than others.

The earliest observed study into donor choice occurred in Scotland by Schlegelmilch and Tynan (1989). They explored the application of market segmentation to the charitable marketplace through quantitative research and concluded that 'people who donate to one charity do not differ from those who donate to another' (p. 8). However, as observed by Bennett (2003), their lack of distinction between supporters of different causes may have been a product of the charitable categories used in the study.

Over a decade then passed before a renewed attempt to explore the area. It was the aforementioned Roger Bennett who was approached by a fundraising professional for guidance on the issue of donor choice, and consequently became the next researcher to explore this subject empirically. His 2003 work intended to investigate if variables which were known to explain donating to charity in general (specifically values and personal tendencies towards materialism, individualism and empathy) could also explain preference for certain charitable types. He concluded 'personal values have the potential to influence the specific genre of charity that an individual might choose to assist' (Bennett, 2003, p. 26), suggesting that when choosing a charitable cause, donors may use it as an opportunity to convey their own personal values. From here, the last decade in particular has seen an increase in research focused upon donor choice. Based on such work, the key drivers of this decision have been summarised in Figure 5.1 which serves as a structure for the subsequent discussion.

Personal experience

It is perfectly logical that an individual's life experiences, and their subsequent exposure to and usage of certain charities, will influence their charitable preferences. Indeed, Small and Cryder (2016) argue that certain charities receive disproportionate amounts of donations because their cause is related to a cause to which many donors

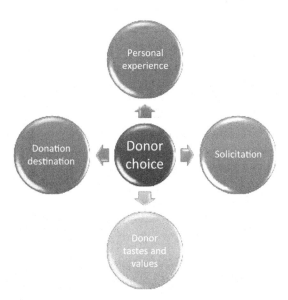

FIGURE 5.1 Key drivers of donor choice

can relate. On a primary level, should a donor utilise a charitable service (e.g. adopting a pet from an animal shelter), their personal gain from that offering may inspire future giving. Similarly, Burgoyne et al. (2005) argued that potential contact with charity beneficiaries and a wider involvement in the local community may make donors more aware of which charities need their support.

In their 2007 focus group-based research, Sargeant and Woodliffe contended that many charities were experiencing a loyalty crisis amongst donors, with a large proportion of passive donors only maintaining their support through inertia. They did however identify that more 'active commitment' to a charity arises from personal links to the cause or the issue that it supports. Here then, we use 'life experiences' to refer to any form of direct or indirect exposure to a charity and/or an observation of how their work benefits either the donor or others. As Wolpert (1995) notes, an individual's propensity to help others increases when they are exposed to someone in need, which may impact on the issue of donating to local versus international charities (as discussed later). Payton and Moody (2008) refer to these life experiences as 'philanthropic autobiographies' which result in a connection with or affinity for a particular cause. This presents an interesting dichotomy between those charities that may frequently find themselves entwined in these biographies (e.g. a charity providing support for a common illness) versus a more niche cause to which fewer individuals are exposed.

Solicitation

According to Bekkers and Wiepking (2011), solicitation refers to the simple act of asking for a donation, and the manner in which this is undertaken will impact the chances of a successful outcome (e.g. Yörük, 2009). They also cite data from various nations which shows that the majority of donations received are a direct result of solicitation. Here we will explore to what extent solicitation may impact actual choice of charity, as opposed to intention to donate in general.

One issue to cite here is the increased amount of donations generated through sponsorship, specifically when friends and family may support someone known to them as they undertake a (often sporting related) challenge. By 2003, such work accounted for around one-fifth of all donations in Canada (Higgins & Lauzon, 2003), and their global proliferation has been noted elsewhere (Palmer, 2016). In these contexts, the solicitation will come directly from a known person who is raising money for a course, and research has demonstrated that such social ties can make it much more difficult to refuse the request (Meer, 2011). This peer-to-peer fundraising (Castillo et al., 2014) can be further intensified when such asks are made on social network feeds, drawing attention to others who have supported the cause in question. The implications of this on donor choice are significant. An individual may in some cases choose to support a cause not because of the charity's purpose/values, but instead because of an obligation to a friend, thus conflating the decisions of whether to donate and to whom. The conclusion here then is that personal experience may drive the fundraiser to select a certain cause to raise money for, but their network will provide sponsorship for altogether more social reasons.

Elsewhere, Barman (2008) noted how in many cases donations often come with 'strings attached'. Here, donors to a charitable cause may then state a preference on where their donation is specifically directed (e.g. The United Way in North America). Whilst offering donors such control has the potential to create a more powerful solicitation message, the shift of power in how donations are used has significant implications for charities. Barman (2008) examined this phenomenon in the context of a US workplace-based giving scheme, identifying that it was younger and well-educated donors who were most likely to expect such control over where their donation was directed. This has clear implications for other charities who may wish to target similar segments but at the same time retain control over how to invest donations.

Donor tastes and values

Much like in more standard consumer scenarios, an individual's choice of charitable cause may be a product of either their personal preferences or values. Breeze (2013) reviewed the limited literature on charitable choice and determined that giving decisions are highly reliant on personal taste, which leads to the notion of some causes being more popular than others. Body and Breeze (2016) provide a fascinating insight into what they describe as 'unpopular causes'. They argue that this is a concept that not only applies to smaller charities (who lack the resources to pitch for donations against more established competitors) but also causes which may struggle to generate sympathy from the wider public, such as those supporting ex-offenders or those fighting addictions. Based on media coverage, their top ten types of unpopular cause covered mental health, refugees, domestic violence and the travelling community. In terms of removing the unpopular tag, the authors suggested communications that aroused greater feelings of sympathy and minimised perceptions that the beneficiaries are responsible for their predicament.

Of course, tastes change. Recent years have witnessed, for example, a surge in awareness of and support for promoting better mental health with a corresponding increase in registered charities, largely inspired by the attention drawn to male suicide rates (e.g. Project84, a guerrilla marketing campaign promoting awareness of male mental health; CALM, 2018) and the impact of lockdown on wider wellbeing (ONS, 2020d). The UK has also witnessed increased (albeit not complete) empathy towards domestic violence and refugee related charities. Recent work by Bennett and Vijaygopal (2019) specifically focused on mental health charities as an example of an unpopular cause. Their research uncovered that whilst stigmas negatively impacted willingness to donate, having close contact with a sufferer of mental illness increased donation intention, as did altruism and empathy.

There is mixed evidence on the issue of whether donor preferences are informed by perceptions of which charities have the greatest need for financial support. Utilising a dictator game experiment (where participants receive a fee for taking part but are then prompted to consider donating some of this payment to charity; Fielding & Knowles, 2015), Bachke et al. (2014, p. 481) concluded that donors give 'most to projects benefitting groups and regions that they perceive as the most vulnerable and poor'. Their experiment attempted to identify preferences for giving based upon recipient group (i.e. the intended charity beneficiary) and project type (loosely mapped the ICNPO classification of charities outlined earlier). What is interesting is that recipient neediness (the notion that donors will direct funds towards those causes where the need is perceived most acute; Singer, 2009) appeared to be the strongest driver of donor preferences, whereas it has elsewhere been observed that the majority of private donors do not align their choices with this principle (Cryder et al., 2017).

Even when a donor is clear on which specific project they wish to support, the plethora of charities requesting assistance to serve said cause can be overwhelming. Zhuang et al. (2014) illustrated this using the example of the devastating 2010 earthquake in Haiti, which took the lives of around 250,000 people. They concluded that the extent to which charities disclosed value-relevant information to donors (such as how previous donations have been utilised and other financial/performance data) positively impacted charitable contributions. Similarly, Williams (2007) identified that younger donors tended to be less concerned with charity efficiency than the 'baby boomers' generation (born between 1946 and 1964), but more concerned with the outcomes of their donation. Such disclosure appears logically linked to the concept of trust, which can be viewed at either a sector-wide or individual-charity level and has been previously demonstrated to correlate with giving (e.g. Bekkers, 2003; Naskrent & Siebelt, 2011).

An individual's values also have the potential to influence donor choice. Values can be viewed as somewhat abstract constructs (Prince et al., 2020), but can translate into specific attitudes and behaviours (Schwartz, 1992). Much as values have been found to influence consumer choice across prosocial behaviours such as sustainable produce (Nguyen et al., 2017), gift giving (Beatty et al., 1991) and responses to CSR activity (Park et al., 2017), 'the type of charitable organisation a person donates to might tell us more about his or her values and preferences than merely whether or not he or she donates at all' (Erlandsson et al., 2019, p. 814).

Bennett (2003) reviewed evidence that values such as harmony and freedom were most prevalent amongst charity volunteers, and in his own empiric work concluded that not only do certain values drive interest in particular charities, but that donors also seek a fit between their personal values and that of the charity itself. More recently, a cross-national study from Sneddon et al. (2020) provides a comprehensive understanding of how values influence donor choice. Their work with both American and Australian samples looked at the role of values (specifically universalism and tradition) on donation intentions towards nine categories of charitable cause, and concluded that values clearly influenced respondent's preferred causes (for example, values surrounding tradition were associated with support for religious causes). Chapman et al. (2020) explored different motives for giving and eventually clustered their resulting nine themes under 'self', which drove donations to religious and research charities, and 'other', which explained support for animal, international and educational causes.

It has also been acknowledged that an individual's political values may impact on their choice of charitable cause (Atkinson, 2009; Winterich et al., 2012). For example, Lee et al. (2020) noted how those with conservative political values prefer charitable messages which focus on individual attributions and failings, whereas liberal voters are more responsive to messages which blame inequalities on societal factors. Indeed, Wiepking (2010) has associated liberal voters with support for more cosmopolitan charitable causes. This appears particular applicable to the following section, where we consider donation destination.

Donation destination

Existing research points to a notable distinction in donor preferences to support causes relative to their geographic distance from recipients. Whilst some make the distinction simply between causes which are domestic versus international in scope, other have split the former into local- and national-level alternatives (Hall et al., 2013; Robson & Hart, 2020a).

Charitable ethnocentrism represents a positive disposition towards domestic donation alternatives compared with a negative viewpoint for international equivalents, whilst charitable cosmopolitanism represents the opposite perspective (Hart & Robson, 2019). In the USA, Lee et al. (2003) indicate that nationalism and internationalism are significant predictors of ethnocentric behaviour from the standpoint of general consumer activity. Demographic factors including age, gender, educational attainment and income influence the extent of this ethnocentrism. In a US–Chinese comparison, Tsai et al. (2013) identify American consumers as the more ethnocentric, with the most significant determinant of consumer ethnocentrism being nationalism across both consumer groups. Country-level differences were also identified as part of a German–Chinese comparative study from Strombach et al. (2014), particularly regarding beneficiaries who are more closely located.

This view of nationalism differs slightly from that reported by Hart and Robson (2019), where donor levels of internationalism relate positively with international charity choice but negatively with respect to domestic equivalents. Greater donor nationalism aligns with disposition towards domestic options, but its links to international charitable options are non-significant (Hart & Robson, 2019). Interestingly, Yildiz et al. (2018) identified that consumers with greater regional commitment have a higher propensity to purchase local produce than others who simply display greater ethnocentrism.

This ethnocentrism–cosmopolitanism spectrum influences charitable destination choice. For charitable options that are 'politically sensitive', donor attitudes toward charity in general influence donation intention, with specific political attitudes offering a relatively limited role in explaining donor behaviour (Robson & Hart, 2020b). Distinct segments of donor exist, differing in their donation intentions, policy perspectives and preferred charitable choices. Evidence does support private donor willingness to donate overseas, but there is an extent to which the actions of government through aid policy can inhibit such private donation, and as such, public policy must be responsive to such donor predisposition (Atkinson, 2009).

In their New Zealand based study, Knowles and Sullivan (2017) identified that a majority of study donors expressed preference for donation to a named local charity ahead of an equivalent international development comparator, with Micklewright and Schnepf (2009) similarly reporting preference for national rather than international alternatives (although the latter suggests that international donations may be less frequent but of higher value). Domestic interventions were also seen to yield greater returns than international causes by Einolf et al. (2013), with appeals responding to natural disasters resonating more than fundraising for human-made concerns.

Whilst relative popularity for domestic campaigns dominates, examples exist of international donation being more popular (Lwin et al., 2014). Donor inclination towards both destinations can be determined by a combination of trust, favoured charitable cause and donation channels. Robson and Hart (2020a) suggest commonality exists in the determinants of intention to donate locally and nationally, with those for international donation being relatively distinct. Much as observed in other countries, national and local alternatives are more popular with UK-based donors than international offerings.

There are various forms of international donation research that merit attention. Charitable research is dominated by work focused on countries with robust donation profiles and assessment is overwhelmingly based on individual donors. In doing so, the effect of social and environmental interventions is relatively underplayed (Denis et al., 2018). There is a call here for work on public policy, the role of institutions and responses to ad-hoc events. Recent examples include government aid allocations that assess donor priorities against beneficiary requirements and capacity for the recipient state to utilise aid allocation effectively (Feeny et al., 2019). There is also assessment of the expectations of individuals from company-level giving, where individuals favour equitable giving by organisations to domestic and international beneficiaries or exclusively to the latter, a perspective at odds with organisational action (Schons et al., 2017).

Notwithstanding the need for more research on policy and institutions, individual donor research still remains prominent. Aligned to this is the extent to which popularity of donation destination relates in various ways to donor demographics. From a US perspective, Casale and Baumann (2015) indicate predisposition to international donation is independent of donor income, but foreign-born donors with postgraduate education and religious beliefs demonstrate greater inclination to give overseas. Higher levels of institutional trust and engagement in activities such as youth volunteering are significantly aligned to relatively greater international donation. Income, donor education and gender influence international destination, with greater contributions from women and the more highly educated (Micklewright & Schnepf, 2009). From a Canadian perspective, Rajan et al. (2009) further indicate that both higher education attainment and religious beliefs drive a preference for international over domestic giving, with international donations being further influenced by perceptions of personal financial security.

Contrasting demographic findings also exist. Whilst Knowles and Sullivan (2017) report no gender or age-band differences and Robson and Hart (2020a) only a partial demographic influence, increases in ethnic diversity are seen to decrease private charitable donation, with equivalent outcomes being identified between greater religious diversity and donation (Andreoni et al., 2016). Lwin et al. (2014) found conflicting findings from their Australian perspective. For an older, less educated and less religion-influenced donor base, international options were more popular, diverging sharply from the studies presented above. Where a donor audience comprises the younger and more educated, international donation support may only be conditionally endorsed and come with expectations (Stevenson & Manning, 2010). There is beneficiary poverty driven by educational deficit identified by young, educated New Zealand non-donors (Dalton et al., 2008). They perceived giving as being limited by donor immunity, further exacerbated by perceptions of recipient self-help and self-responsibility, aligning to the donor-held international priorities (natural versus non-natural) reported by Einolf et al. (2013).

Whilst stakeholder segmentation underpins successful not-for-profit relationship marketing, demographics contribute, but so does the capture of additional psychographic and attitudes-based characteristics (Rupp et al., 2014). Whilst charitable giving relates to donors' preferences and individual attributes, Breeze (2013) indicates that donors may recognise giving focused on recipients with greater need but show propensity to support organisations aligning with personal preferences and will champion causes that chime with personal experiences. The overriding choice to donate and associated destination are driven by compatibility between donor values and those set out by the not-for-profit beneficiary (van Dijk et al., 2019). Whilst financial investment remains insignificantly different according to political ideology, differences emerge for breadth and depth of giving, although these actions can be fluid (Farmer et al., 2020). Neumayr and Handy (2019) suggest subjective measures including empathy, trust and religious belief determine donation occurrences, with income and donor education influencing donation values.

Summary and implications

Our review of existing knowledge on donor choice highlights three key conclusions:

1.   Whilst work in understanding donor choice is developing, there appears much still to learn.
2.   There is however ample evidence to suggest that donor choice is driven by multiple factors and thus further complicates the charitable giving decision-making process.

3.   Charities (particularly those without huge fundraising budgets) need further guidance on how to convert this learning into effective fundraising activity.

The key to addressing the final point appears to be effective donor segmentation, a vehicle used to improve fundraising efficiency for charitable organisations (De Vries et al., 2015). An ability to segment donors (or potential donors) on shared characteristics allows for critical decisions around which groups to target with limited budgets (Boenigk & Scherhag, 2014; Tsiotsou, 2007). The creation of donor segments is useful not only for nurturing existing donor relationships but also for the targeting of 'lookalike donors', as successfully employed by social media advertisers such as Facebook. Some donors may be responsive to the donation decisions of their peers and can be attracted accordingly (Drouvelis & Marx, 2020).

Previous work on donor segmentation ranges from using demographic and behavioural data through to more lifestyle, psychographic and values-based approaches. Whilst demographic data is naturally easier to obtain and charities may have behavioural data of previous donors at hand, it is often the more values-based data that is key to effective segmentation. For example, Sargeant et al. (2004) argued that understanding a donor's motive for donating was the single most important issue.

Robson and Hart (2019) undertook what appears an interesting piece of donor segmentation research that has notable implications for practitioners. Their work on a nationally representative UK sample sought information on respondent's charitable giving (covering past donations, preferred causes, trust and future intention), political attitudes, newspaper readership and various demographic factors. Their resultant cluster analysis revealed six distinct donor segments as outlined in Table 5.2.

TABLE 5.2 Donor segments based on political attitudes (Source: Adapted from Robson & Hart, 2019)

Cluster name	Size	Core characteristics
Educated Liberals	124	Typically highly educated, with a global perspective on politics and charity and left-wing political tendencies
Young Urban Altruists	149	Remain voters, aged 18–44, with positive attitudes towards both domestic and international charities and highest donation intentions
Cautious Pragmatists	327	Usually report higher levels of nationalism, give modest amounts to charity but have negative views on overseas development aid
Disengaged Cynics	100	Tend to distrust all charities, hold more right-wing political beliefs but are less likely to be politically engaged
Home-first Casuals	119	Display a clear preference for domestic over international charities but typically do not donate large amounts to any charity
Anti-EU Nationalists	185	A group dominated by men with the strongest 'pro-country' tendencies, readership of right-wing newspapers and mistrust of international charities

Of course, such detailed psychographic segmentation is difficult to achieve for the vast majority of charities. There remains though some more tactical implications of such work that charities may wish to employ as part of their fundraising activity:

- If donors can indeed be segmented by their political attitudes, this may assist charities in effective targeting. Even without individual-level data, charities may wish to target activity towards specific regions/political constituencies based upon recent voting behaviour. For example, an area in the UK which voted strongly in favour of Brexit and has higher support for right-wing political parties is a more logical target for local or domestic causes, particularly surrounding health or animal welfare.
- Linked to the above, it is pertinent not to underestimate the value of the social network. Extensive research has demonstrated that social media users often operate in so-called 'echo chambers', where they deliberately seek ties with users who share their values and political beliefs and thus provide opinion reinforcement (Garrett, 2009; Wollebæk et al., 2019). The opportunity here then is not necessarily around paid social content but encouraging more organic sharing of a cause by existing donors that may naturally reach like-minded individuals.
- Whilst political values may drive donor segmentation, the safest way to ensure charities do not alienate potential donors is by staying clear of political messaging. In an age where political 'affective polarisation' is clearly on the rise (Reiljan, 2020), any references that allude to political leanings may risk putting off donors who may otherwise have been potentially interested. An interesting case here surrounds the growth in foodbanks across the UK, which some argue have become a more necessary resource owing to various austerity measures (Loopstra et al., 2015). Major food bank charities such as the Trussell Trust strike a delicate balance between identifying the growth in food poverty that acted as the catalyst for their growth, whilst stopping short of attributing blame to government policy.
- According to the Charity Commission (2018b), trust in charitable causes is decreasing and this impacts donation behaviour. Research also suggests that trust is highest for smaller local causes (Robson & Hart, 2020a), which may be attributed to perceptions that they do not waste money on expensive marketing activity or highly paid executives. This has clear implications for solicitation messaging: whilst smaller charities can play on their 'local' status by showcasing credible volunteers and beneficiaries in the community, larger charities clearly have a bigger challenge in changing perceptions through demonstrating impact and providing full disclosure of how donations are distributed, especially for those with an international remit.

In summary, it is heartening to see an emerging body of knowledge that not only considers why people donate to charity but their choice of donation destination. There are no signs of the charitable sector becoming any less competitive in the short- to medium-term future, so a fuller understanding of donor choice is of potentially critical value to academics and practitioners alike. The sector would especially benefit not only from more understanding of what drives donor choice, but guidance on how to best target the most promising prospective donors, and what messaging will provide the greatest return on their fundraising investment.

Chapter discussion questions

1. The academic literature suggest that some causes will always be less attractive to donors than others. Consider what social stigmas or other environmental factors may lead to a charitable cause being perceived as 'less worthy'.

2. Working in groups, conduct your own 'dictator game' style experiment, where each participant has a hypothetical £100 to donate. Compile of list of ten possible charities covering different causes and ask each person to split their money across the causes as they see fit. Use the findings of this experiment to discuss what drives donations in some charitable areas more than others.

3. In the chapter we discuss the differences between donors that support domestic versus international charities. What advice would you give to a charity that supports both domestic and international projects (for example, Comic Relief) to allow them to effectively target donors for both aspects of their work?

References

Andorfer, V.A. & Otte, G. (2013). Do contexts matter for willingness to donate to natural disaster relief? An application of the factorial survey. *Nonprofit and Voluntary Sector Quarterly*, 42(4), 657–688.

Andreoni, J., Payne, A.A., Smith, J. & Karp, D. (2016). Diversity and donations: The effect of religious and ethnic diversity on charitable giving. *Journal of Economic Behavior & Organization*, 128, 47–58.

Andreoni, J., Rao, J.M. & Trachtman, H. (2017). Avoiding the ask: A field experiment on altruism, empathy, and charitable giving. *Journal of Political Economy*, 125(3), 625–653.

Atkinson, A.B. (2009). Giving overseas and public policy. *Journal of Public Economics*, 93(5), 647–653.

Bachke, M.E., Alfnes, F. & Wik, M. (2014). Eliciting donor preferences. *VOLUNTAS: International Journal of Voluntary and Nonprofit Organizations*, 25(2), 465–486.

Barman, E. (2008). With strings attached: Nonprofits and the adoption of donor choice. *Nonprofit and Voluntary Sector Quarterly*, 37(1), 39–56.

Beatty, S.E., Kahle, L.R. & Homer, P. (1991). Personal values and gift-giving behaviors: A study across cultures. *Journal of Business Research*, 22(2), 149–157.

Bekkers, R. (2003). Trust, accreditation, and philanthropy in the Netherlands. *Nonprofit and Voluntary Sector Quarterly*, 32(4), 596–615.

Bekkers, R. & Wiepking, P. (2011). A literature review of empirical studies of philanthropy: Eight mechanisms that drive charitable giving. *Nonprofit and Voluntary Sector Quarterly*, 40(5), 924–973.

Bennett, R. (2003). Factors underlying the inclination to donate to particular types of charity. *International Journal of Nonprofit and Voluntary Sector Marketing*, 8(1), 12–29.

Bennett, R. & Vijaygopal, R. (2019). Towards a model of donor behaviour relating to mental disability charities. *Social Business*, 9(3), 248–271.

Body, A. & Breeze, B. (2016). What are 'unpopular causes' and how can they achieve fundraising success? *International Journal of Nonprofit and Voluntary Sector Marketing*, 21(1), 57–70.

Boenigk, S. & Scherhag, C. (2014). Effects of donor priority strategy on relationship fundraising outcomes. *Nonprofit Management and Leadership*, 24(3), 307–336.

Breeze, B. (2013). How donors choose charities: The role of personal taste and experiences in giving decisions. *Voluntary Sector Review*, 4(2), 165–183.

Burgoyne, C.B., Young, B. & Walker, C.M. (2005). Deciding to give to charity: A focus group study in the context of the household economy. *Journal of Community & Applied Social Psychology*, 15(5), 383–405.

CALM. (2018). Project84. Available at www.projecteightyfour.com/ (accessed 15 May 2021).

Casale, D. & Baumann, A. (2015). Who gives to international causes? A sociodemographic analysis of US donors. *Nonprofit and Voluntary Sector Quarterly*, 44(1), 98–122.

Castillo, M., Petrie, R. & Wardell, C. (2014). Fundraising through online social networks: A field experiment on peer-to-peer solicitation. *Journal of Public Economics*, 114, 29–35.

Chapman, C.M., Masser, B.M. & Louis, W.R. (2020). Explanations for charity preferences from a global donor survey. *Psychology & Marketing*, 37(9), 1277–1291.

Charities Aid Foundation. (2020). Charities likely to reduce services as lockdown bites. Available at   www.cafonline.org/about-us/media-office-news/charities-likely-to-reduce-services-as-lockdown-bites (accessed 15 May 2021).

Charity Commission. (2018a). Charity register statistics. Available at www.gov.uk/government/statistics/charity-register-statistics (accessed 15 May 2021).

Charity Commission. (2018b). Trust in charities 2018. Available at www.gov.uk/government/publications/trust-in-charities-2018 (accessed 15 May 2021).

Cryder, C., Botti, S. & Simonyan, Y. (2017). The charity beauty premium: Satisfying donors' 'want' versus 'should' desires. *Journal of Marketing Research*, 54(4), 605–618.

Dalton, S., Madden, H., Chamberlain, S., Carr, S. & Lyons, C. (2008). 'It's gotten a bit old, charity': Young adults in New Zealand talk about poverty, charitable giving and aid appeals. *Journal of Community and Applied Social Psychology*, 18(5), 492–504.

de Vries, N.J., Reis, R. & Moscato, P. (2015). Clustering consumers based on trust, confidence and giving behaviour: Data-driven model building for charitable involvement in the Australian not-for-profit sector. *PloS One*, 10(4). doi:10.1371/journal.pone.0122133.

Denis, E., Pecheux, C. & Decrop, A. (2018). Segmenting the Belgian charitable sector: The impact of environmental factors on households' generosity. *International Journal of Nonprofit and Voluntary Sector Marketing*, 23(3), 1–9.

Drouvelis, M. & Marx, B.M. (2020). Dimensions of donation preferences: the structure of peer and income effects. *Experimental Economics*, 1, 1–29.

Einolf, C.J., Philbrick, D.M. & Slay, K. (2013). National giving campaigns in the United States: Entertainment, empathy, and the national peer group. *Nonprofit and Voluntary Sector Quarterly*, 42(2), 241–261.

Erlandsson, A., Nilsson, A., Tinghög, G., Andersson, D. & Västfjäll, D. (2019). Donations to outgroup charities, but not ingroup charities, predict helping intentions toward street-beggars in Sweden. *Nonprofit and Voluntary Sector Quarterly*, 48(4), 814–838.

Fajardo, T.M., Townsend, C. & Bolander, W. (2018). Toward an optimal donation solicitation: Evidence from the field of the differential influence of donor-related and organization-related information on donation choice and amount. *Journal of Marketing*, 82(2), 142–152.

Farmer, A., Kidwell, B. & Hardesty, D.M. (2020). Helping a few a lot or many a little: Political ideology and charitable giving. *Journal of Consumer Psychology*, 30(4), 614–630.

Feeny, S., Hansen, P., Knowles, S., McGillivray, M. & Ombler, F. (2019). Donor motives, public preferences and the allocation of UK foreign aid: A discrete choice experiment approach. *Review of World Economics*, 155(3), 511–537.

Fielding, D. & Knowles, S. (2015). Can you spare some change for charity? Experimental evidence on verbal cues and loose change effects in a Dictator Game. *Experimental Economics*, 18(4), 718–730.

Fuentenebro, P. (2020). Will philanthropy save us all? Rethinking urban philanthropy in a time of crisis. *Geoforum*, 117, 304–307.

Garrett, R.K. (2009). Echo chambers online? Politically motivated selective exposure among internet news users. *Journal of Computer-Mediated Communication*, 14(2), 265–285.

Hall, D., Jones, S.C., Andrews, K. & Cridland, L. (2013). Community perceptions of and suggested fundraising strategies for local charities. In R. Brodie (ed.), *ANZMAC 2013 Conference Proceedings*. University of Auckland.

Hart, D.J. & Robson, A. (2019). Does charity begin at home? National identity and donating to domestic versus international charities. *Voluntas: International Journal of Voluntary and Nonprofit Organizations*, 30(4), 865–880.

Hibbert, S.A. & Home, S. (1997). Donation dilemmas: A consumer behaviour perspective. *International Journal of Nonprofit and Voluntary Sector Marketing*, 2(3), 261–274.

Higgins, J.W. & Lauzon, L. (2003). Finding the funds in fun runs: Exploring physical activity events as fundraising tools in the nonprofit sector. *International Journal of Nonprofit and Voluntary Sector Marketing*, 8(4), 363–377.

Knowles, S. & Sullivan, T. (2017). Does charity begin at home or overseas? *Nonprofit and Voluntary Sector Quarterly*, 46(5), 944–962.

Lacetera, N. & Macis, M. (2010). Social image concerns and prosocial behavior: Field evidence from a nonlinear incentive scheme. *Journal of Economic Behavior & Organization*, 76(2), 225–237.

Lee, W.N., Hong, J.Y. & Lee, S.J. (2003). Communicating with American consumers in the post 9/11 climate: An empirical investigation of consumer ethnocentrism in the United States. *International Journal of Advertising*, 22(4), 487–510.

Lee, Y. & Chang, C.T. (2007). Who gives what to charity? Characteristics affecting donation behavior. *Social Behavior and Personality: An International Journal*, 35(9), 1173–1180.

Lee, Y., Seo, J.Y. & Yoon, S. (2020). Charity advertising: Congruence between political orientation and cause of need. *International Journal of Advertising*, 39(7), 943–962.

Legacy Fundraising Market. (2019). UK legacy fundraising market 2019. Available at www.rememberacharity.org.uk/media/8d82cb82603f68e/uk-legacy-marketplace-summary-report-apr-2019-final-v2.pdf (accessed 15 May 2021).

Loopstra, R., Reeves, A., Taylor-Robinson, D., Barr, B., McKee, M. & Stuckler, D. (2015). Austerity, sanctions, and the rise of food banks in the UK. *British Medical Journal*, 350, 1775.

Lwin, M., Phau, I. & Lim, A. (2014). An investigation of the characteristics of Australian charitable donors. *Journal of Nonprofit & Public Sector Marketing*, 26(4), 372–389.

Maher, C.S., Hoang, T. & Hindery, A. (2020). Fiscal responses to COVID-19: Evidence from local governments and nonprofits. *Public Administration Review*, 80(4), 644–650.

Meer, J. (2011). Brother, can you spare a dime? Peer pressure in charitable solicitation. *Journal of Public Economics*, 95(7–8), 926–941.

Micklewright, J. & Schnepf, S.V. (2009). Who gives charitable donations for overseas development? *Journal of Social Policy*, 38(2), 317–341.

Naskrent, J. & Siebelt, P. (2011). The influence of commitment, trust, satisfaction, and involvement on donor retention. *Voluntas: International Journal of Voluntary and Nonprofit Organizations*, 22(4), 757–778.

National Center for Charitable Statistics. (2019). The non-profit sector in brief. Available at https://nccs.urban.org/project/nonprofit-sector-brief (accessed 15 May 2021).

NCVO. (2020). UK civil society almanac (2020). Available at https://data.ncvo.org.uk/?gclid=EAIaIQobChMI0-uI7fmq7wIVREiRBR1dQgEwEAAYASAAEgKTkfD_BwE (accessed 15 May 2021).

Neumayr, M. & Handy, F. (2019). Charitable giving: What influences donors' choice among different causes? *Voluntas: International Journal of Voluntary and Nonprofit Organizations*, 30(4), 783–799.

Nguyen, T.N., Lobo, A. & Greenland, S. (2017). The influence of cultural values on green purchase behaviour. *Marketing Intelligence & Planning*, 35, 377–396.

Office for National Statistics. (2020a). Coronavirus and the impact on the economy: October 2020. Available at www.ons.gov.uk/economy/grossdomesticproductgdp/articles/coronavirusandtheimpactonoutputintheukeconomy/october2020 (accessed 15 May 2021).

Office for National Statistics. (2020b). Labour market overview: December 2020. Available at www.ons.gov.uk/employmentandlabourmarket/peopleinwork/employmentandemploueetypes/bulletins/uklabourmarket/december2020 (accessed 15 May 2021).

Office for National Statistics. (2020c). HMRC Coronavirus statistics. Available at www.gov.uk/government/collections/hmrc-coronavirus-covid-19-statistics (accessed 15 May 2021).

Office for National Statistics. (2020d). Coronavirus and the social impacts on Great Britain: June 2020. Available at www.ons.gov.uk/peoplepopulationandcommunity/healthandsocialcare/healthandwellbeing/bulletins/coronavirusandthesocialimpactsongreatbritain/5june2020 (accessed 15 May 2021).

Palmer, C. (2016). Research on the run: Moving methods and the charity 'thon'. *Qualitative Research in Sport, Exercise and Health*, 8(3), 225–236.

Park, E., Kim, K.J. & Kwon, S.J. (2017). Corporate social responsibility as a determinant of consumer loyalty: An examination of ethical standard, satisfaction, and trust. *Journal of Business Research*, 76, 8–13.

Payton, R.L. & Moody, M.P. (2008). *Understanding Philanthropy: Its Meaning and Mission*. Indiana University Press.

Peloza, J. & Hassay, D.N. (2007). A typology of charity support behaviors: Toward a holistic view of helping. *Journal of Nonprofit & Public Sector Marketing*, 17(1–2), 135–151.

Piersma, T.W., Bekkers, R., de Kort, W. & Merz, E.M. (2019). Blood donation across the life course: The influence of life events on donor lapse. *Journal of Health and Social Behavior*, 60(2), 257–272.

Prince, M., Yaprak, A., Cleveland, M., Davies, M.A., Josiassen, A., Nechtelberger, A., Nechtelberger, M., Palihawadana, D., Renner, W., Supekova, S.C. & Von Wallpach, S. (2020). The psychology of consumer ethnocentrism and cosmopolitanism: A five-country study of values, moral foundations, gender identities and consumer orientations. *International Marketing Review*, 37(6), 1013–1049.

Rajan, S.S., Pink, G.H. & Dow, W.H. (2009). Sociodemographic and personality characteristics of Canadian donors contributing to international charity. *Nonprofit and Voluntary Sector Quarterly*, 38(3), 413–440.

Reiljan, A. (2020). 'Fear and loathing across party lines' (also) in Europe: Affective polarisation in European party systems. *European Journal of Political Research*, 59(2), 376–396.

Robson, A. & Hart, D. (2019). The post-Brexit donor: Segmenting the UK charitable marketplace using political attitudes and national identity. *International Review on Public and Nonprofit Marketing*, 16(2), 313–334.

Robson, A. & Hart, D.J. (2020a). Understanding the correlates of donor intention: A comparison of local, national, and international charity destinations. *Nonprofit and Voluntary Sector Quarterly*, 50(3), 506–530.

Robson, A. & Hart, D.J. (2020b). Feed the world or help the heroes? Exploring how political attitudes influence charitable choice, *Journal of Marketing Management*, 36(17–18), 1680–1706.

Rupp, C., Kern, S. & Helmig, B. (2014). Segmenting nonprofit stakeholders to enable successful relationship marketing: A review. *International Journal of Nonprofit and Voluntary Sector Marketing*, 19(2), 76–91.

Salamon, L.M. & Anheier, H.K. (1996). *The International Classification of Nonprofit Organizations: ICNPO-Revision 1, 1996*. Working Papers of the Johns Hopkins Comparative Nonprofit Sector Project, No. 19. The Johns Hopkins Institute for Policy Studies.

Sargeant, A. & Woodliffe, L. (2007). Building donor loyalty: The antecedents and role of commitment in the context of charity giving. *Journal of Nonprofit & Public Sector Marketing*, 18(2), 47–68.

Sargeant, A., West, D.C. & Ford, J.B. (2004). Does perception matter? An empirical analysis of donor behaviour. *The Service Industries Journal*, 24(6), 19–36.

Schlegelmilch, B.B. & Tynan, A.C. (1989). The scope for market segmentation within the charity market: An empirical analysis. *Managerial and Decision Economics*, 10(2), 127–134.

Schons, L.M., Cadogan, J. & Tsakona, R. (2017). Should charity begin at home? An empirical investigation of consumers' responses to companies' varying geographic allocations of donation budgets. *Journal of Business Ethics*, 144(3), 1–18.

Schwartz, S.H. (1992). Universals in the content and structure of values: Theoretical advances and empirical tests in 20 countries. *Advances in Experimental Social Psychology*, 25, 1–65.

Sharfuddin, S. (2020). The world after Covid-19. *The Round Table*, 109(3), 247–257.

Singer, P. (2009). *The Life You Can Save: Acting Now to End World Poverty*. Random House.

Small, D.A. & Cryder, C. (2016). Prosocial consumer behavior. *Current Opinion in Psychology*, 10, 107–111.

Sneddon, J.N., Evers, U. & Lee, J.A. (2020). Personal values and choice of charitable cause: An exploration of donors' giving behavior. *Nonprofit and Voluntary Sector Quarterly*, 49(4), 803–826.

Stevenson, C. & Manning, R. (2010). National identity and international giving: Irish adults' accounts of charitable behaviour. *Journal of Community and Applied Social Psychology*, 20(4), 249–261.

Strombach, T., Jin, J., Weber, B., Kenning, P., Shen, Q., Ma, Q. & Kalenscher, T. (2014). Charity begins at home: Cultural differences in social discounting and generosity. *Journal of Behavioral Decision Making*, 27(3), 235–245.

Tsai, W.H., Lee, W.N. & Song, Y.A. (2013). A cross-cultural study of consumer ethnocentrism between China and the US. *Journal of International Consumer Marketing*, 25(2), 80–93.

Tsiotsou, R. (2007). An empirically based typology of intercollegiate athletic donors: High and low motivation scenarios. *Journal of Targeting, Measurement and Analysis for Marketing*, 15(2), 79–92.

van Dijk, M., Van Herk, H. & Prins, R. (2019). Choosing your charity: The importance of value congruence in two-stage donation choices. *Journal of Business Research*, 105, 283–292.

Wall Street Journal. (2020). While Covid-19 donations soar, other charities see a big hit to funds. Available at www.wsj.com/articles/while-covid-19-donations-soar-other-charities-see-a-big-hit-to-funds-11596913200 (accessed 15 May 2021).

Wiepking, P. (2010). Democrats support international relief and the upper class donates to art? How opportunity, incentives and confidence affect donations to different types of charitable organizations. *Social Science Research*, 39(6), 1073–1087.

Williams, S.R. (2007). Donor preferences and charitable giving. *International Journal of Educational Advancement*, 7(3), 176–189.

Winterich, K.P., Zhang, Y. & Mittal, V. (2012). How political identity and charity positioning increase donations: Insights from Moral Foundations Theory. *International Journal of Research in Marketing*, 29(4), 346–354.

Wollebæk, D., Karlsen, R., Steen-Johnsen, K. & Enjolras, B. (2019). Anger, fear, and echo chambers: The emotional basis for online behavior. *Social Media + Society*, 5(2), 1–14.

Wolpert, J. (1995). Giving and region: Generous and stingy communities. *New Directions for Philanthropic Fundraising*, 7, 11–30.

Yildiz, H., Heitz-Spahn, S. & Belaud, L. (2018). Do ethnocentric consumers really buy local products? *Journal of Retailing and Consumer Services*, 43, 139–148.

Yörük, B.K. (2009). How responsive are charitable donors to requests to give? *Journal of Public Economics*, 93(9–10), 1111–1117.

Zhuang, J., Saxton, G.D. & Wu, H. (2014). Publicity vs. impact in nonprofit disclosures and donor preferences: A sequential game with one nonprofit organization and N donors. *Annals of Operations Research*, 221(1), 469–491.

6

FUNDRAISING ACROSS DIFFERENT CAUSES[1]

Alison Body and Beth Breeze

Introduction

There is an extensive literature exploring why people give to charity, but less discussed is the destination of those donations. Britain itself is a generous country, with most people (57%) reporting that they gave to charity in the past year, and a third (31%) within the previous four weeks (CAF, 2019), but that generosity is not equally spread amongst all the tens of thousands of good causes seeking financial support, leaving many charities feeling that their cause is 'neglected', 'a Cinderella cause' and particularly difficult to fundraise for. Given this widespread belief amongst charities that not enough people care about their beneficiaries or 'get' what they do, it is useful to try to understand why some causes appear to more easily attract widespread support whilst others struggle to raise any significant donated income, in order to help all charities maximise their philanthropic reach.

To start, it is important to note that charitable giving varies widely between both causes and individual charities. For example, within the top 100 most popular causes by fundraised income there are 12 animal charities compared to only one mental health charity, and some causes do not feature at all: in the top 100 there is not a single charity supporting ex-offenders, or refugees and asylum seekers (Pharoah, 2020). The CAF (2019) UK giving survey offers further insight into this distribution, highlighting that the two most popular causes in the UK were animal welfare and children and young people, with 26% of donors saying they had given to each; this was closely followed by medical research (25%), hospitals and hospices (20%), and homeless people, housing and refuge shelters in the UK (18%). These top five cause areas have remained relatively stable over the past five years. Whilst data on private financial support for different types of causes in the UK shows that some cause areas dominate, further analysis also shows that not every charity working in the same area achieves similar fundraising success. For example, Cancer Research UK, the UK's most

DOI: 10.4324/9781003134169-9

successful fundraising charity, attracted almost as much fundraised income in 2019 as all the other cancer charities in the top 100 fundraising charities added together.

Charitable giving is a voluntary act – the freedom to choose which causes to support is an essential element of donor autonomy, and the ability to align personal and philanthropic preferences is an important factor in encouraging giving amongst donors (Frumkin, 2006). Yet normative conceptions of 'worthiness' and cultural factors aligning certain causes with elite preferences creates an 'unequal playing field' for fund-seeking charities that fall – or believe themselves to fall – outside the charmed circle of causes that are popular with potential donors. In addressing this, this chapter first seeks to understand donor choice behaviour, reviewing insights from research and literature into how donors choose charities. We then consider two theories which each help us to better understand the distributional pattern of donations, 'crowding out' (Andreoni & Payne, 2011; Payne, 1998) and 'socio-emotional economy' (Clark, 1997). Next we reflect on what good practice looks like at the donor, organisational and societal level, drawing on case studies to illustrate our argument. Finally, we suggest five implications for practice that are relevant to all types of charities, wherever they perceive themselves to be on the 'popularity spectrum'.

Overview: How do donors choose charities?

The most widely cited research exploring why people give is Bekkers and Wiepking's (2011) meta-review of over 500 studies of philanthropic activity, which identifies eight core mechanisms that drive giving behaviours, as summarised in Table 6.1.

While these mechanisms can help us to understand why individuals donate to charity, they are less helpful in aiding us to understand why donors choose one cause over another among the plethora of good causes (Neumayr & Handy, 2019). However, research suggests that solicitation may be the key driver, as one of the few consistent findings in research into charitable giving is that asking matters. The common-sense wisdom 'if you don't ask, you don't get' turns out to be the closest thing the field has to an iron law (Andreoni, 2006). Despite assumptions that giving is driven by individual-level factors and qualities, such as how much wealth one has, or how compassionate one is, it turns out that whether or not one is asked to donate is the factor with the highest explanatory power regarding the incidence of giving across all causes (Neumayr & Handy, 2019, p. 783). The reason this matters so much is because being asked creates opportunities to donate, and some degree of social pressure to do so (Meer & Rosen, 2011). In the absence of an ask, people may be willing to give but that is less likely to be put into action.

Turning to the few studies that attend to the question of the distribution of philanthropic donations, a common conclusion is that giving decisions are not entirely rational and tend to be highly reliant on donor taste and preferences. Breeze (2013) identifies four non-needs based factors: donor tastes, personal experiences, perceptions of charities' competence and desire for personal impact:

- *Donor tastes:* Donor taste is a key factor in the selection of charitable beneficiaries. Donors state that they typically support 'things that happen to appeal
  to me', causes that are 'close to my heart', things that 'touch a chord' and
  charities 'that I admire' and 'am comfortable giving to'. This approach is collectively termed 'taste-based giving', as opposed to 'needs-based giving', and is
  exemplified by donors who say they prefer to support one sort of animal over
  another, those who support causes aligned with their hobbies or those who
  give financial support to charities they are heavily involved with as volunteers,
  such as a scout group or their local theatre.
- *Personal experiences:* personal preferences are a factor in giving decisions, even
  when donors perceive themselves as motivated by needs. Nonetheless, tastes
  develop because of the individual's socialisation, which includes their
  upbringing, education, personal and professional experiences. People draw on
  their own life experiences to create what have been called 'philanthropic
  autobiographies' (Payton & Moody, 2008) which affects their choice of charitable
  recipients as they give to causes they feel some connection to, or affinity with, as a
  result of experiences and incidents that occur in their personal and professional
  lives, for example donors who support a medical charity after a loved one is
  affected by the illness it researches or supports, or donors who support sea-rescue
  charities because they live or grew up living near the sea.
- *Perceptions of charities' competence:* The third non-needs-based criteria evident in
  giving decisions concerns donors' judgements regarding the competence of
  recipient organisations, such that charities are selected for support based on
  being 'well-run' and 'efficient', or 'charities that don't pay their staff too
  much' and 'charities that have low overheads'. There is a consensus that
  charity competence, as demonstrated in the efficient use of money, is highly
  attractive and likely to prompt greater donations. However, as most donors
  lack the time or resources to obtain and compare robust metrics in order to
  assess organisational competence, they often rely on word of mouth, media
  coverage or proxies such as the apparent cost of fundraising materials or subjective experience of competency such as the misspelling of their name on
  fundraising communications (Breeze, 2010, p. 35).
- *Desire for personal impact:* The fourth non-needs based criteria for giving is a
  desire for donations to make an impact that is not 'drowned out' by support
  from other donors or the government. Donors are particularly keen to avoid
  their donations becoming a substitute for government spending. A preference
  for 'additionality' is widespread, such that donors are keen to ensure that their
  contribution enhances, rather than replaces, the funding available for a particular
  cause. This is especially relevant in the areas of spending on human welfare, as
  studies show that very high proportions of the public believe that meeting social
  need is primarily the job of government rather than philanthropy (Breeze &
  Mohan, 2020).

TABLE 6.1 The eight mechanisms that drive charitable giving (source: Breeze 2019, based on Bekkers and Wiepking, 2011)

Mechanism	Explanation
Awareness of need	People give when they are aware that an organisation needs funds – this awareness is raised through the media and word of mouth as well as through the charities' own efforts in fundraising and communication.
Solicitation	Most giving is prompted by an 'ask', so actively soliciting donations is more effective than passively presenting opportunities to give.
Costs/benefits	Donors are incentivised when the 'price of giving' is lowered by tax breaks and matched funding, and by receipt of benefits such as invitations to events and access to interesting relationships and unusual experiences.
Altruism	Caring about the beneficiaries, and a belief that donations will have a positive effect on their welfare, is a driver of giving.
Reputation	Donations are more likely when giving is viewed as a positive thing to do, and donors are rewarded socially by public approval and an enhanced reputation.
Psychological benefits	In addition to social benefits, donors seek psychological benefits: these include feeling good, alleviating guilt, opportunity to express gratitude and avoiding the cognitive dissonance that occurs when values and actions are not aligned.
Values	When personal values (such as belief in the value of heritage) align with organisational values (such as a charity that exists to protect heritage) there is a greater probability of a donation occurring.
Efficacy	Donors want their contribution to make a meaningful difference. Demonstrating efficacy to the donor can be formal (e.g. through evaluation reports and financial information) or informal (e.g. through anecdotes in charity communications, participating in a 'seeing is believing' trip, and modelling by high status people whose actions are emulated).

In addition, Robson and Hart (2020) show that whilst political identity impacts on charitable choice, it also influences perceptions of need. For example, a liberal donor is more likely to respond positively to solicitations that blame external societal factors for issues such as poverty, whereas conservatives instead prefer messages which focus on individual attributes and failings (Lee et al., 2020). This is further supported by van Dijk et al. (2019), who show that donors look for synergies between their personal values and those of charities they wish to support. Chapman et al. (2018a) support this, highlighting that donors like to give to their 'in-group', meaning they select charities that reflect the priorities of the group they feel they belong too, for example identifying as Christian and giving to Christian organisations.

This overview of the existing research context establishes that philanthropic behaviour is complex and motivated by a multiplicity of factors, that donors choose causes that resonate with their personal experiences and values, and that – crucially – most charitable gifts have to be asked for before they are given. However, there is a surprising lack of confidence amongst charities about asking people for donations (Thelkelsen, 2011). Charities often rely on their work to 'speak for itself' rather than directly 'making the ask'. Nonetheless as various studies suggest that some causes are inherently more popular than others (Body & Breeze, 2016; Robson & Hart, 2020), consideration of how different causes can maximise their philanthropic reach is important.

Theoretical approaches to understanding popularity of causes

Whilst there are few studies focused on the relationship between the types of causes and their fundraising success, there is a larger body of work exploring the organisational behaviours of charities and their relationships with donors. Here we draw on this literature to present two theoretical approaches which may be helpful in making sense of the meaning of popular and unpopular causes: crowding out theory, and the social construction of sympathy.

Crowding out theory: The concept of 'crowding out' comes from the discipline of economics, and occurs when increased government funding leads to a reduction in income from other sources, such as fundraised donations from private individuals and institutions. The research evidence is mixed, with studies showing that the impact of government funding on other income sources is not consistent across time and place (De Wit & Bekkers, 2017; Jilke et al., 2019). Indeed, Horne et al. (2005) show that most donors do not know how much government support charitable organisations receive, and thus are unlikely to use this indicator in their decision-making. Nonetheless, what is clear is that certain causes receive more statutory support than others, for example charities providing support services for children services receive more tax-funded support than do charities rehoming dogs. Therefore, charities rehoming dogs, being entirely reliant on voluntary income from private donors, must focus a great deal of effort on donor fundraising activities. Thus, Andreoni and Payne (2011) suggest that another version of this phenomenon, known as 'internal' crowding out, occurs within organisations when charities reduce their own fundraising efforts as a result of new income success; this presents a plausible hypothesis for why some causes may be more 'popular' (as measured by success in fundraising) than others.

Other possibilities to explain the internal 'crowding out effect' include Weisbrod's (1988) suggestion that charities do not set out to maximise their income, but rather aim to raise enough money to meet identified needs or to address a particular issue; once this target has been met, they do not continue fundraising efforts even if it were possible to raise more money from other sources. Alternatively, if a charity views itself as unpopular and likely to be overlooked by donors the charity may alter its own behaviour by not making substantive efforts to seek support and therefore crowd themselves out of receiving voluntary income. If a charity decides the cause it represents is too unpopular to receive donated income and does not ask, it becomes a self-fulfilling prophecy. The result in this scenario is also a reduction in fundraising efforts because of securing 'sufficient' funds elsewhere. As the popularity of a cause is related to the amount of voluntary income it attracts, the 'crowding out effect' can create circumstances within which a seemingly successful cause in terms of delivery and income is perceived as unpopular with donors.

The social construction of sympathy: A second theoretical approach that is useful in understanding the topic in question comes from a different discipline, psychology, and draws on Clark's (1997) notion of the construction of sympathy, or the 'socio-emotional economy'. This concept understands sympathy, and giving priorities, as something the donor subjectively and socially constructs based upon their own experiences and the social world they live in (Sneddon et al., 2020), thereby suggesting that the popularity of any cause is governed by the level of sympathy it can attract at any given time. Although sympathy may be considered a natural, reflexive reaction, people are not born knowing how and when to distribute it appropriately. We know that personal experience increases sympathy, leading to bigger charitable donations (Small et al., 2007), and that individuals also use external guides to modify their thoughts and behaviours by learning elaborate rules for the expression of sympathy that are considered appropriate to the time and social context. For example, research suggests that people, based on their personal experiences, priorities and characteristics, automatically create conceptual categories that place different groups of people in four quadrants of moral evaluation – these are termed by Fiske et al. (2002) as warm or cold, and competent or incompetent. The warmth dimension includes traits like (dis) honesty, (un)trustworthiness, and (un)friendliness. These can be considered as traits which help people assess whether someone will help or harm you. The competence dimension contains traits like (un)intelligence, skilfulness, persistence, laziness, clumsiness, etc. These traits tell people how effectively someone is at achieving their goals. According to Fiske et al. (2002) there is an underlying pattern to the way we attribute these personality traits to groups and our subsequent responses, each of which ascribe to a particular stereotype as shown in Figure 6.1.

The first quadrant (top right), social reference stereotype, includes those who we view as being both warm and competent and 'people like us'. The second, paternalistic stereotype, we view as being warm but incompetent, they are similar to us but have fallen on hard times or are experiencing difficulties (for example if

		Competence	
		Low	High
	High	Paternalistic stereotype *Traits*: Low status, in-group, honest, unintelligent *Responses*: Pity, sympathy, caring	Social reference stereotype *Traits*: High status, in-group, honest, dominant, intelligent *Responses*: Pride, admiration
Warmth	Low	Contemptuous stereotype *Traits*: Selfish, low status *Responses*: Competitive contempt, anger, resentment	Envious stereotype *Traits*: High status, intelligent, selfish, dishonest *Responses*: Competitive envy, jealousy

FIGURE 6.1 The stereotype content model (Source: Adapted from Fiske et al., 2002)

someone falls ill). These first two quadrants are 'in-groups' and more likely to be considered 'deserving' of our sympathy. As Smith (1976) notes, sympathy and feelings of moral responsibility are easier to elicit when presenting donors with situations which they are familiar with. The third quadrant, envious stereotype, is the first 'out-group', those we are more likely to view as 'undeserving' of our sympathy, who we view as competent but we feel cold towards. The fourth out-group we neither view warmly nor view as competent. According to Murphy (2019) this group are then targeted with particularly harsh, often dehumanising, framing. For example, this can help us understand the frequent negative media attention concerning asylum seekers and immigrants (Drywood & Gray, 2019). As research tells us that sympathy plays a key role in decision-making when help is required (Batson, 2011), the social construction of those we will feel sympathy for and those who we will not is a likely strong predictor as to who we will give donations to and who we will not. This leads us to question whether the concept of popular and unpopular causes really exists beyond that of the individual donor's sympathetic preferences, societal identification of the 'in-group' and 'out-group' and the context at any given time.

Examples of good practice

In 2016, the authors of this chapter carried out research analysing how 'unpopular' causes have been defined in media outlets in the last two decades. We began by analysing 20 years of UK media coverage in order to identify the ten most 'unpopular' charitable cause areas, as shown in Table 6.2.

We then conducted a thorough examination of publicly available material on ten successful fundraising charities working in each of these cause areas in order to demonstrate that 'unpopularity' is not a necessary barrier to raising funds from individual donors.

TABLE 6.2 'Unpopular' causes as defined in UK media coverage 1994–2014 (Source: Body & Breeze, 2016)

Rank	Cause area
1	Mental health (including suicide and eating disorders)
2	Refugees and asylum seekers
3	Offenders/ex-Offenders
4	Children with behavioural problems (including young offenders)
5	Travellers/Gypsies
6	AIDS/HIV
7	Domestic violence and child abuse
8	Sex workers
9	LGBTQ rights
10	Drug and alcohol addiction

In the next section we identify good practice in asking at three different levels of the fundraising process: (1) the organisational level of the charity; (2) the interaction between the donor and the cause; and (3) wider societal norms and values.

Good practice at the organisational level

A culture of philanthropy: A charity is said to have a 'culture of philanthropy' when

> most people in the organisation (across positions) act as ambassadors and engage in relationship building. Everyone promotes philanthropy and can articulate a case for giving. Fundraising is viewed and valued as a mission-aligned programme of the organisation. Organisational systems are established to support donors. The chief executive/director is committed and personally involved in fundraising.
>
> *(Belle & Cornelius, 2013, p. 3)*

Embedding a commitment to fundraising throughout organisations creates a 'culture of philanthropy' that has a proven connection to successful fundraising (Gibson, 2016). Creating a culture of philanthropy extends beyond the staff and volunteers of a charity, embracing cheerleaders and donors as well. According to Ferguson (2017) 'it is not just about maintaining past donors and acquiring new ones; it is about viewing all individuals as a vital part of your organization who can bring more to the table than just money' (p. 2).

For example, in 2016, our research identified mental health as the topmost 'unpopular cause' in the UK as defined by UK media outlets (Body & Breeze, 2016). Indeed, as Mind's (2015) own research highlighted, stigma against people with mental health illness occurs across all socio-economic groups, potentially making this a difficult to cause to fundraise for. In efforts to combat this, the mental health charity purposefully placed fundraising at the heart of the charity's communications strategy and has worked with all staff and supporters to ensure fundraising is understood as a key strategic priority. Since 2015, they have more than doubled their fundraised income through donations and legacies, from £10.4 million in 2015 to £26.4 million in 2020.

Cultivating celebrity cheerleaders: Research has highlighted that charities who actively celebrate and engage celebrity and well-known supporters experience positive impacts on their donations (Peterson et al., 2018). Celebrities are most effective as cheerleaders when they can speak from authentic personal experience to a large following, thus effecting donations (Knoll & Matthes, 2017). For example, the Terrence Higgins Trust, a charity aiming to end HIV cases in England by 2030, is promoted by a multitude of global names including pop-star Elton John and actress Dame Judy Dench, whose support raises the charity's profile and helps them gain access to major donors in their networks.

Good practice at the donor level

Arousing donor sympathies: Research shows that the successful framing of a cause is linked to better fundraising outcomes. Examples of the importance of framing include the finding that donors respond more generously to one 'identifiable victim' than they do to hearing statistics about large numbers of unknown yet similarly affected people (Dickert et al., 2016). This finding explains why disaster relief appeals tend to be 'fronted' by one face, usually that of a sympathy-provoking child. Multiple other studies highlight how individuals are more likely to feel sympathy for an image of a sad child, and thus more likely to donate, than they are if presented with an image of a happy child (Allred & Amos, 2018; Small & Verrochi, 2009). Whereas other research suggests that videos which highlight the differences between donors' situation and the beneficiaries' situation also have a positive effect on fundraising amounts (Van Rijn et al., 2017). However, there are moral sensitivities to balance here. Research has suggested charities need to take care to not use imagery which reinforces negative stereotypes and instead should adopt longer-term strategies which seek to educate donors about the wider issues which sit behind a cause, such as food poverty, to help achieve longer-term social change (Bhati & Eikenberry, 2016; Body et al., 2020).

Charities that deliberately and carefully frame their key message and reinforce that framing through all their communication activity, including carefully chosen images (still and videos), are more likely to elicit the attention and sympathy of donors. For example, Storybook Dads, a charity which works with parents in prison to produce CDs and DVDs of themselves reading a book to their children, frames its beneficiaries as the innocent children with an in-prison parent. Their website material in 2020 leads with the statement: 'Prisoners' children haven't committed a crime'. They use videos to illustrate this message, primarily of sad children made happy by listening to their storybook or reconnecting with family. The website, social media and marketing material reflect a child-focused approach with a range of drawings and doodles, giving the impression that children have helped design the brand and are directly asking the donor for support. As a small charity, they have more than doubled their fundraised income between 2017 and 2019.

Minimising perceptions of culpability: Clark's (1997) notion of the 'socioemotional economy' suggests donors prefer beneficiaries whose needs arise through little or no fault of their own and hence are perceived to be free – or more free – of culpability. Research has highlighted the importance of educating donors by bringing more voices of beneficiaries into fundraising and telling more complete stories, particularly about needy or marginalised people, rather than just overwhelmingly focusing on donor motivation to give (Bhati & Eikenberry, 2016). For example, Refugee Action, a charity supporting refugees and people seeking asylum in the UK, notes on their website[2] that refugees face 'hatred, isolation and destitution… when they arrive in the UK', and seek to challenge this narrative by highlighting that 'everyone who's had to flee their home deserves a chance to live again', and offering insight into individuals' stories highlighting stories of persecution. Alongside these stories, fundraising materials show pictures of families and children, reinforcing the message that the donor and beneficiaries have shared values and networks, and that beneficiaries are victims of persecution and war, and thus need our support. Between 2015 and 2019 the charity's fundraised income has increased by 34%, which is likely supported by such messaging, coupled with increased media and political attention.

Good practice at a societal level

Attracting positive media coverage: Media discourses are widely understood to be directly reflexive of public opinion (Ewart, 2000, p. 2). Mass media acts as a gate-keeper at two levels: first deciding which social issues make it onto the public radar, and second shaping how they are presented which impacts on how people are encouraged to think about an issue rather than just whether the topic appears in the media (Hale, 2007). The recent rise of social media has dented the power of the mass media to some extent and greatly benefitted charities as communication messages can now be spread more democratically through diverse networks of individuals lacking traditional media power. For example, The Lucy Faithful Foundation, a charity working with child abusers or those at risk of abusing, has received ongoing public criticism because of its client group. Despite attracting 'bad press' it has invested in facilitating supporters prepared to champion the cause in television and radio interviews, and has proactively used social media, such as blogs and twitter, to promote the value of their work direct to the public. Their social media campaign 'It's time we talked about it' launched in March 2019 saw Twitter impressions increase by 539% in the first three months. In the same year fundraised income increased by 40%.

Implications for practice

In drawing this chapter to a close we identify five key areas that directly impact on successful fundraising.

Asking: We conclude that asking donors to donate is the single biggest factor affecting giving. We know that almost all donations occur in response to a solicitation. Asking for donations means investing in fundraising, not just in financial terms but also by strategically placing fundraising at the heart of the organisation, including establishing a culture of philanthropy. Such investment can pay dividends, regardless of the size of the charity.

Framing the cause: Framing the cause effectively to both capture donors' sympathies and appeal directly to donors' personal tastes is key to securing donations. Personalising the message of the charity through storytelling and individual case studies is more likely to appeal to donors' sympathies. Examples of good practice discussed in this chapter offer good examples on their websites, highlighting personal and compelling stories of individuals that help donors emotionally connect to the cause and feel empathy with the beneficiaries. Such approaches allow donors to understand and visualise the impact of their gift, whilst simultaneously overcoming issues associated with the cause being labelled as unworthy or unpopular.

Illustrating the cause: Choosing the right images to illustrate a cause in print, online and broadcast media is essential to supporting the chosen framing of a cause. Imagery should focus on fostering empathy and connection. However, there are several moral sensitivities to consider when considering illustrations used to frame a cause, and charities should take care not to reinforce negative stereotypes which can be counterproductive to long-term change.

Empowering supporters: Successful fundraising charities make the most of all available resources including employees, volunteers, beneficiaries, donors and celebrity supporters who can use their networks and influence to reach and empower people who are unaware of the need and may be motivated to donate. Empowering the people at the heart of a cause – beneficiaries, former beneficiaries, their parents and loved ones, as well as volunteers and staff – to ask their social networks to support the cause, is an efficient and effective way to secure donations (Yörük, 2012). Donors are known to respond positively to the person who is doing the asking, as well as to the cause they are asking on behalf of. This phenomenon, known as 'relational altruism', or the 'champion effect', underlines the importance of supporting volunteer fundraisers who can efficiently and effectively reach large numbers of potential donors (Chapman et al., 2018b; Scharf & Smith, 2016).

Making good use of celebrities is another way of extending reach and influence, as some donors look to well-known supporters as a shorthand method for assessing a charity's calibre (Breeze, 2013). Engaging such individuals can be difficult for smaller charities with fewer resources, but cheerleaders do not need to be famous as social media enables anyone who is connected to other people to promote the work of a charity.

Raising cause profile: Opportunities to raise a charity's profile can be created through calculated marketing efforts, or they can be opportunistic. Accepting that the visibility of a cause is largely influenced by wider social factors means that a charity needs to remain vigilant for opportunities to discuss and promote the work of their organisation at all times. Many charities lack the funds, resources and networks to launch significant media campaigns, and their supporters and leadership may not endorse significant spending on non-frontline activities. Social media has helped redistribute some of this power, meaning some charities have launched successful donor education and fundraising campaigns. However, it is often beneficial for charities to work together to raise the profile of specific causes and use their combined resources and networks to secure sufficient media support for the effort to be fruitful.

Conclusion

This chapter has explored the topic of fundraising across different causes by focusing on the question of how donors choose causes, and the implications of this for charities' marketing and fundraising activities. We argue that good fundraising at an organisational level is primarily concerned with internal investment in, and advocacy of, fundraising. Investment in fundraising is not tied to success or otherwise in generating other types of income – the search for philanthropic support is viewed as a valid task that is owned and supported by the whole organisation and is not at risk of internal crowding out. Good practice at the donor level in the charity–donor relationship is exemplified by successfully arousing sympathy and minimising perceptions of culpability amongst the beneficiary group. Charities that invest in the 'ask' and frame their cause effectively position themselves more favourably with donors. Empowering cheerleaders and advocates can further enhance this relationship. And finally, at the societal level, successful fundraising depends to some extent on successfully influencing media coverage of the beneficiary group as well as the work of the organisations working in that area. We note that the rise of social media is helping to redistribute some power into the hands of charities and their supporters, but they do remain reliant on favourable depiction of their work in the main news outlets.

In summary, we conclude that the UK is a generous country, but this generosity is not evenly distributed or allocated according to objective criteria of 'worthiness', so all charitable organisations need to work hard to attract voluntary support. The landscape of charitable activity is increasingly filled with well-framed, emotive causes competing for donors' support. Whilst we know that an individual's decision to donate is hugely influenced by subjective experience and personal taste, we also know that they are unlikely to seek out charitable causes beyond their normal frame of reference or experiences. This means charities, especially those that perceive themselves to be unpopular and/or working in cause areas beyond typical donors' experiences, must create an organisational culture of philanthropy, consider carefully how they frame their cause and its beneficiaries and be proactive in drawing attention to their work. As such we recognise that they sometimes need to work harder to ensure they make their cause as visible and compelling as possible for donors. However, this is not an impossible task as demonstrated by the examples given above. Whilst we recognise that some causes are undoubtedly a tougher 'ask' than others, none should pre-emptively write themselves off as 'unpopular' and therefore unlikely to attract private support.

Chapter discussion questions

1.   How does Fiske et al.'s (2002) Stereotype Content Model help us understand why some causes may be perceived to be more popular than others?
2.   What steps can fundraisers take to overcome perceived unpopularity?
3.   How do perceptions of unpopular causes change over time (e.g. mental health, refugees)?

Notes

1   This chapter is based upon an updated version of our previously published article Body, A. and Breeze, B. (2016). What are 'unpopular causes' and how can they achieve fundraising success? *International Journal of Nonprofit and Voluntary Sector Marketing, 21(1)*, 57–70.
2   www.refugee-action.org.uk/about/facts-about-refugees/

References

Allred, A. & Amos, C. (2018). Disgust images and nonprofit children's causes. *Journal of Social Marketing*, 1(8), 120–140.

Andreoni, J. (2006). Philanthropy. In S.-C. Kolm and J.M. Ythier (eds), *Handbook of the Economics of Giving, Reciprocity and Altruism*. Elsevier.

Andreoni, J. & Payne, A. (2011). Is crowding out due entirely to fundraising? Evidence from a panel of charities. *Journal of public Economics*, 95(5–6), 334–343.

Batson, C.D. (2011). *Altruism in Humans*. Oxford University Press.

Bekkers R. & Wiepking P. (2011). A literature review of empirical studies of philanthropy: Eight mechanisms that drive charitable giving. *Nonprofit and Voluntary Sector Quarterly* 40(5), 924–973.

Belle, J. & Cornelius, M. (2013). *Underdeveloped: A National Study of Challenges Facing Nonprofit Fundraising*. Compasspoint.

Bhati, A. & Eikenberry, A.M. (2016). Faces of the needy: The portrayal of destitute children in the fundraising campaigns of NGOs in India. *International Journal of Nonprofit and Voluntary Sector Marketing*, 21(1), 31–42.

Body, A. & Breeze, B. (2016). What are 'unpopular causes' and how can they achieve fundraising success? *International Journal of Nonprofit and Voluntary Sector Marketing*, 21(1), 57–70.

Body, A., Lau, E. & Josephidou, J. (2020). Engaging children in meaningful charity: Opening-up the spaces within which children learn to give. *Children and Society*. doi:10.1111/chso.12366.

Breeze, B. (2010). *How Donors Choose Charities*. Centre for Giving and Philanthropy.

Breeze B. (2013). How donors choose charities: The role of personal taste and experiences in giving decisions. *Voluntary Sector Review*, 4(2), 165–183.

Breeze, B. (2019). Individual giving and philanthropy. In H. Anheier and S. Toepler (eds), *Routledge Companion to Nonprofit Management*. Routledge.

Breeze, B. & Mohan, J. (2020). Sceptical yet supportive: Understanding public attitudes to charity. *History & Policy*, 28 April. Available at www.historyandpolicy.org/policy-papers/papers/sceptical-yet-supportive-understanding-public-attitudes-to-charity (accessed 18 August 2021).

CAF (Charities Aid Foundation) (2019). *UK Giving 2019*. Charities Aid Foundation.

Chapman, C.M., Louis, W.R. & Masser, B.M. (2018a). Identifying (our) donors: Toward a social psychological understanding of charity selection in Australia. *Psychology and Marketing*, 35(12), 980–989.

Chapman, C.M., Masser, B.M. & Louis, W.R. (2018b). The champion effect in peer-to-peer giving: Successful campaigns highlight fundraisers more than causes. *Nonprofit and Voluntary Sector Quarterly*, 48(3), 572–592.

Clark, C. (1997). *Misery and Company: Sympathy in Everyday Life*. University of Chicago Press.

De Wit, A. & Bekkers, R. (2017). Government support and charitable donations: A meta-analysis of the crowding-out hypothesis. *Journal of Public Administration Research and Theory*, 27(2), 301–319.

Dickert, S., Kleber, J., Västfjäll, D. & Slovic, P. (2016). Mental imagery, impact, and affect: A mediation model for charitable giving. *PLoS ONE*, 11(2), e0148274.

Drywood, E. & Gray, H. (2019). Demonising immigrants: How a human rights narrative has contributed to negative portrayals of immigrants in the UK media. In M. Farrell, E. Drywood and E. Hughes (eds), *Human Rights in the Media: Fear and Fetish*. Routledge.

Ewart, J. (2000). Capturing the heart of the region: How regional media define a community. Transformations. Available at www.cqu.edu.au/transformations (accessed 10 July 2016).

Ferguson, A. (2017). *Creating a Culture of Philanthropy in Nonprofit Arts Organizations*. Virginia Commonwealth University Scholars Compass.

Fiske, S.T., Cuddy, A.J., Glick, P. & Xu, J. (2002). A model of (often mixed) stereotype content: Competence and warmth respectively follow from perceived status and competition. *Journal of Personality and Social Psychology*, 82(6), 878–902.

Frumkin, P. (2006). *Strategic Giving: The Art and Science of Philanthropy*. University of Chicago Press.

Gibson, C. (2016). *Beyond Fundraising: What Does it Mean to Build a Culture of Philanthropy?* Evelyn and Walter Haas, Jr. Fund and CompassPoint.

Hale, M. (2007). Superficial friends: A content analysis of nonprofit and philanthropy coverage in nine major newspapers. *Nonprofit and Voluntary Sector Quarterly*, 36, 464–486.

Horne, C., Johnson, J. & Van Slyke, D. (2005). Do charitable donors know enough – and care enough – about government subsidies to affect private giving to nonprofit organizations? *Nonprofit and Voluntary Sector Quarterly*, 34, 136–149.

Jilke, S., Lu, J., Xu, C. & Shinohara, S. (2019). Using large-scale social media experiments in public administration: Assessing charitable consequences of government funding of nonprofits. *Journal of Public Administration Research and Theory*, 29(4), 627–639.

Knoll, J. & Matthes, J. (2017). The effectiveness of celebrity endorsements: A meta-analysis. *Journal of the Academy of Marketing Science*, 45(1), 55–75.

Lee, Y., Seo, J.Y. & Yoon, S. (2020). Charity advertising: Congruence between political orientation and cause of need. *International Journal of Advertising*, 39(7), 943–962.

Meer, J. & Rosen, H. (2011). The ABCs of charitable solicitation. *Journal of Public Economics*, 95, 363–371.

Mind. (2015), *Time to Change: Attitudes to Mental Illness 2014 Research Report*. Mind.

Murphy, E. (2019). *The Politics of Compassion: The Challenge to Care for the Stranger*. Rowman and Littlefield International.

Neumayr, M. & Handy, F. (2019). Charitable giving: What influences donors' choice among different causes? *Voluntas: International Journal of Voluntary and Nonprofit Organizations*, 30(4), 783–799.

Payne A. (1998). Does the government crowd out private donations? New evidence from a sample of non-profit firms. *Journal of Public Economics*, 69, 323–345.

Payton, R. & Moody, M. (2008). *Understanding Philanthropy: Its Meaning and Mission*. Indiana University Press.

Peterson, N., Tripoli, E., Langenbach, K. & Devasagayam, R. (2018). Celebrity endorsements and donations: Empirical investigation of impact on philanthropic giving. *Business Perspectives and Research* 6(2), 79–89.

Pharoah, C. (2020). Top 100 fundraisers spotlight annual report. Charity Financials, April. Available at: www.charitychoice.co.uk/charity-reports (accessed 9 September 2020).

Robson, A. & Hart, D. (2020). Understanding the correlates of donor intention: A comparison of local, national, and international charity destinations. *Nonprofit and Voluntary Sector Quarterly*, 50(3), 506–530.

Scharf, K. & Smith, S. (2016). Relational altruism and giving in social groups. *Journal of Public Economics*, 141, 1–10.

Small, D. & Verrochi, N. (2009). The face of need: Facial emotion expression on charity advertisements. *Journal of Marketing Research* 46(6), 777–787.

Small, D., Loewenstein, G. & Slovic, P. (2007). Sympathy and callousness: The impact of deliberative thought on donations to identifiable and statistical victims. *Organizational Behavior and Human Decision Processes*, 102(2), 143–153.

Smith, A. (1976). *The Theory of Moral Sentiments*. Liberty Fund.

Sneddon, J., Evers, U. & Lee, J. (2020). Personal values and choice of charitable cause: An exploration of donors' giving behavior. *Nonprofit and Voluntary Sector Quarterly*, 49(4), 803–826.

Thelkelsen, A. (2011). Encounters with philanthropic information: Cognitive dissonance and implications for the social sector. *Voluntas: International Journal of Voluntary and Nonprofit Organizations*, 22, 518–545.

van Dijk, M., Van Herk, H. & Prins, R. (2019). Choosing your charity: The importance of value congruence in two-stage donation choices. *Journal of Business Research*, 105, 283–292.

Van Rijn, J., Barham, B. & Sundaram-Stukel, R. (2017). An experimental approach to comparing similarity and guilt-based charitable appeals. *Journal of Behavioral and Experimental Economics*, 68, 25–40.

Weisbrod, B. (1988). *The Nonprofit Economy*. Harvard University Press.

Yörük, B. (2012). Charitable solicitations matter: A comparative analysis of fundraising methods. *The Journal of Applied Public Economics*, 33(4), 467–487.

7

CONTEMPORARY PERSPECTIVES ON CHARITY AND NONPROFIT ARTS MARKETING

From creative economy towards a public realm

Athanasia Daskalopoulou and Chloe Preece

> In short, theatre and the arts are a giant economic growth engine. That is not because the arts keep us alive (thank you to the NHS for that) but because they give us something worth staying alive for.
>
> *Sam Mendes (2020)*

Introduction

This chapter offers an overview of some contemporary issues in charity and nonprofit arts marketing. Unfortunately, the current situation is somewhat bleak. Given the financial hit of the Coronavirus pandemic and years of government funding reductions as well as the social, political and economic unrest around Brexit, the arts are struggling to survive in the UK. Indeed, the pandemic has aggravated pre-existing funding inequities in the UK arts sector. Although many arts organisations are supported by the Arts Council England (ACE), they have seen either a stagnation or reduction of public funding for the 2018–2022 period (ACE, 2018). At the same time, grassroots arts organisations and freelance, independent artists have slipped through the cracks of Covid-19 government support. This workforce is characterised by freelance precarious workers who have found themselves in 'pandemic insolvency', unprotected by employment regulations, unable to afford a basic standard of life or plan for the future (Freelancers Make Theatre Work, 2020). This perfect storm requires radical new approaches. In investigating some possible alternative models of funding, we first consider the need for diversification before providing an overview of individuals' motivations and giving practices to the arts. We then uncover the ideological underpinnings on which the arts sector is built in the UK and finally conclude by looking at some innovative responses by arts organisations to broaden their audiences despite financial pressures.

DOI: 10.4324/9781003134169-10

Is diversification the answer?

The result of the reduction (or in some cases, complete loss) in government grants, footfall and box-office returns presented above is that many artists and arts organisations have had to (continuously) diversify their revenue base (Lee et al., 2017; Moraes et al., 2020). Relying on diverse sources of funding allows arts organisations to mitigate financial risks by grasping different funding opportunities (Mollick & Nanda, 2016). Diversification also connotes an arts organisation's flexibility (Hager, 2001); when an organisation receives all its funding from one source (e.g. the government) the funding can be highly concentrated, as compared to a highly diversified organisation which receives its funding from multiple sources (e.g. government grants, donations, etc.). In other words, arts organisations with diversified sources of funding are more flexible than organisations with concentrated sources of funding because they can balance the loss of one funding source (e.g. the loss of a grant) by increasing their intake from and appeals to another funding source (e.g. appeal to individual donors) (Hager, 2001). It is worth noting, however, that diversification requires additional effort in managing different stakeholders and supplementary bureaucracy. Furthermore, many of these funding mechanisms are based on discourses of instrumental measures of value, burdening artists and arts organisations with having to evidence extraneous outcomes using spurious metrics (Belfiore & Bennett, 2007).

New models to generate additional income, such as crowdfunding, can, however, provide an antidote to some of these concerns. For example, the music industry has incorporated crowdfunding into the development of business models for artists, labels and live music companies (Gamble et al., 2017). In the performing arts crowdfunding is also used as a fundraising substitute and empirical research shows that it benefits both younger and more established nonprofit performing arts organisations (Alexiou et al., 2020). Additional benefits of diversifying funding strategies for arts organisations by embracing crowdfunding include promoting audience loyalty and the fact that crowdfunding serves as a legitimation signal (Alexiou et al., 2020). Another example is fundraising membership schemes. Audience members participate voluntarily in these schemes and when they do so, they receive exclusive perks for their participation. Prior studies show that the following benefits are particularly desirable for audience members; exclusive passes to attend rehearsals or exhibition openings, reduced ticket fees, priority passes/bookings, discounts and exclusive offers (Pitts et al., 2020), social gatherings and networking opportunities with like-minded individuals, fostering meaningful and lasting relationships with staff and artists and the opportunity to engage in a local cultural scene (Bussell & Forbes, 2006). These include both tangible and intangible benefits that illustrate both audiences' philanthropic inclinations and cost-saving attitudes. Philanthropy or voluntary giving refers to private giving for public purposes (Barman, 2017). As such, individuals desire to support the arts but are also keen to be rewarded for their support and loyalty. This type of horizontal philanthropy can provide mutual benefit (versus vertical where the very wealthy give to the less wealthy).

However, there is a risk of this becoming a purely transactional relationship; to avoid this, and to promote philanthropic citizenship, the purpose of fundraising needs to be extremely clear so as not to trivialise involvement (Body et al., 2020).

Diversifying the revenue base of arts organisations proved useful during lockdowns when many took to Instagram to reach their audiences and appeal for funds such as the Manchester Craft and Design Centre, a crafts collective in Manchester, that organised pop-up sales to gather funds for its creatives. Appealing to individual (voluntary) donors is common for arts organisations and audiences tend to respond well, especially during times of crises, such as when government cuts threaten organisations that are important to them (De Wit & Bekkers, 2020) or when they need to mobilise to save venues that are a part of their local heritage (Bennett & Strong, 2018). According to a recent report from the Charities Aid Foundation about giving during Covid-19, although the number of individuals that donated funds has not changed dramatically compared to previous years, between January and June 2020, there was £5.4 billion worth of donations to charity (CAF, 2020). In comparison to the same period in 2019, this was an increase of £800 million in donations (CAF, 2020).

Although diversifying funding sources is therefore integral for arts organisations, it also raises a number of questions: How can arts organisations continue to be viable? And at the same time what is their responsibility for the well-being of their local community (Kim, 2017)? How can arts organisations balance the expectations (or even demands) of different funders (e.g. the government and individual donors)? For example, empirical studies show that funding sources have an impact on arts organisations' performance and activities; performing arts organisations take more risks when they have secured funding (McDonald & Harrison, 2002), museums' financial arrangements impact their managerial decision-making (Frey & Meier, 2002) and even for independent cultural spaces that are largely autonomous, their marketability is linked to their revenue sources and stakeholders (Murray, 2019).

A balancing act

As we have seen, diversification of revenue is increasingly a necessity for arts organisations and often for individual artists as well, yet this requires a delicate balancing act in order to satisfy multiple stakeholders who have different giving practices and motivations. In differentiating between these, we provide an overview of recent research on voluntary giving from micro-, meso- and macro-level perspectives.

Individuals' giving practices depend on a number of factors: first, micro-level approaches to voluntary giving have focused on individual donors' sociodemographic characteristics in order to understand their giving practices. A considerable number of studies have explored the role of gender in voluntary giving, although findings have not been consistent across studies (Wiepking & Bekkers, 2012). For example, in a study of Dutch households, De Wit & Bekkers (2016) found that women are more likely to give than men and to a wider variety of sectors, whereas men donate higher amounts than women. Much of this research follows a 'gender-as-a-variable' perspective (Haynes, 2008) which measures essential sex differences between men's and women's charitable behaviour. This is not without problems, as it has been noted that without careful methodology this type of study can result in a literature of contradiction (Rich-Edwards et al., 2018), but it does still provide some general takeaways worthy of consideration. Similarly, a number of studies have explored the role of education, marital status, age, social class, income and religious conviction among other 'individual' characteristics that make some individuals give more than others. For example, Bennett (2012) studied low-income charitable giving in inner London and found that individuals' level of education positively influenced their giving choices (e.g. to arts and cultural heritage) despite their constrained financial position. Other motives to give according to micro-level approaches include altruism and the 'feel good' factor. Altruistic giving is 'motivated mainly out of a consideration for another's needs rather than one's own' (Piliavin & Charng, 1990, p. 30). Altruism is seen as an innate trait that drives certain individuals to donate to cause-based (rather than arts) organisations – regardless of whether driven by self-serving motives (Bekkers & Wiepking, 2011; Bennett, 2012). There is also a relationship between giving and 'happiness' or the 'feel good factor': giving has emotional meaning and it is linked to positive emotions, wellbeing and personal happiness (Liu & Aaker, 2008).

A second body of research has followed a meso-level, relational approach in order to understand voluntary giving. According to this perspective, charitable behaviour is shaped by individuals' embeddedness in dynamic social fields and by their social relationships (Barman, 2017). For example, giving circles have emerged in many countries, including the UK, as a response to mainstream, professionalised and bureaucratic philanthropy (Eikenberry, 2009). Giving circles bring together individuals who collaborate in order to financially support or in some cases volunteer time to different organisations and individuals (Eikenberry & Breeze, 2018). This form of organising relies on small groups and 'loose' networks and mainly aims to address community problems, thus giving choices might favour cause-based charities rather than (community) arts organisations which are not typically perceived as sufficiently 'essential'. There are various types of giving circles in the UK and Ireland and the various reasons to form and participate in them include responding to a problem, aiming to perform a 'different' type of philanthropy (i.e. making voluntary giving more meaningful and personal, contributing to positive social changes, moving away from transactional approaches), becoming aware of organisations' needs through relational networks and thus making donations where/when needed, and networking and socialising (Eikenberry & Breeze, 2015). Similarly, Friends groups are a very important source of support for arts organisations (e.g. funding support, volunteering, PR, sponsorship, etc.). Bussell and Forbes (2006) find that Friends groups are an important resource for provincial theatres in the North of England, helping them to generate revenue; for example, Friends groups can cover the cost of improvements in a theatre or donate gifts to it. Typically, Friends groups work closely with theatre management in order to make decisions regarding funding (Bussell & Forbes, 2006).

Apart from active and conscious participation in organised giving circles and Friends groups, voluntary giving is also shaped and socially shared with co-workers, friends and family. Individuals respond to direct 'word-of-mouth' fundraising appeals that offer palatable, clear messages and instructions in the workplace (Moraes et al., 2020). These appeals are often framed around the needs of cause-based charities, whereas arts organisations' needs and their solicitation styles do not always resonate with givers (Bekkers & Wiepking, 2011; Body & Breeze, 2016). For example, Breeze and Wiepking (2018, p. 461) find that employees might dis-agree with the types of organisations that corporate leaders decide to support with arguments such as: 'theatre is like a luxury, you can live without a theatre'. It is evident in this comment that some causes, such as the theatre, are associated with elite tastes and that makes them perceived to be less 'worthy' of support than others (e.g. hospices). Finally, according to the meso-level approach, individuals' embeddedness in social fields shapes how, where and how much they donate (Barman, 2017). Following a practice theory perspective, Moraes et al. (2020) illustrate that voluntary giving towards different causes, and more specifically the arts, is influenced by individuals' affinity identification with the arts. Individuals develop affinity with the arts (and other causes) through their lived experience in social fields such as through primary socialisation in childhood, hobbies, formal and informal education, normative influences and professionally. According to this perspective, individuals are more likely to support causes with which they share an affinity, a sense of belonging, rather than others that do not necessarily share the same values or congruence with their identity:

> affinity identification, thus, implies that identity can illuminate the meanings and emotions connected to voluntary giving, as well as those linked to 'not giving' and non-identification objects; a type of counter or non-affinity that may include a specific nonprofit organisation or an entire sector, such as the arts.
>
> *(Moraes et al., 2020, p. 73)*

Similarly, Pitts et al. (2020) found that audience members were more likely to sup-port contemporary music commissioning when their values and ethos aligned with that of the contemporary music organisation. Affinity identification can be impacted by how long someone has been a part of an arts organisation, whether they support other similar organisations or other cause-based charities, and also by how their contribution is recognised by the arts organisation (Pitts et al., 2020). In other words, the degree of an individual's affinity identification with an arts organisation impacts their willingness to be emotionally and financially attached to it.

Finally, a third body of research has followed a macro-level approach to understand voluntary giving. According to this perspective, individuals' embeddedness in broad societal and geographical configurations hinder or encourage giving practices (Barman, 2017). For example, the existence of formalised and organised opportunities to donate positively influence individuals' giving (Healy, 2010). This is often a problem for arts organisations because many lack the formal infrastructure to solicit donations and thus individual donors often do not know how to donate. As a result, individuals are not always aware of the funding needs of arts organisations and the result is that well-established organisations (e.g. museums, art galleries) tend to receive the majority of donations via for example donation boxes in highly-visible areas; yet, it is the smaller-scale, community arts organisations – without audience-facing venues and thus without donation boxes – that more likely need financial assistance (Moraes et al., 2020). Research in the arts sector also shows that funding sources are mutually interdependent (Grasse et al., 2016). Institutional and legal arrangements in different countries influence the scale of individual and corporate giving. Federal government in the United States, for example, legitimised and encouraged voluntary giving by offering tax incentives (e.g. deductions) for individual donors and corporate philanthropy initiatives (Barman, 2017). Recognising nonprofit organisations as charitable foundations also permits and encourages philanthropy (Guthrie & McQuarrie, 2008). However, because giving is selective, individuals often feel that alternative funding sources such as public, government funding are sufficient in order for those organisations with charitable status to survive, and hence their relatively smaller donations are seen as irrelevant – acquiring charitable status can then have a crowding-out effect for certain donors (De Wit et al., 2017). At the same time, in the nonprofit arts sector, government support can also confer legitimacy to the organisation and its activities (Alexiou et al., 2020) such as in the context of dance companies (Smith, 2003), theatres (Borgonovi, 2006) and symphony orchestras (Brooks, 1999). A recent study also shows that when individuals are presented with information about government funding cuts to an organisation, they are more likely to support that organisation financially (and even donate more) (De Wit & Bekkers, 2020). Similarly, art lovers and frequent gallery-goers are more likely to donate when they are 'nudged' in order to not 'lose' an existing exhibition, whereas non-frequent gallery-goers respond better to opportunities to 'gain' a new exhibition (Lee et al., 2017). This often makes it difficult for arts organisations to attract revenue to cover basic running costs which has profound implications for arts organisations that are currently in a detrimental financial position due to reductions in government funding and the adverse financial impact of Covid-19-related closures and restrictions.

The arts in crisis

A recent study shows that the cultural and creative industries contributed (pre-Covid-19) over £100 billion to the UK economy, exported £46 billion in goods and services, were growing at twice the rate of the rest of the economy and employed more than two million people (Chung et al., 2018). However, due to the structure of the sector, consisting of mainly small, under-capitalised organisations and a freelance, uncertainly employed workforce, it has been decimated by the pandemic.

In response to the emergency of the pandemic, many arts institutions fell back on what was a 'broadcast mode', that is, broadcasting what they do digitally, online, in order to get the work they have created out to audiences. This has been particularly the case with larger institutions, what Oliver Dowden, the Culture Secretary, called the 'crown jewels of our national life' which have been the focus of the £1.57 billion emergency support package provided by the government. The National Theatre's NT at Home scheme, for example, was one of the biggest virtual successes of lockdown; it screened 17 productions and garnered more than 15 million views from audiences in more than 170 countries (Akbar, 2020). It was free of charge with an option to donate, providing entertainment for the masses who perhaps are not in the usual elite bubble. While this is not to be sneered at, the National Theatre also made 400 casual staff redundant in the same period (Bakare, 2020). A recent report revealed that 36% of freelancers were ineligible for government support of any kind and it is therefore not surprising that one-third of freelancers are considering leaving the industry (Freelancers Make Theatre Work, 2020). If we accept that the arts do make an economic contribution, there is a need to better distinguish between an individual act of creation and the industrial mechanisms devised to exploit it. That is, how do financially insecure artists make a contribution to this economy and how can they be better rewarded? While a Universal Basic Income has been heavily contested by many, it could provide a short-term solution although, as of yet, there is no sign that this is likely. In the longer term, there is a need for a welfare reform which would consider the particularities of insecure creative labour and portfolio working.

This crisis is particularly problematic given that theatre freelancers comprise 86% of all people of colour employed by national portfolio organisations; in contrast, 82% of all permanent staff are white (Thompson, 2020). The pandemic is turning back the clock on the minute equality gains which were starting to make progress in the sector, for gender, racial and ability equality. In the face of these concerns, phrases such as the 'crown jewels' are at best misplaced and at worst have colonial undertones. The implications are clear: the biggest and richest (and therefore mostly London-based) institutions are first in line for bailout. Saving buildings and administrative jobs is pointless, however, without protecting the artists that make the work, it is therefore worth reflecting on the wider ecology of the sector to stop reinforcing the old fashioned and alienating hierarchies which do not reflect the true reach and public value of the arts sectors.

Industry or charity?

The crux of the matter is that the arts are struggling as they are built on a hybrid corporate model. The quote at the start of the chapter by Sam Mendes illustrates this clearly – there are two discourses at work here, the powerhouse industry, which is central to the economy, and historic models of benevolence. That the arts can provide both market value and social value is evident; however, the discourses underpinning these values need disentangling. The creative economy emerged from the Thatcher government of the 1980s, where we saw the argument for the economic importance of the arts surface in response to threats to public funding (Littler, 2000). Soon, this evolved into cultural production and consumption becoming central to Thatcher's neoliberal post-industrial model for the economy; artists were no longer not-for-profit but rather could create profit through copy-rightable ideas and images which were to be commercially exploited. New Labour shifted the discourse somewhat by focusing on a social inclusion agenda, whereby the arts could solve all problems as embodied in their mantra of 'what art can do for society'. This further muddied the waters but was still underpinned by a neoliberal vision of the market. Indeed, Claire Bishop (2012, p. 14) warned that the whole social inclusion agenda resulted not in shifting the structural conditions of inequality but rather in building resilient 'self-administering, fully functioning consumers who do not rely on the welfare state and who can cope with a deregulated, privatised world'. It is due to this discourse that arts institutions now need to pit themselves against other vital life-saving and life-giving organisations. While there is no doubt that arts organisations can be powerful social actors, they do not provide direct, urgent, practical benefits in terms of housing, finances, healthcare, etc. although they have been pushed to define the value of their work in these ways. This is deeply problematic at a time when vital community resources are being dismantled.

The result of these neoliberal ideologies, which have been framing our thinking about the economy for over 40 years, is that the arts have become a commodity like any other. As public funding has been progressively driven down, arts institutions have had to partner with ethically and environmentally dubious commercial sponsors, had to become shopping malls themselves, and often had to raise ticket prices out of the reach of the very people public funding was intended to encourage to participate. By turning into an industry with a focus on maximum corporate profitability and return on investment, it is not surprising that the cultural sector has become increasingly unequal, with super profits at the top of the pyramid and low waged precarity at its base, as illustrated by the streaming services – Netflix, Amazon Prime, etc. making millions in lockdown while the arts ecosystem that nurtured the very actors, producers and directors involved is allowed to collapse.

The other side of the equation is the nonprofit model of the arts as an offering or a service (even within a market economy). Art history attests to the significance of the arts and the meaning they can provide outside of their cash value. In fact, it can be argued that it is cultural value which results in economic value (Belfiore & Bennett, 2007; Preece et al., 2016). By thinking of the arts as part of the public realm, we move towards building more inclusive institutions where the public good can drive the discourse rather than just a focus on profits, where private and public interests can meet, where the local and national can co-exist and where audiences become participants, part of a collective of a common imaginative space. However, where we are now is in a cultural sector which is deeply confused. On the one hand it has to position itself as an industry, supported by statistics of employment growth and profitability in order to impress politicians (Oakley & Banks, 2020). At the same time, it must present itself as worthy of public subsidy, invoking 'market failure' and the significance of creativity beyond its economic weight. This cutting-edge industry/public service dilemma results in the needs of the cultural sector being overlooked; ambiguity is not something the Treasury appreciates.

Moving forwards

Despite this disheartening outlook, the sector is fighting back. For some smaller organisations the crisis has been a chance to reconsider subsidy, support artists more directly and, most significantly, take an inclusive approach towards audiences. To exemplify this, we turn to two theatres in London, who, rather than just adopting a broadcast model, are moving towards a hyper-local approach, asking their communities what they need and what their cultural emergency might be in order to create more inclusive structures.

Battersea Arts Centre (BAC), in South-West London, has been a community arts centre since 1974, pioneering creative change particularly in the performing arts. It has recently announced a radical shift in terms of its fundraising model, replacing fixed ticket prices with a 'pay as you can' pricing model from Spring 2021. While the venue has previously operated a 'pay as you can' model for Tuesday performances, the move will now make every performance at BAC accessible to all. This is part of a wider transformation of the overall business model in order to embed access and inclusivity across all activities, having already become the world's first entirely 'relaxed' venue (benefitting a huge range of audiences including autistic people, those with learning disabilities, movement disorders or dementia by considering – and normalising – difference from the outset).

The venue receives its funding, as is typical for arts organisations in the UK, from multiple sources. Pre-Covid-19 pandemic, this consisted of 15% of the budget from the Arts Council, 25% from fundraising activities, 40% from commercial enterprise and 20% from the box office. This financial model was upended by the pandemic, as was the case for all performing arts venues. While the lockdowns were devastating, they prompted a renewed focus on finances and some difficult decisions and cost-cutting needed to be made. This was certainly challenging, as Tarek Iskander (2020), CEO and Artistic Director of BAC discussed: 'the year has thrown difficulties and hardships at everyone, and we've been forced to make some hard decisions'; however, 'this disruption of "normal life" [also gave] BAC the space to do some radical thinking about how we can best support our community and inspiring people we work with'. In conversation at a conference on 'art, audiences and money' Iskander suggested that the pandemic offers an opportunity to think about things again: 'in the context of losing 20% of our income in the first place, it's an opportunity for us to say: "what if we never revive that 20% of income?"'.

The 'pay as you can' model signals that the engagement of the audience is more valuable to the organisation than the money paid for the tickets, as befits a community-focused organisation. In practice, it will mean shifting the commercial enterprise income into artists' fees in order to ensure they are not disadvantaged. While this is by no means easy, the decision has been made in line with the mission of the organisation to 'inspire change' (bac.org.uk). In a financial landscape which has become increasingly difficult for arts organisations since the 2008 recession, where there is never enough money to go around, the pandemic has forced arts organisations to reconsider their purpose. It has never been clearer that change is needed if the sector is to survive and it seems evident that local audiences will be at the heart of this, at least for the near future. The decision BAC has made allows the organisation to re-value the relationship they have with their audience. Rather than the tail wagging the dog, that is, the mission being at the mercy of fundraising, this new approach means the fundraising model selected serves the mission. This purpose-driven approach is clear: the organisation is not interested in 'art for art's sake' but rather in provoking change in the audience and their communities. In practice, this results in a radical revisioning of shorter-term economic value towards longer-term social value; the value of the audience is not about the ticket prices but about their attention and how they are affected by what they see and what this can result in. This type of long-term, relational approach is very much aligned to recent arts marketing theory (e.g. Walmsley, 2019).

Whether this new approach will work is still unclear, but it is sure to allow the work to reach new audiences. This is inspiring at a time when West End theatre is increasingly unattainable to the majority of the population. Figures from the Society of West End Theatre show that the average ticket price increased by 5.8% from 2018 to 2019 at a cost of £52.17 (SOLT, n.d.). It will be important for BAC to closely monitor their audiences going forward. This will be challenging but not impossible. They could do so by, for example, selling online tickets for free in advance and then giving these tickets to audiences on arrival in envelopes with a unique order number, perhaps with feedback forms included, in which the money they choose to pay can be deposited. Such monitoring could then allow them to identify how many first-time visitors return as a result of 'pay as you can' and ascertain those audience members whose average spend increases, providing an opportunity to build them into regular donors or ambassadors for the organisation. This may also allow for a chance to disprove any theories that certain classes or age groups are not interested in theatre and to nurture future audiences.

The Donmar Warehouse (DW) is another not-for-profit theatre, situated at the heart of London in Covent Garden with a very different funding model. It receives only 6% of its funding from the Arts Council, with 50% coming from fundraising and the rest from box office. This means that, in normal times, fundraising has to raise about £3 million a year. Half of this is raised from individuals and the rest from corporates. As a result of this model, the organisation is geared primarily towards fundraising and 90% of the audience have traditionally been donors who are predominantly over 55 and white. This also means that the programming has needed to appeal to the core donors. However, since the appointment of Mike Longhurst, artistic director, and Henny Finch, executive director, in 2019, the venue is now trying to move away from its reliance on individual donors in order to diversify its audiences (Finch, 2020).

To support this new vision, the fundraising model needs to change. This means reducing the costs of the operation, driving up commercial revenues and, in order to make space for new audiences, dissuading lower-level, transactional giving; trying to develop more philanthropic motivations and higher profile participants from fewer donors; and introducing more support from trusts and foundations. In doing so, care needs to be taken in transitioning existing audiences to new, more diverse and participatory work.

It is clear that if arts institutions need to raise million-pound budgets, it is hard to do so without turning arts institutions into engines that directly benefit wealthy donors and centre around their needs. This business model is extremely efficient in terms of getting large donations; however, what is clearly needed in the future, as the DW has bravely put forward, is a broad and novel range of financial support. Indeed, research (Reich, 2018) has shown that philanthropy can be, in many cases, a symptom rather than a solution to an unequal economy. Recent scrutiny around, for example, the Sackler donations coming at the price of an opioid crisis which has claimed thousands of deaths illustrates some of the dangers for arts institutions on relying heavily on certain individuals (Marshall, 2019). Big philanthropy, Reich (2018) shows, is often used as an exercise of unaccountable power, converting private assets into public influence. Reich does, however, make a case for private foundations if these foundations operate in roles that neither market nor state can undertake (as they do not need to be accountable to shareholders or voters), that is, by taking an 'experimentalist, long-time horizon approach to policy innovation' (2018, p. 197). The solution is positioning art as a public resource so that the direct beneficiaries of arts projects which have concrete social value will have an increased hand in paying for it. This means taking more nuanced approaches to reconceptualise value as created collaboratively, changing the power dynamics (Preece et al., 2016) and creating a direct relationship whereby community members are directly investing in art, no longer mere consumers but contributors.

New models required

The arts ecosystem in the UK was not a healthy, diverse place, even before the pandemic. In fact, it was characterised by a bloated, predatorial and over-industrialised art complex. In the visual arts, for example, this resulted in speculative collecting and a systematic erosion of the lower levels of the arts ecosystem. This dynamic of destructive consolidation is apparent across art forms, and, as we have examined, results in a preoccupation by the government with only the largest, most prestigious arts institutions. The language of the market led to mergers and acquisitions with many communities left underserved. Even before Covid-19, it was clear change was needed; now it has been forced. There is a need to rethink the relationship between the private and the public sector: while the government clearly values the creative economy (at least to a certain extent, as the bailout shows), it is restricting its growth at the roots, in public education, where creative thinking and the arts are being squeezed out of the system.

What is evident is that the health and vitality of the sector is dependent on the bottom of the food chain, the artists. Recent research (Belfiore, 2021) demonstrates the unacknowledged costs shouldered by socially engaged and independent practitioners/artists working on participatory projects pointing to 'a clear moral failure of cultural policy'. Yet it is these artists whose work is organic, local and responsive who are most vital to the sector. Indeed, the larger arts institutions should look to the independent sector for expertise in running alternative, efficient, flexible and resourceful operations. These artists are used to taking risks, experimenting and making art with few resources – they have the resilience to reimagine (Daskalopoulou & Skandalis, 2019). Perhaps, in this sense, the pandemic will allow for local, grassroots, community arts organisations to redress the balance. Although there is no doubt that the pandemic will cause huge attrition to the sector (and some of the damage has already been done), perhaps, in the 'new normal', we can become more connected to our local scenes. We are now at a crossroads which offers an opportunity to reimagine the infrastructure of the arts, especially at the local level. Although both our case studies are situated in London, there is a need to think outside the capital, to consider the 80% or more of the population who are not regular arts-goers. To engage with these audiences, collaboration will be key and the gap and inequality between arts institutions and those who make art must be narrowed.

Chapter discussion questions

1. What are the pros and cons of a diversification approach?
2. Compare and contrast the approaches of Battersea Arts Centre and the Donmar Warehouse in widening access; how could micro-, meso- and macro-level approaches to voluntary giving practices provide them with the financial security they need to operate?
3. What more radical approaches to arts funding could the government adopt in a post Covid world?

References

ACE. (2018). Our national portfolio in numbers, 2018–2022. Available at https://bit.ly/2WLWN9Z (accessed 12 December 2020).

Akbar, A. (2020). The next act: How the pandemic is shaping online theatre's future. *The Guardian*, 21 September. Available at www.theguardian.com/stage/2020/sep/21/future-of-live-theatre-online-drama-coronavirus-lockdown (accessed 12 December 2020).

Alexiou, K., Wiggins, J. & Preece, S.B. (2020). Crowdfunding acts as a funding substitute and a legitimating signal for nonprofit performing arts organizations. *Nonprofit and Voluntary Sector Quarterly*, 49(4), 827–848.

Bakare, L. (2020). National Theatre tells 400 casual staff they will lose their jobs. *The Guardian*, 3 July. Available at www.theguardian.com/stage/2020/jul/03/national-theatre-tells-casual-staff-they-will-lose-their-jobs (accessed 12 December 2020).

Barman, E. (2017). The social bases of philanthropy. *Annual Review of Sociology*, 43, 271–290.

Bekkers, R. & Wiepking, P. (2011). A literature review of empirical studies of philanthropy: Eight mechanisms that drive charitable giving. *Nonprofit and Voluntary Sector Quarterly*, 40(5), 924–973.

Belfiore, E. (2021). Who cares? At what price? The hidden costs of socially engaged arts labour and the moral failure of cultural policy. *European Journal of Cultural Studies*. doi:10.1177/1367549420982863.

Belfiore, E. & Bennett, O. (2007). Determinants of impact: Towards a better understanding of encounters with the arts. *Cultural Trends*, 16(3), 225–275.

Bennett, A. & Strong, C. (2018). Popular music heritage, grass-roots activism and Web 2.0: The case of the 'Save the Palace' campaign. *Cultural Sociology*, 12(3), 368–383.

Bennett, R. (2012). Why urban poor donate: A study of low-income charitable giving in London. *Nonprofit and Voluntary Sector Quarterly*, 41(5), 870–891.

Bishop, C. (2012). *Artificial Hells: Participatory Art and the Politics of Spectatorship*. Verso Books.

Body, A. & Breeze, B. (2016). What are 'unpopular causes' and how can they achieve fundraising success. *International Journal of Nonprofit and Voluntary Sector Marketing*, 21(1), 57–70.

Body, A., Lau, E. & Josephidou, J. (2020). Engaging children in meaningful charity: Opening-up the spaces within which children learn to give. *Children & Society*, 34(3), 189–203.

Borgonovi, F. (2006). Do public grants to American theatres crowd-out private donations? *Public Choice*, 126, 429–451.

Breeze, B. & Wiepking, P. (2018). Different drivers: Exploring employee involvement in corporate philanthropy. *Journal of Business Ethics*, 165, 453–467.

Brooks, A.C. (1999). Do public subsidies leverage private philanthropy for the arts? Empirical evidence on symphony orchestras. *Nonprofit and Voluntary Sector Quarterly*, 28 (1), 32–45.

Bussell, H. & Forbes, D. (2006). 'Friends' schemes in arts marketing: Developing relationships in British provincial theatres. *International Journal of Arts Management*, 8(2), 38–49.

CAF. (2020). UK giving during Covid-19: A special report. Available at www.cafonline. org/docs/default-source/about-us-publications/caf-uk-giving-2020-covid-19.pdf. (accessed 5 January 2021).

Chung, C., Yang, L. & Cauldwell-French, E. (2018). Growing the UK's creative industries. Available at www.creativeindustriesfederation.com/sites/default/files/2018-12/Creative% 20Industries%20Federation%20-%20Growing%20the%20UK's%20Creative%20Indus tries_0.pdf (accessed 13 December 2020).

Daskalopoulou, A. & Skandalis, A. (2019). Consumption field driven entrepreneurship (CFDE): How does membership in the indie music field shape individuals' entrepreneurial journey. *European Journal of Marketing*, 53(1), 63–82.

De Wit, A. & Bekkers, R. (2016). Exploring gender differences in charitable giving: The Dutch case. *Nonprofit and Voluntary Sector Quarterly*, 45(4), 741–761.

De Wit, A. & Bekkers, R. (2020). Can charitable donations compensate for a reduction in government funding? The role of information. *Public Administration Review*, 80(2), 294–304.

De Wit, A., Bekkers, R. & Broese van Groenou, M. (2017). Heterogeneity in crowding-out: When are charitable donations responsive to government support? *European Sociological Review*, 33(1), 59–71.

Eikenberry, A.M. (2009). *Giving Circles: Philanthropy, Voluntary Association, and Democracy*. Indiana University Press.

Eikenberry, A.M. & Breeze, B. (2015). Growing philanthropy through collaboration: The landscape of giving circles in the United Kingdom and Ireland. *Voluntary Sector Review*, 6(1), 41–59.

Eikenberry, A.M. & Breeze, B. (2018). Growing philanthropy through giving circles: Collective giving and the logic of charity. *Social Policy and Society*, 17(3), 349–364.

Finch, H. (2020). Art, audiences, Money. Achtates Philanthropy Foundation Conference, 12 November. Available at www.youtube.com/watch?v=MWt7g-qeZfU (accessed 13 December 2020).

Freelancers Make Theatre Work. (2020). Covid-19: Routes to recovery. Available at http s://freelancersmaketheatrework.com/wp-content/uploads/2020/07/Routes-To-R ecovery.pdf. (accessed 5 January 2021).

Frey, B.S. & Meier, S. (2002). Museums between private and public: The Case of the Beyeler Museum in Basle. Available at https://papers.ssrn.com/sol3/papers.cfm?abstract_ id=316698. (accessed 12 December 2020).

Gamble, J.R., Brennan, M. & McAdam, R. (2017). A rewarding experience? Exploring how crowdfunding is affecting music industry business models. *Journal of Business Research*, 70, 25–36.

Grasse, N., Whaley, K. & Ihrke, D. (2016). Modern portfolio theory and nonprofit arts organizations. *Nonprofit and Voluntary Sector Quarterly*, 45(4), 825–843.

Guthrie, D. & McQuarrie, M. (2008). Providing for the public good: Corporate-community relations in the era of the receding welfare state. *City Community*, 7, 113–139.

Hager, M.A. (2001). Financial vulnerability among arts organizations: A test of the Tuck-man-Chang measures. *Nonprofit and Voluntary Sector Quarterly*, 30(2), 376–392.

Haynes, K. (2008). Moving the gender agenda or stirring chicken's entrails: Where next for feminist methodologies in accounting? *Accounting, Auditing and Accountability Journal*, 21 (4), 539–555.

Healy, K. (2010). *Last Best Gifts: Altruism and the Market for Human Blood and Organs*. University Chicago Press.

Iskander, I. (2020). Art, audiences, Money. Achtates Philanthropy Foundation Conference, 12 November. Available at www.youtube.com/watch?v=MWt7g-qeZfU (accessed 13 December 2020).

Kim, M. (2017). Characteristics of civically engaged nonprofit arts organizations: The results of a national survey. *Nonprofit and Voluntary Sector Quarterly*, 46(1), 175–198.

Lee, B., Fraser, I. & Fillis, I. (2017). Nudging art lovers to donate. *Nonprofit and Voluntary Sector Quarterly*, 46(4), 837–858.

Littler, J. (2000). Creative accounting; Consumer culture, the 'creative economy' and the cultural policies of New Labour'. In J. Gilbert & T. Bewes (eds), *Cultural Capitalism: Politics after New Labour*. Lawrence & Wishart.

Liu, W. & Aaker, J. (2008). The happiness of giving: The time-ask effect. *Journal of Consumer Research*, 35, 543–557.

Marshall, A. (2019). Museums cut ties with Sacklers as outrage over opioid crisis grows. *The New York Times*, 25 March. Available at www.nytimes.com/2019/03/25/arts/design/sa ckler-museums-donations-oxycontin.html (accessed 13 December 2020).

McDonald, H. & Harrison, P. (2002). The marketing and public relations practices of Australian performing arts presenters. *International Journal of Nonprofit and Voluntary Sector Marketing*, 7(2), 105–117.

Mendes, S. (2020). How we can save our theatres. *Financial Times*, 5 June. Available at www.ft. com/content/643b7228-a3ef-11ea-92e2-cbd9b7e28ee6 (accessed 13 December 2020).

Mollick, E. & Nanda, R. (2016). Wisdom or madness? Comparing crowds with expert evaluation in funding the arts. *Management Science*, 62(6), 1533–1553.

Moraes, C., Daskalopoulou, A. & Szmigin, I. (2020). Understanding individual voluntary giving as a practice: Implications for regional arts organisations in the UK. *Sociology*, 54(1), 70–88.

Murray, C. (2019). Funders and stakeholders matter: A case study analysis. *Arts and the Market*, 9(2), 219–234.

Oakley, K. & Banks, M. (2020). Cultural industries and environmental crisis: An introduction. In K. Oakley & M. Banks (eds), *Cultural Industries and the Environmental Crisis*. Springer.

Piliavin, J.A. & Charng, H.W. (1990). Altruism: A review of recent theory and research. *Annual Review of Sociology*, 16, 27–65.

Pitts, S.E., Herrero, M. & Price, S.M. (2020). Understanding the liminality of individual giving to the arts. *Arts and the Market*, 10(1), 18–33.

Preece, C., Kerrigan, F. & O'Reilly, D. (2016). Framing the work: The composition of value in the visual arts. *European Journal of Marketing*, 50(7/8), 1377–1398.

Reich, R. (2018). *Just Giving: Why Philanthropy is Failing Democracy and How It Can Do Better*. Princeton University Press.

Rich-Edwards, J.W., Kaiser, U.B., Chen, G.L., Manson, J.E. & Goldstein, J.M. (2018). Sex and gender differences research design for basic, clinical, and population studies: Essentials for investigators. *Endocrine Reviews*, 39(4), 424–439.

Smith, T. (2003). The effect of NEA grants on the contributions to nonprofit dance companies. *Journal of Arts Management, Law, and Society*, 33(2), 98–113.

SOLT. (n.d.). Facts and figures. Available at https://solt.co.uk/about-london-theatre/facts-and-figures/ (accessed 5 January 2021).

Thompson, T. (2020). The real 'crown jewels' of the arts? An unprotected freelance workforce. *The Guardian*, 22 July. Available at www.theguardian.com/stage/2020/jul/22/the-real-crown-jewels-of-the-arts-an-unprotected-freelance-workforce (accessed 13 December 2020).

Walmsley, B. (2019). The death of arts marketing: A paradigm shift from consumption to enrichment. *Arts and the Market*, 9(1), 32–49.

Wiepking, P. & Bekkers, R. (2012). Who gives? A literature review of predictors of charitable giving. Part 2: Gender, marital status, income, and wealth. *Voluntary Sector Review*, 3, 217–245.

8

DIGITAL MARKETING FOR CHARITIES

Reflections from a collaborative project

Emma Reid

> I didn't think charities had a big marketing footprint, I assumed consumers would know what they're looking for and engage with them whenever they wanted. I had never seen digital marketing for charities before, mostly television adverts, and partnerships with stores for Red Nose Day etc. I always thought because it was nonprofit, they wouldn't have access to finances to be able to get creative with marketing.
>
> *(M, 2018 cohort)*

Introduction

The UK government report a total of 168,186 charities in England and Wales (UK Government, 2018) with a total annual income of £77.404 billion. To be classified as a charity in England and Wales, the organisation must be 'established for charitable purposes only… and is subject to the control of the High Court's charity law jurisdiction' (UK Government, 2017) These 'purposes' can focus on a number of diverse areas include poverty relief, advancing education, religion, health, citizenship, the environment, animal welfare, youth, disability and so on (UK Government, 2017). In Scotland, the setting for this chapter, there are over 24,000 charities regulated by the Independent Office of the Scottish Charity Regulator (OSCR), who set up and regulate the legal framework around Scottish charities. Research has highlighted that charities often lack the skills and expertise required to allow them to take full advantage of the opportunities offered by developments in digital marketing.

This chapter will discuss an ongoing collaboration between marketing lecturers at a university in Scotland and MH Charity (a pseudonym), a national charity for Mental Health in Scotland. As part of a university student assessment, groups of students were asked to critically analyse the current digital tools, techniques and

DOI: 10.4324/9781003134169-11

capabilities of the charity sector in Scotland. Students were then asked to use this information to create a five-minute video pitch and proposal to the charity which would present ideas around a new digital strategy.

The chapter begins with an overview of the digital challenges facing charities in the United Kingdom, and especially during Covid. It then presents a narrative of this partnership between the university and MH Charity. The chapter will also refer to student reflections and interviews to contextualise the impact of the project on students, considering the digital skills developed, the greater understanding of the third sector and some suggestions from former students as to how charities can approach life post-Covid.

What counts as a charity in the United Kingdom?

Organisations must fit the criteria set by the 'charity test', a legal test regulated by OSCR which states that charities must:

- Have only charitable purpose
- Provide public benefit
- Use their funds and property only for charitable purposes
- Allow fair access to the benefit they provide
- To be, or exist to advance, a political party.

(OSCR, 2021)

The value of the Scottish charity sector stands at £14 billion per annum. Funds can be raised through grants and awards, legacies and donations. Marketing for charities and not-for-profits faces challenges compared to marketing within commercial organisations. The UK House of Lords 'Select Committee on Charities' 2017 published a report entitled 'Stronger charities for a stronger society' in 2017 which stated:

> Charites are also facing change as a result of the ways that digital technologies have reshaped society particularly in terms of how people give their time and their money. These changes bring challenges but also considerable opportunities for charities, with new ways to raise money, to mobilise support and to communicate more effectively.
>
> *(House of Lords, 2017, p. 6)*

The 'House of Lords' report suggested some potential areas where digital could be beneficial for charities, including digital fundraising, raising awareness and encouraging engagement with supporters, donors and service users. The same report outlines challenge for charities being more digital focused including a lack of investment in web infrastructure. This included poor quality websites which were unattractive/unprofessionally designed and not mobile responsive websites. The report also noted that many charities missed the opportunity to allow people to donate via the site. As we move toward a 'mobile first' world (Medium, 2017) there is a need for websites to have a responsive web design to ensure that content automatically fits screens for different device sizes and operating systems.

The size and maturity of the charity generally had an impact on the quality of the digital offerings. One point raised was micro charities, for example toddler groups or Brownies, where there was rarely any web presence for individual groups. The report highlighted issues for smaller charities including 'lack (of) capacity, skills and confidence to fully benefit from this technology' (p. 76), reduced funding or grants from local authorities or other sources, lack of creative or digitally savvy talent in-house, a reliance on volunteers, levels of risk, flexibility and time were all reasons cited as challenges facing the charity sector.

Furthermore, the House of Lords report suggested actively searching for board members and trustees for charities with digital skillsets and encouraging the technology sector to work directly with the charity sector to improve skills and confidence. The author of this chapter spent several years volunteering with a local pre-school group which employed three members of staff to run the group. Income was raised through entrance fees and local authority grants which rarely covered the rent of the local church hall, insurances and basic equipment such as a small snack and art supplies. The remainder of costs to run the playgroup, including staff salaries, came from local fundraising such as sponsored events and Race Nights. In 2013, the author worked with the playleaders to write applications for competitive grants from lottery bodies and other commercial organisations (such as Tesco Community funds). This allowed the group to access funds for basic technical equipment such as a laptop and printer, however there were issues with the premises not having access to broadband, and of course minimal time for volunteers to access training to improve digital skills, build websites or keep information up to date. Data security was also an issue as the team members worked with vulnerable children but received no training on how to store personal data securely. The team were confident in using Facebook and as a result used their own phones and data to set up a private group to share children's activities with parents, as well as a public page to raise awareness of the group to potential new members.

Lloyds Bank (2020) reported that 111,000 charities (56% of all UK charities) had what they describe as 'full Essential Digital Skills' in 2019, which were mainly the ability to communicate with and respond to stakeholders using digital, up to date software. The study also highlighted the need for employees that have digital skills and capabilities, however there is a lack of understanding of the technologies and skills required to implement these processes. Furthering the concerns raised from the House of Lords report, the study highlighted a lack of accessibility built into their websites, something of great importance when working with people with disabilities, and in fact would be against UK disability laws. While many large organisations including Google and Lloyds Bank offer free or reduced-price skills training and access to software for charities there remains a need to ensure charities were aware that this was on offer and had the capacity to participate in training.

Baird (2017) presents some examples of best practice in applying marketing to the not-for-profit sector, suggesting that marketers should 'start with strategy', making it clear that there is an organisational understanding of what the objectives, goals and KPIs should be when implementing digital. Charity marketers should focus on the call to action, in what Baird describes as 'motivating people to take an action'. She then moves on to examine the importance of content, specifically using storytelling to appeal to audiences and then being clear on what you expect your audience to do with this content (share, donate, raise awareness?). She highlights the importance of convenience for consumers, for example donations via mobile devices, and ensuring measurement through social media metrics and engagement rates to understand what is working and what isn't. She concludes that 'online marketing provides a powerful set of tools that can be harnessed. The keys are being strategic, thoughtful, authentic and willing to invest resources' (p. 379). Quinton and Fennemore's (2013) work in adopting social media networks by UK charities found that how consumers interact with social networks is useful when creating relevant digital marketing strategies, however their research found there was an emphasis on broadcasting messages and content rather than interactivity with consumers and followers. Quinton and Fennemore (2013) highlighted the increased use of social networks to build brand awareness, and to participate in growing online conversations about the charity. The same research highlighted resistance to adopting social media including a perceived loss of control around the brand, a lack of specialist skills and lack of awareness around the need for strategy and measurement. While this article is slightly dated, the key messages are still relevant for many charities for the reasons discussed earlier in this chapter.

Leonhardt and Peterson (2019) examine the importance of direct marketing (both online and offline) for charities and focus on the ability of organisations to adapt messaging to appeal to different types of donors dependent upon their previous behaviours and levels of involvement and was in favour of the use of 'altruistic' appeals as part of a charity's integrated marketing communications campaigns, particularly where consumers do not currently have an involvement or relationship with the charity. They highlight the potential benefits of consumer-to-consumer sharing of altruistic campaign messaging to build brand awareness and conversions.

Digital Doughnut's (2018) study on the charity sector illuminated digital moving away from being perceived as channel and a movement towards a core element of a charity's strategy, with a focus on digital from the board level down. However, the study outlined some confusion at all levels of the organisation around the meaning of digital. This study again highlighted the main concern being staff training and confidence in using technology, rather than the technology itself. The future of the sector appeared to lead towards a focus on engagement rather than purely using channels for fundraising and awareness. The study also highlighted a movement towards transparency to build trust and relationships, using the example of VR lab tours shared by Cancer Research UK. While this chapter does not look specifically at the potential of virtual and augmented reality in marketing for charities, rather focusing on covering less advanced areas of digital marketing, VR, AR, predictive analytics and automation all have an important role and provide opportunities for digital marketing charities now and in the future.

Young people and charity

Dean's (2020) study uncovers the challenges of encouraging 16–25-year-olds (the largest user group of social media) to donate online, explaining that this group are less likely to donate, and when they do, they tend to give almost half of what 25 and overs donate. The study explains that the 16–24-year-old group appear to be more interested in volunteering, protesting, demonstrating and other forms of online activism. While digital helps to encourage donor behaviour, young people are more motivated by charities which appeal to their own experiences and those which impact on those they are closely connected to. Further, a lack of trust and 'cynicism' towards larger charities, with participants describing the 'unreasonable, inauthentic, low quality asks' compared to a more 'personal connection or direct connection' to the person asking for the donation. This paper highlights the 'personal experiences, practices and decisions made in everyday life' and also the ease of use of social media of encouraging friends, family and wider networks to contribute to or donate to the individual's own charity efforts. Based on this, some participants in Dean's study highlighted 'peer pressure' to donate due to the strong 'social ties' between their social media connections. This study proposes that the voluntary sector needs to be aware that young people frequently have a social media led way of engaging with friends and family and that they are 'peer motived' in that they will support friends and family when asked to donate, and suggests that charities should work with young people when proposing new campaigns.

Moving into 2020 and a Covid world

Skill Platform (2020) conducts an annual survey into digital trends in charities. The 2020 survey studied 429 charity professionals between 3 March and 24 May 2020 – which includes the period of the first UK lockdown – with responses from all over the UK. Key findings illustrated the moving to delivering work remotely and online, with two-thirds of respondents moving to online service. There were challenges around funding raised, particular the increased need to invest in essential tech and software, which was made more difficult due to the lack of funding for investment in both digital and staff training. Staff lack of confidence in accessing and utilising technology is also an issue and there is a need to change the culture within organisations. A need for strong digital leadership was highlighted, especially in encouraging leaders to drive digital investment. Concerns were raised that a lack of investment in digital technologies and skills in helping those in need could lead to an impact on digital fundraising and an overall impact on brand image. A lack of understanding of digital technologies including analytics, data and security and digital fundraising was raised as a challenge, and overall, a lack of understanding about audience behaviours around digital was also raised as a challenge. Other areas of concern highlighted included email marketing, SEO and digital advertising and delivering services online. Emerging tech including AI, horizon scanning and automation were all raised as areas where there was a lack of skills and knowledge or an understanding of the relevance to their business. Overall, there was a lack of digital strategies. Although 39% of charities reported that their organisational strategy now includes digital as a priority. In terms of skills sets, social media and basic file management skills (cloud computing) were seen as the most common skillsets ranked as excellent in terms of levels of confidence. In May, Medium (2020) highlighted the top ten concerns for those working in charities focusing on three main areas: technology, services and ways of working. This reference to enforced changing working practices, due to government requirements for people to work from home, brought its own challenges to those who already had limited access to technology and lacked digital skills. This highlighted additional concerns for this already under-resourced sector and we are yet to see the full impact that this has had on the running and survival of charitable organisations across the United Kingdom.

Overall, as the literature has shown, charities appear to be open to adopting digital tools and technologies. However, challenges continue to emerge around leadership and digital direction for the charity. Limited IT skills, access to equipment and training and a failure to build digital into the strategy for the charity remain an issue. As we are yet to see the full impact of Covid on charities, it is clear that there is an urgent need to move the main services, including fundraising, onto digital platforms while continuing to provide services to those in need. Indeed, many of the micro-charities such as toddler playgroups are yet to re-open due to Covid regulations, and these services cannot be recreated digitally.

We now move on to the next stage of this chapter, which presents a case study around an honours marketing class in Scotland. In 2017, 2018 and 2019 students in the class were asked to work directly with Scotland's national mental health charity to propose new digital marketing campaigns for the charity. To familiarise herself with the charity and its current digital practices, the author worked on a summer long consultancy project at SAMH in 2017, using a range of social media and website analytical tools to conduct a digital audit for the organisation, outlining best practice, challenges and the need for additional resources for this charity. The author then collaborated with Lauren, the Communications Manager for the charity, to design a student assessment which encouraged experiential learning while developing theoretical and practical digital marketing skills. Lauren worked with the author to deliver a briefing lecture and Q&A session with students, and then viewed the completed video pitches in class together with the students on the project. Written proposals were also shared with the charity, and in 2020 a student project idea was used in SAMH digital communications.

Stage 1: Conducting a social media audit of the charity's platforms

In 2017, the author and a digital marketing consulted worked on a summer long paid project with the charity to carry out a digital marketing audit for the organisation. The research team analysed the existing social media platforms. Demographics Pro, a tech company specialising in Twitter demographics, analysed the current Twitter audience profiles and behaviours and provided a highly detailed analysis of the audience free of charge. Most interestingly, the breakdown of the main followers was found to be mainly local, female professionals, particularly nurses and teachers aged between 25 and 45. This indicated that the current engaged Twitter audience were more likely to be people who supported mental health as part of their employment roles. Brand affinities were also included, and it seemed that this audience had affinities with specific travel, cosmetic and soft drinks brands. Analytics produced by Twitter were carefully analysed by the research team to understand which posts performed well and, more importantly, why they performed well.

Facebook was used and updated most frequently. The team also used Facebook Insights and Analytics to gain an understanding of the engaged Facebook audience. Again, it was found that the most engaged audiences were women in Scotland in the same age bracket as the Twitter audience. Here it became apparent that young people in Scotland were less likely to engage with the charity on Facebook and that the audience profile was 78% female and 21% male. While the charity regularly posted on Facebook, there was no clear strategy around when to post and how to measure engagement. Lookalike audiences and competitor analysis was also carried out with charities of a similar size and focus. The MH Charity Instagram (the most popular platform at the time for 16–25-year-olds) account was used irregularly and without a planned strategy in place.

The social media pages were run by the small communications team comprising 1.5 members of staff. The team were also responsible for all communications, marketing and PR activity, crisis response, planning and other marketing-related activities for the charity. While the team were professionally qualified as marketers, they lacked the time to invest in design skills or plan social media content in the way that they would like. There was internal awareness of analytics, but staff had not spent time fully analysing the platforms, engagement and audiences. Therefore, much of the content posted on social media was responsive and ad hoc rather than planned. The team did have support at board level; however, the board were not keen to invest in permanent digital-focused staff at that point.

An additional challenge emerged that service users of the charity (those currently experiencing mental health issues) regularly attempted to use the private message function on the charity social media pages to try to reach the charity for urgent support, however this messaging would go to the communications team first who were not qualified to deal with such important issues. Furthermore, the social media pages were not manned 24 hours a day which could lead to life-threatening issues with service users if those needing care felt ignored by the charity or did not receive immediate support.

As the charity is relatively large in size employing a large number of staff, there were enough resources in place to engage with external agencies to look after the website, however the social media pages were operated completely in-house. The computers and software used were good quality and there was a fixed office space used by the team. There were conflicts between other in-house teams such as fundraising and those engaging with service users who placed demands on the communications team to post on social media on their behalf with little notice or planning. This made it difficult to design and implement an agreed digital marketing strategy.

As shown by Dean (2020) above, young people were also recognised as a missing audience on social media, despite being the biggest users of social media overall. Moreover, research conducted by MH Charity found that the number of students presenting with serious mental health issues was steadily increasing year on year. This finding is supported by the Office for Students (2020) who have recognised the urgent need for increased mental health support. Work carried out by the charity also found issues with school aged children being unable to access child and adolescent mental health services due to demand and insufficient support available. Additional research carried out by the charity found that tragically, men were 2.5 times more likely to die by suicide than women in Scotland. The team also recognised the urgent need to utilise their social media channels to try to reach men in Scotland to encourage them to talk about mental health. It was therefore difficult for the communications team to prioritise campaigns and targeted messaging to ensure the right content was seen by the intended target audience at the right time while continuing to promote other fundraising activities, calls to action, responses to media and news stories and to communicate with current service users.

Taking into consideration the findings from the social media audit, coupled with recognised mental health priorities, the charity recognised that there was a need to utilise their digital platforms to increase the number of engaged male and young people followers in the hope of creating targeted strategies and campaigns to address the complex needs of these target audiences. Lauren (Communications Manager) and the author met to discuss how this might be possible and the idea for the student project was formed.

Stage 2: Working with the students – 2017

In September 2017, the author created an assignment for honours year digital marketing students. There were three elements to the assessment: an individual report which focused on analysing the challenges facing charities in Scotland around accessing and using digital tools and technologies, including a critical analysis of MH Charity's existing digital platform. The second part of the assessment asked the students to work in groups to propose a new digital strategy for MH Charity that would appeal to students in Scotland, and which also highlighted challenges facing men in Scotland. To provide context and to encourage the students to think of this as a live project, Lauren from MH Charity delivered a guest lecture to the students to give them an overview of the charity and the challenges facing MH Charity overall, and specifically from a digital perspective. As the author of this chapter had supervised the social media audit, she was also very familiar with the charity and particularly the digital channels.

Over the next 12 weeks, students worked on the coursework in class and independently. Each group was asked to create a five-minute video to explain their new digital strategy and to prepare a written report which would go into more detail about the specifics of their strategy. The project was structured around the SOSTAC framework where students would carry out a situational analysis (based around their first assessment), the outline Objectives, Strategy, Tactics, Actions and Controls. The instructions given to students allowed creativity and flexibility in how students would present their findings. As well as offering guidance to students for their assessment, Lauren also left materials focusing on supporting students with mental health issues in the classroom.

As discussed, this was a completely new project and the author and Lauren had very little idea what to expect from students. The videos were submitted at the end of term and viewed by the author and Lauren at MH Charity. Not only had the students highlighted innovative uses of social media such as targeted paid-for campaigns, improved SEO techniques and the use of shock advertising and viral content, but they also suggested offline campaigns that would complement the online activities and realistic timescales for implementation. Some groups even researched agencies and organisations that would provide funding for such a campaign. The author realised the talent of and efforts that had been made by students to create short creative films, to integrate different forms of media and to focus on storytelling and content creation. Some groups created short films featuring members acting out challenges facing those with mental health issues before introducing their campaign, complete with measurable objectives and a clear implementation plan. Overall, there was a real passion about the project. The author recognised this and created, with students' permission, a YouTube playlist of the videos which was shared with senior management team members in the university. The playlist was also used to promote the marketing programme at open days and events.

Stage 3: Working with the students – 2018

The module ran again in 2018, and in Lauren's introductory lecture to the class, it was clear that the work undertaken by the research team and carried out by the students in 2017 was being utilised within the charity as there was a big focus on analytics, engagement, social media planning, increased strategic use of Instagram, targeted hashtags and planned social media campaigns. However, there was still a lack of investment in digital at the board level. This year, Lauren and the author decided to widen the parameters of the project and allow students to focus on a target group of their choice. Many of the student groups decided to focus on men in Scotland, recognising the growing need to address men's mental health. There were also video submissions focusing on the dangers of Instagram and cyber bullying with young women; issues around sexuality and gender identity and again student mental health were also chosen as areas where digital campaigns could be developed.

The author also introduced a new element to the project, where all students were invited to watch the videos together at an event (similar to a mini film festival), alongside the lecturers, students from the previous year, representatives from MH Charity and other academic staff. While some students felt nervous around showcasing their work, most were proud of their videos and keen to show them to others. Receiving immediate formative feedback from lecturers and MH Charity also allowed students to improve their written proposals prior to submitting the final assessment.

Stage 4: Working with the students – 2019

Due to a change in the university programme structure, 2019 was the last year that the module would run in its current format. Lauren left the company prior to the project starting in 2019 and a new manager took over the project. Jacqueline, the new manager, had also worked on the project in 2018 and was aware of how the students had approached the work. This year, MH Charity had a new idea, to focus on developing a campaign that could be launched around Valentine's Day 2020, targeted at an audience of the group's choice. The student submissions were again of excellent quality, focusing on issues around sexuality, loneliness and negative self-image, the dangers around Instagram's 'perfect life' ideas, men's mental health and a focus on the loving relationship between people in Scotland and their dogs (based on insights from Twitter that most MH Charity followers were also interested in or owned dogs). Again, a video showcase event took place with guests from the charity and other academic staff invited. Former students were also invited to attend this showcase. One project was chosen by MH Charity to be featured as part of their Valentine's Week social media campaign.

What impact did this project have on the charity?

Charities in Scotland face challenges around adopting digital due to lack of skills, access to technology or lack of organisation buy-in. By participating in this project. MH Charity was able to have a full audit of its digital channels and was directed to different tools that could be used to gain a greater understanding of their digital audiences. For a very small investment of time, the communications team gained access to 50 different student projects across three years, each of which utilised existing digital marketing strategy models and provided ideas for objectives, tactics and measurable outputs. Furthermore, the charity had access to high-quality videos that demonstrated highly creative well-planned campaigns that were timely and completely relevant to the charity and chosen audience, and which could be used as inspiration for campaigns and content in the future. Furthermore, MH Charity used the project to speak directly to students, a group that they had previously struggled to reach, and gained support and increased awareness of mental health issues from this particular group.

What impact did this project have on the students?

Every student was asked to complete a short individual reflective piece as part of their assessment, with most commenting on their feelings of pride in being able to create innovative work and a real sense of achievement in working on the project. In addition, many students showed the videos they created in job applications and interviews, and these were mentioned by potential employers who contacted the author for character references. Perhaps more importantly, in working on the projects, students began to feel more comfortable in discussing their own mental health and that of others, and this led to greater support and stronger friendships formed within the module, something which is particularly important in the final year of study. In 2021 the author contacted students and asked them to reflect on their experience in taking this module and some quotes from the students are below.

Knowledge of marketing for charities prior to taking this module

The responses demonstrated that there was a lack of knowledge and understanding around the area of not-for-profit marketing, especially in terms of digital. In fact, many students had not considered charity to be a sector.

> As marketing in this sector was an area I was both really interested in and keen to work in this was a dream class for me… How do you create a campaign that was focused on awareness and not sales? I didn't know how a lot of the skills we had gained transferred or were valued in this sector. How did you prove your worth?
>
> *(D, 2017 cohort)*

> I didn't think charities had a big marketing footprint, I assumed consumers would know what they're looking for and engage with them whenever they wanted… I always thought because it was nonprofit, they wouldn't have access to finances to be able to get creative with marketing.
>
> *(M, 2018 cohort)*

> I had never thought about charities using social media to their advantage. But after doing the class I understood the approaches charities can take and the types of appeals they can use.
>
> *(S, 2018 cohort)*

> What I knew was that charities mainly relied on the emotional marketing such as showing starving kids, disabled people to gain support from donors.
>
> *(R, 2019 cohort)*

> My knowledge of the charity sector was more in how they used tactics and offline marketing to get donations or for example using shock or sadness and playing on people emotions to get donations.
>
> *(B, 2019 cohort)*

Skills and learnings from the assessment

Students were asked to reflect on what they felt they had learned from participating in the assessment. A range of soft skills were mentioned around empathy and communication, as well as increased understanding and application of technical skills.

> I took a lot away from this assessment... how to apply consumer behaviour knowledge to encourage behavioural change... I discovered social marketing and it became my absolute passion... I can now perform a detailed SOSTAC – I have used this a lot at work.
>
> *(D, 2017 cohort)*

> During the class I came to realise that charities have an interest in becoming digital, some were digital already. I learned that they do receive support, and a following from social media, and it's actually a cost-effective way for them to process messages, and keep consumers updated with events etc. Communication and creativity were developed. Empathy was a huge factor for me as a person, I'm not very good at it and I figured it was something that charities need to have to be able to communicate.
>
> *(B, 2019 cohort)*

> It allowed me to understand how charities use social media in greater detail. The skills I learned were the types of appeals used, SEO, keywords, editing, and story writing.
>
> *(S, 2018 cohort)*

> I learned how to film and edit a short movie, I learned how to use clip grab and Touch Cast then how to edit it all together. My creative skills were also brought on as it was all about coming up with a new idea nobody had done before. Learning to take constructive criticism was also a skill presented in the assessment as we got real live feedback.
>
> *(B, 2019 cohort)*

> I re-learned my skills on shooting videos and having to come up with creative ideas for the video project. Also, my group has been absolutely phenomenal, we split the work equally and everybody did their parts. I also dusted off my video editing skills and had to put them to use again.
>
> *(R, 2019 cohort)*

Did the class alter your career path?

The interviewees all graduated in the last three years. Several of the students went on to undertake further study in digital marketing, achieving an MSc in the subject. Some students went on to work for charities or work freelance.

100%. After this class, I knew that this is what I wanted to do and fixated on this sector. I secured a job before I graduated, and I am still there today.

(D, 2017 cohort)

It has given me valuable knowledge of the industry challenges and opportunities, therefore my employability increases. I would work for charities even before, but after the assessments and campaigns it was clearer how the sector looks and what threats it is facing, moreover how could I contribute.

(A, 2019 cohort)

I learned that good organisation skills are invaluable – with often very limited budgets, there is no margin for wasting time or money. Good communication and people skills as well as enthusiasm and a dedication to the cause are also vital. I now work for a charity, with this class opening my eyes to a new career path – working on the assessment for SAMH I knew this was a route I would like to explore further.

(E, 2017 cohort)

MH Charity's presentation about their activities opened my eyes to see there's much more to charities than what is being presented to us and begging for money. My perception slightly changed on charities. I think charities should work closely with government bodies to gain a better public trust.

(R, 2019 cohort)

Finally, students were asked their opinions on what charities could do differently with digital, especially during and post-Covid. While the class was completed long before Covid was an issue, students used their skills and knowledge to reflect on how charities could adapt, suggesting ways to adapt current campaigns and taking the opportunity to implement new forms of digital such as VR and AR into their digital offerings.

What do you think charities could do differently with digital, especially during and post-Covid?

I think a balance needs to be found between budgets and expectations… a lot of pressure is put on digital while it remains one of the lower paid roles in organisations… there is not a lot of understanding of the role and the potential of digital. I think Covid pushed charities to take risks and try new things and forced some organisations to value digital and its role more. As an individual (who works in digital for a charity) I had to create strict boundaries between work and personal time. The biggest obstacle is getting work notifications through personal devices, especially when working from home.

(D, 2017 cohort)

Even though Covid-19 has been a challenge for every organisation, I feel that charities can take advantage of the situation by developing their skills, strategies, and ideas. It'll provide them with the opportunity to take over platforms that their competitors haven't had the chance to.

(M, 2018 cohort)

During and post-Covid charities could use digital tools to naturally expand their reach for both support and donations. They could use digital for new and trendy fundraising methods and raising awareness to people who will be spending more time online during lockdowns.

(J, 2018 cohort)

Charities who had been embracing digital transformation before Covid-19 had advantages to engage their audiences. The organisational culture however needs to be open to changes as Covid-19 has showed how uncertain the future is. Agility and Continuity can be enhanced by strategic planning. Half of the charities have no digital strategy to follow. Digital content creation is ever evolving, and user experience becomes immersive. These especially with mental health prevention work greatly. VR is used in the NHS to enhance therapy, moreover the gaming market capitalisation on VR is widespread. Transforming services and products offered to be digital is a vital part, as people are more isolated than ever before. Apps and XR content development would be preferable as that is what the newer generations grow up with, therefore reaching them via new platforms and digital realms seems the only root to ultimate efficiency in the long term.

(A, 2019 cohort)

In terms of what charities could do? Get away from this fake filmed campaign nonsense. Utilise short video content of all emotions and feelings. Perhaps consider using TikTok as a creative platform and most definitely ensure their website has a good UX experience and is easy to search through. There's a distrust towards charities in the UK especially and where the money goes so charities should be using digital to put that message out to people 'we're not taking your money and giving it to the big CEO, it's going to this project and that.

(B, 2019 cohort)

During Covid-19 digital delivery is the biggest (perhaps only) way of communicating for many charities – I would withdraw any outdoor advertising and advertise only on digital platforms.

(E, 2017 cohort)

They definitely need to push for more digital activities, such as creative videos, PPC and better online presence and engagements. One thing Covid has taught us is to move online and don't take face to face interactions and events for granted. I'd like to see them run more online events or raise awareness of any cause in a more effective way on their digital channels. The digital channels can be used effectively, and the cost is less compared to running an actual event.

(R, 2019 cohort)

Conclusion

This chapter has outlined the digital challenges facing charities in the UK, and particularly Scotland, today. Resources, skills and organisational buy-in all remain key challenges. Covid has also led to additional issues around working remotely, access to software and technology, and being able to continue to engage service users and stakeholders. Online digital platforms can be used to encourage donations as can online word of mouth via social networks as a way for sharing involvement with charities via sponsorship.

Encouraging charities to work with external parties such as consultants, technology companies, academics and students can help provide a new insight into the charity's digital activities. Charities of all sizes should be encouraged to apply for and access digital skills-based training, grants and other forms of funding.

Working in collaboration with universities and colleges can lead to student projects with charities. These projects improve student technical skills and allow students to apply traditional and digital marketing models to real-world issues. In addition, projects like the partnership between MH Charity and the university can also lead to greater engagement with the charity, something which can be lacking for that particular age group. Working with charities can improve student employability and encourage them to consider the not-for-profit sector as a potential career.

Chapter discussion questions

1. What challenges have UK charities faced in adopting digital marketing techniques?
2. How can charities encourage board of directors/trustees to support investment in digital marketing?
3. Can you identify any charities who have taken innovative approaches to attract fundraising during Covid using digital marketing techniques? How successful have these campaigns been? What would you do differently?

References

Baird, A. (2017). How digital marketing can galvanise nonprofit supporters. *Journal of Digital & Social Media Marketing*, 4(4), 374–379.

Dean, J. (2020). Student perceptions and experiences of charity on social media: The authenticity of offline networks in online giving. *Voluntary Sector Review*, 11(1), 41–57.

Digital Doughnut. (2018). How digital trends are shaping the future of charities. Available at www.digitaldoughnut.com/articles/2018/november/how-digital-trends-are-shaping-cha rities (accessed 15 January 2021).

House of Lords. (2017). Stronger charities for a stronger society – Select Committee for Charities. Available at https://publications.parliament.uk/pa/ld201617/ldselect/ldchar/133/133.pdf (accessed 15 January 2021).

Leonhardt, J.M. & Peterson, R.T. (2019). Should charity promotions appeal to altruism? *International Journal of Nonprofit and Voluntary Sector Marketing*, 24(1), e1629.

Lloyds Bank. (2020). Essential digital skills. Available at www.lloydsbank.com/banking-with-us/whats-happening/consumer-digital-index/essential-digital-skills.html (accessed 15 January 2021).

Medium. (2017). What is mobile first design? Available at https://medium.com/@Vincent xia77/what-is-mobile-first-design-why-its-important-how-to-make-it-7d3cf2e29d00 (accessed 15 January 2021).

Medium. (2020). Top ten digital challenges facing charities. Available at https://medium. com/wethecatalysts/the-top-ten-digital-challenges-facing-the-charity-sector-2144789a ec14highlighted (accessed 15 January 2021).

Office for Students. (2020). Supporting students' mental health. Available at www.officefor students.org.uk/publications/coronavirus-briefing-note-supporting-student-mental-health/ (accessed 15 January 2021).

OSCR. (2021). What we do. Available at www.oscr.org.uk/about-oscr/about-oscr/ (accessed 15 January 2021).

Quinton, S. and Fennemore, P. (2013). Missing a strategic marketing trick? The use of online social networks by UK charities. *International Journal of Nonprofit and Voluntary Sector Marketing*, 18(1), 36–51.

Skills Platform. (2020). Charity digital report. Available at http://report.skillsplatform.org/ charity-digital-report-2020 (accessed 15 January 2021).

UK Government. (2017). What makes a charity? Available at https://assets.publishing.ser vice.gov.uk/government/uploads/system/uploads/attachment_data/file/637648/CC4.pdf (accessed 15 January 2021).

UK Government. (2018). Charity Commission for England and Wales. Available at www. gov.uk/government/organisations/charity-commission (accessed 15 January 2021).

9

RELATIONSHIP MARKETING IN CHARITIES

So much more than just 'tea and sympathy'

Fran Hyde

Introduction

The core principles of Relationship Marketing are deeply rooted in the marketing practice of nonprofit organisations. Through an examination of the nationally recognised Suffolk-based charity the Rural Coffee Caravan (RCC), this chapter will examine how building trust, gaining commitment and maintaining an authentic dialogue with diverse stakeholders are necessities for nonprofit organisations. Successful nonprofit organisations, like the RCC, understand that alignment must be clearly maintained between an organisation's mission statement and its operations. For charities, it is the daily work of ensuring that their organisation's values are shared by their wide range of stakeholders which powers a flourishing organisation. Effective and viable charities, such as the RCC, focus on their relationships with distinct stakeholders – service users, donors, volunteers, employees and trustees – who together comprise a charity. For charities it is not enough to just maintain a relationship, because the ongoing support of a wide range of stakeholders is essential to the charity's existence. To sustain operations a charity must simultaneously develop an extensive network of contacts and accommodate a large number of single contacts, whilst also investing time and effort into identifying, building and maximising key relationships.

To explore Relationship Marketing 'in action' – how Relationship Marketing has been employed and deployed effectively in the charity sector – this chapter will draw on a relationship established between the author, Ann the Chief Executive Officer (CEO) of the RCC and Helen the owner of Suffolk-based Public Relations (PR) agency Affinity PR who is also a key stakeholder in the RCC. This relationship began when the author (Deputy Dean of Suffolk Business School, University of Suffolk) was talking to Helen in her capacity as Visiting Fellow for the University of Suffolk. During a conversation exploring the difficulties of

DOI: 10.4324/9781003134169-12

finding a suitable case study organisation for a third year strategic marketing module, Helen suggested the RCC. Having explained to Helen that students needed the chance to demonstrate their ability to examine marketing theory in practice, and in particular the managing and building of relationships with customers or service users, Helen suggested that the RCC would make an ideal case study. What subsequently transpired over two years was not only an engaging case study assessment for a cohort of students, but the opportunity for the author to explore and reflect on charity Relationship Marketing in action, and it is this work and these conversations which have formed the case study.

This chapter begins with an overview of the key aspects of Relationship Marketing theory; next the RCC is introduced. The chapter then uses the tacit and pragmatic marketing practice of the RCC as a case study from which to explore the application, successes and challenges of charity Relationship Marketing in practice. The chapter ends by considering a number of unresolved issues for charities and sets some key questions for readers to consider with regard to charity Relationship Marketing in action.

Relationship marketing: an overview

The identification of Relationship Marketing as a topic of academic study in marketing, and as an area of focus by marketing practitioners, emerged in the early 1980s. Originating in the areas of industrial or business-to-business marketing, Relationship Marketing developed as a field of study as economies moved from being dominated by the mass marketing of products in the post-war years through the 1950–1960s, to the more service-based economies of the 1970–1980s, and as those involved in marketing awoke to the need of serving the requirements of customers (Gummesson, 2017; O'Malley & Tynan, 1998; Payne & Frow, 2017). An early definition of Relationship Marketing by Berry (1983) states that Relationship Marketing is about 'attracting, maintaining and – in multi-service organisations – enhancing customer relationships' (p. 25). Berry went on to outline five strategies to encourage the practice of Relationship Marketing to become a core focus of organisations. His suggestions included building and customising the relationship, augmenting the core services with extra benefits and being aware of the need for internal marketing to employees because of the impact of this on the employees' interactions with customers (Berry, 1995). Evert Gummesson, a constant and key academic voice on Relationship Marketing, around the same time sought to capture the 'soul' (2017, p. 17) of Relationship Marketing with a more conceptual definition which focused on the interactions of relationships in the complex networks between organisations and customers (Gummesson, 1983). By the 1990s, Relationship Marketing was a well-established topic in the marketing curriculum with terms such as customer relationship management, together with technological developments in data capture and analysis, driving marketing practitioners to focus on developing digitally enabled Relationship Marketing strategies and, then, tactics using a variety of software and digital platforms. Looking back over the past 30 years, and considering the developments in Relationship Market-ing, it is significant and relevant to this chapter to note that human activity, and the need to keep this in balance with fast-developing technological aspects of Rela-tionship Marketing, continues to be considered a vital area of debate within a successful overall orientation of an organisation and for those involved in marketing (Gummesson, 2017).

Relationship Marketing is usually contrasted to a more transactional and the less 'relationship-building' approach taken in marketing practice. In a relational approach, marketers focus on the end user or customer and, seeking to understand their customers' needs and wants, work towards building a 'relational exchange'. This marketing approach requires organisations to consider the exchange with a customer or service user as much more than a one-off, 'one and done' discrete transactional event. Expanding marketing thinking around what was involved, or could be involved, in and around 'the exchange', Relationship Marketing has also caused some revaluation of that most popular of marketing concepts, 'the market-ing mix'. Writing about the dominance and influence which the marketing mix has held over marketing practice and thought since the 1960s, Christian Gronross (1996) suggested that the marketing mix, or the 4 Ps as it is sometimes known, encouraged a generation of marketers to focus on what organisations can do *to* customers rather than *for* customers (p. 6). The weakness of this transaction-focused marketing concept is further explored by Constantinides (2006). Identifying one limitation of this popular marketing concept as its lack of personalisation, Con-stantinides discusses Relationship Marketing as one driving force within the recognition that the marketing mix can perpetuate a lack of customer orientation. Indeed, it is Constantinides's view that the acknowledgement of the importance of focusing on consumer interactivity with an organisation has driven many develop-ments of this popular mnemonic (p. 413). Whilst many marketing students may be quick to cite the addition of the 'P' of People in the extended marketing mix, or 7 Ps, it is also interesting to note how many more of the extensions of, and propositions to extend, the marketing mix over the last 20 years have acknowledged the absence of the human within the original mix, whether customer, service user, employee or, indeed, volunteer. This seems to have become one of the most essential and popular of additions and developments to this most well-known marketing concept (ibid.).

Relationship Marketing advocates that marketing practice in organisations puts the interactions with people, whether customers, service users, employees or volunteers, at the core of marketing strategy and tactics. For this focus to be suc-cessful, a dedication to building trust and a demonstration of commitment is required (Morgan & Hunt, 1994). Commitment and trust could be considered as the antecedents to the practice of 'cooperative behaviours' (Morgan & Hunt, 1994, p. 22) and possibly even to a productive relationship between an organisation and an individual. This is in contrast to 'opportunistic' marketing activity which involves activities which are not considered to be either productive or effective, or indeed 'beneficial' for all parties involved (Sweeney & Webb, 2002). Focusing on a sustained and planned approach to building relationships, Dwyer et al. (1987)

proposed that relationships between a 'buyer and seller' (individual and organisation) evolve through five stages, or a 'relationship development process of (1) awareness, (2) explorations, (3) expansion, (4) commitment, and (5) dissolution' (p. 15). It is important to note that this idea of stages, and the possibility of progressing an individual, has since been developed to help marketing practitioners in the area of loyalty (Christopher et al., 1991), and with the advent of social networks, the impact and influence of social media on Relationship Marketing practice has also been examined (Harridge-March & Quinton, 2009). How trust and commitment can be operationalised, and whether relational stages, progression and loyalty can be directly applied within successful charity marketing practice, has been less extensively considered by marketing scholars but has some consideration in this chapter through the examination of the work of the RCC.

The planning of activities is based on the concepts of trust, commitment, mutuality, promise keeping and dialogue (Gronross, 1996), as the focus of Relationship Marketing practice can build greater 'value' for all involved in the 'relationship'. A consideration of what is of value in the exchanges made between charitable organisations and their stakeholders is multifaceted. The complex nature of the exchanges of charities and their stakeholders means identifying what is of value to both an individual and the organisation. It is an involved and complex process and requires considering 'non-economic' aspects which are important in this exchange, such as social benefits, participation and emotional satisfaction. For instance, with a key aspect of the work of charitable organisations identified as securing funding for services, without the consideration of what is of 'value' to those involved in giving, donating and fundraising for charities, how is an organisation to achieve success and, moreover, to know and be able to strategise around the behaviours or tactics which are needed to continue to secure vital funds through the building of relations with key supporters and donors (Bennett & Barkensjo, 2004; MacMillan et al., 2005; Sargeant & Lee, 2004)?

Drawing this brief overview of the academic study of Relationship Marketing to a conclusion, it is important to acknowledge that for many organisations the aim of Relationship Marketing, the steps or stages, tactics and practices put in place by organisations to build relationships with stakeholders, may make possible an emotional and social bond between individual and organisation (O'Malley & Tynan, 1998). Indeed, over time the vocabulary of Relationship Marketing seems to have drawn heavily on ideas of human relationships and interpersonal relationships, including marriage (Dwyer et al., 1987; Pressey & Mathews, 2003). More recently Relationship Marketing has been described as shifting thinking from 'share of wallet to share of heart' (Sheth, 2017, p. 7) with the suggestion that, in their dealings with their customers, organisations need to be transcending a 'business relationship' to something more demonstrative and sensitive more akin to friendship (ibid.). This expressive and demonstrative language, and translating this into steps or stages, tactics and practices, might be a somewhat daunting prospect for those involved in marketing practice outside the nonprofit sector. Indeed, to operationalise and maintain, as well as to achieve with some degree of sincerity, such 'relations' could be challenging (Mitussis et al., 2006). However, for charities such 'emotions' in their marketing practice are the very essence of their existence and, although not without their own set of challenges, it is this openness and sensitivity which underpins much of the daily work of charities, and this can be seen in both the philosophy and practices of many organisations within this sector. Indeed, it is through examining how the RCC have embedded the core principles of Relationship Marketing into their everyday work, whilst taking note of the opportunity for social as well as emotional bonds to be formed, that we now consider how they have successfully used Relationship Marketing.

The Rural Coffee Caravan

The Rev. Canon Sally Fogden supported (emotionally and in practical ways) Suffolk's farmers after the devastating foot and mouth and swine fever outbreaks in 2001. Seeing an ongoing need to promote community spirit, in 2003 Sally founded the Rural Coffee Caravan with a mission to ensure that 'all people in rural Suffolk have the connections and community they need to be happy and healthy'.[1] The vision Sally had was to connect rural communities and end loneliness. Initially the Rural Coffee Caravan was born from a partnership between Citizens Advice, Age UK and Suffolk Farm Support Network, with the aim of targeting people from outlying rural villages and hamlets. Networking and working collaboratively with over 60 agencies and organisations, the RCC continues to hold mobile pop-up café events in villages and rural communities, making on average 200 village visits to pour over 71,000 cups of coffee a year (Osborn, 2019). More recently the RCC have created a network called 'MeetUpMondays', an initiative inspired by Mick Dore of The Alexandra pub, London SW19, in January 2018. Based on encouraging publicans and café owners/managers to host free coffee mornings in their venues, led by RCC and aided by Community Action Suffolk in 2019–2020, this helped facilitate activities which connected over 46,000 people who joined community events and entered into the social life of their communities (Osborn, 2020).

Even before the recent devastating impacts of the 2020 Covid pandemic on communities and individuals, in the last decade loneliness had become a topic of national concern and discussion (House of Commons, 2017). In an 'age of loneliness' it has been suggested that the United Kingdom has become a nation of strangers with social bonds, networks and connections increasingly focused on our immediate families and friends, and less on our neighbours and wider communities (Gov.uk, 2018). A gap has appeared in communities as a result of the loss of community social spaces through the closing of pubs and local libraries that has been well documented (CAMRA, 2018). Indeed, in October 2018, Teresa May launched the first cross-government strategy to tackle loneliness and, whilst being lonely can affect anyone at any age, an isolated and ageing population are key issues in the current loneliness debate, with many people just not knowing their neighbours anymore (Gov.uk, 2018). In 2019 the RCC received The Queens Award for Voluntary Service. The work of the RCC has become nationally recognised, with agencies and charities in other areas of the UK, such as Lincoln-shire and Leicestershire, contacting the RCC for help and advice on how to set up in their area. Even in the 2020–2021 lockdowns of the Covid pandemic, the RCC continued to facilitate community meetings and networks by supporting people to move online, to use telephone trees and, where possible, meet albeit in socially distanced settings (ibid.).

For Rev. Canon Sally Fogden and the team which has continued to take her vision forward, the ambition for the RCC has always been of doing much more than organising for volunteers to arrive and set up in a village to serve coffee (and tea) from a caravan (Osborn, 2019, 2020). Ann, the current CEO, explains that for her team at the RCC 'every visit must matter' because the RCC aims to be the catalyst to initiate or reinvigorate the community by bringing people who live near each other, but have never met, together. Importantly, rather than offering to stay on and 'solve' (ibid.) community issues or an individual's problems, the RCC has always aimed to facilitate connections within, and indeed between, communities. Ann and Helen explained that the RCC might be contacted by a concerned vil-lage vicar, priest, publican, member of the Parish Council or a village resident. Concern may have arisen from villagers seeing underused communal facilities such as a village hall, through a villager hearing about the work of the RCC in a nearby village, or from a local councillor or member of a specialist agency being con-cerned about the welfare of a group of residents. Whilst over the past 17 years requests for help to the RCC have been made through several channels, those leading the RCC have always been clear from the outset that ultimately their aim is to leave, and leave behind a community in contact with each other, and a net-work in place which will continue and develop the regular meet ups which the RCC helped to establish between residents (ibid.).

Achieving the vision: relationship marketing in action

No 'quick fix' is promised by the RCC. Over the course of several meetings with the author, Ann explained that for each village or community what is needed will be different and it is essential to establish 'what is of value to a community' (Osborn, 2020). Certainly, it is clear that the RCC is working at building what Sweeney and Webb (2002) discussed in their examination of successful Relation-ship Marketing as the 'longevity of relationships, mutual respect, a win win strategy and the acceptances of the customer [for the RCC "the community"] as a partner' (p. 78). For instance, Ann gave an example of the RCC working with a commu-nity which was 'broken' (Osborn, 2020) and how in the first instance the RCC needed to simply help re-establish community communications. Responding to a first contact which, as previously stated, might come from a vicar, someone on a village hall committee, the parish council or a citizen living in the village, the RCC know that, if they want their involvement to be successful, they first need to plan to engage with and support a community for a year by going in every month, but always ensuring that they begin with a clear outline of what it is that they can offer, as well as what they cannot. It is through interacting in this way in this first 'stage' of building relationships that the RCC operationalises its vision of bringing people together and empowering and strengthening rural communities. Working in an active manner to expand the traditional understanding of 'what is the exchange', the work of the RCC shows how 'value' to all involved is achieved over time and through active participation.

A secondary aim of the work of the RCC has been in identifying vulnerable people living in rural isolation and signposting and referring them to specialist agencies, such as the Suffolk County Council housing team, for help and advice. As many health and social care organisations in the public, charity and private sectors move their services and communications online, Helen noted that it has become harder and harder for those people who are not online, as well as those living in areas with poor broadband and WiFi connection, to know about what might be available as well as where to seek out help (Oldfield, 2020). Furthermore, the range of resources being offered by the public, charity and private sectors is continually changing (ibid.). So what might emerge over the exchange facilitated by the RCC and 'promoted' by the RCC as an opportunity for a 'coffee and chat' can at times become much more significant than the opportunity for a chat or a hot beverage. For example, Ann explained that working in the way they do the RCC 'is more likely to bring forward confidences' (Osborn, 2020). Helen gave an example of an RCC volunteer picking up that someone was living in a cold house and not eating hot meals because they were concerned about the cost of fuel, thus not turning on the heating or using their cooker. Through sensitively discussing this situation, the knowledgeable RCC volunteer could then signpost this individual to a range of support services, encouraging this individual to seek help and support. This 'exchange' might also involve facilitating the first contact with the agency by using the RCC caravan WiFi to access a resource or ensuring the individual leaves with a range of leaflets and contact telephone numbers. What is more, the volunteer will then also follow up, discreetly, when the next RCC meet up takes place in that village.

For the RCC to have impact, Ann explains that the RCC must 'be real' (Osborn, 2020). Rarely anonymous and always holistic, the RCC 'exchange' between volunteer and individual requires sensitive handling and discretion. The RCC exchange is clearly more complex than a transactional exchange, and many times in conversation Ann and Helen outlined their essential ingredients at the RCC as being trust and commitment, which this chapter has already identified as key aspects of Relationship Marketing and identified within the academic study of Relationship Marketing (Morgan & Hunt, 1994). Indeed, the relationships the RCC builds with individuals include many of the traditional aspects of for-profit Relationship Marketing, such as understanding customers, their individual preferences, expectations and changing needs (Mitussis et al., 2006, p. 576). But to understand the key difference between the Relationship Marketing practice of organisations such as the RCC as compared to those within the for-profit sector, it is perhaps necessary to look beyond the operational detail to the overriding philosophy of an organisation. The work of O'Malley and Tynan (1998) considered that many organisations use the appropriate terminology of relationships in their marketing approach, whilst not really adopting the necessary philosophy, suggesting that in many organisations Relationship Marketing is more 'rhetoric than reality' (p. 810). Understanding the depth and significance of the relational exchange for the RCC, it was clear that such grandiloquence would be impossible to practice and sustain unless it was a real and genuine guiding principle.

So how does Ann, in her role as CEO, embrace but more importantly operationalise a philosophy of trust and commitment ensuring she avoids empty 'rhetoric'? Ann readily admits that she embarked on her role with passion, enthusiasm and commitment but with no formal training and no marketing knowledge, feeling that this ensured that she was not confined or 'indoctrinated' (Osborn, 2020) into a way of doing things. For instance, she said during one conversation, 'you'll laugh when I tell you that it took me forever to stop putting kisses at the bottom of my emails' (ibid.). Ann feels she sets the tone at the RCC through example, practising 'good old fashioned good manners' (Osborn, 2020) in all her communications. For example, to all her team as well as other stakeholders she recognised 'I need to say thank you… I need to say I couldn't do this without your support' (ibid.). Ann ensures that all her team know the 'ethos' (Osborn, 2020), mission and what is expected of them. But Ann doesn't want to control 'how they do it and when they do it' (ibid.), feeling that if those involved with the RCC 'need to know how and when on everything this is more of a problem' (ibid.). Ann regularly explains to her team that 'they need to figure out what it is the village or community needs' (Osborn, 2020) and be a catalyst in empowering this local dialogue to take place. Whilst Ann believes in 'creating a culture of trust' (Osborn, 2020) and seems to have arrived at a way to do this within the RCC, it is interesting to note that this has not been without challenges. Ann acknowledged that for some individuals who want to become involved in the RCC 'the transition from a corporate hierarchy background might be difficult' (Osborn, 2020), and that 'this has been a hard lesson [for her] to learn at times' (ibid.). Ann goes on to explain that she has now understood the need for 'regular chats' (ibid.) with all her team. Alongside Ann's clear commitment to give her team autonomy, it seems time in her role as CEO of the RCC has also impressed upon Ann the need for structured support and the regular supervision of her team. This demonstrates the need for a planned and organised approach, even if what is being aimed for is autonomy and a degree of freedom within the work of the team in building relationships with clients or service users.

Significance of stakeholders

Like many charities, to achieve their vision and sustain their operations, the RCC is dependent on paid employees as well as a large number of volunteers. The RCC currently has over 50 volunteers, with a paid part-time project manager, a paid project officer and a paid part-time administrator (Osborn, 2020). In addition, a board of trustees provide the governance required by charitable organisations in the UK. Drawing on Gummesson (2017) who suggested 'life is interaction in networks of relationships' (p.16), it is clear to see that, in line with many charities, to continue to operate the RCC relies on a complex network of relationships with a wide range of different stakeholders. For instance, to ensure that the organisation remains up to date in areas such as digital marketing techniques, Ann has developed a range of key relationships achieving a range of pro bono work from experts. Ann recognises that the RCC need to be 'canny' (Osborn, 2020)) in building and maintaining such vital relationships. As one such expert, Helen explained that she was happy to work on this basis with Ann because Ann was always 'mindful of the commercial value of relationships' (Oldfield, 2020). Having experienced undertaking pro bono work for other charities, Helen explained that, if not managed well, this work can become 'disrespectful and exhausting' (ibid.). Helen explained that some charities 'keep coming back and keep coming back saying can I pick your brain… one and half hours later… they are still talking!' (Oldfield, 2020)). Helen explained that what you really want to do is offer 'something more sustainable' (ibid.). Here Helen highlights a challenge for charities who, in operating within what might be considered as a less formal and commercially negotiated 'relationship' with their stakeholders, may be in danger of damaging key stakeholder relationships if these are not structured and maintained carefully.

To secure the time of a volunteer, or the money of a corporate sponsor, Ann and the team at the RCC know that they need to be clear about what the RCC 'does'. Ann believes it is only through her complete 'openness and transparency' (Osborn, 2020) that she has secured key operational resources for the RCC such as 'the partnership with a local organisation who supply all the coffee' (ibid.). Exploring the significance of stakeholder relationships, Sargeant and Lee (2004) emphasised that nonprofit organisations need to be credible and legitimate to secure funding, and that it was only on this basis they would develop long-term support rather than one-off donations or offers of support. Explaining how she has worked to establish the RCC as a trustworthy operation, Ann recounted that 'some people have been quite shocked at the amount of information we are prepared to share' (Osborn, 2020). Ann sees this openness and transparency as key to building trust, believing that it is only through showing exactly what the RCC does very explicitly to those who enquire that she can build the relationships which the RCC needs to exist. Helen went further and discussed Ann's role over the past few years as educating funders and explained how important 'educating as part of relationships' (Oldfield, 2020) was to charities such as the RCC. Helen and Ann discussed that this had come about from being faced, over the years, with very lengthy, and what they felt were 'unhelpful' (Oldfield, 2020), application forms for funding. It was through trying to work out how to get what the RCC needed from a funder, what was of value to the RCC, that the strategy of complete openness had become established. Discussing the reputation which the RCC had established, and Ann had worked hard to establish, Ann saw this as a key reason as to why very recently a grant had been awarded to the RCC to promote the uptake of the Covid vaccination programme within rural communities across Suffolk.

It was through their commitment to the need to build relationship through education that Ann and Helen worked with the University of Suffolk students, setting the students a brief to achieve the objectives of recruiting volunteers and securing resources. The semester of work involved the opportunity for the students to meet Ann, Helen and other RCC volunteers, who gave time to the students as well as arranging to bring an RCC caravan onto campus so students could see as well as go inside it for themselves (see Figure 9.1). The students developed a marketing plan to meet each objective, but this authentic learning experience achieved much more than a 'real life' case study experience for the cohort. Several students from this cohort took on volunteering opportunities in their local communities which they attributed to the understanding they had developed of challenges of isolation which RCC had revealed. A further two students in this cohort went on to work in charities after graduating; one used their work with RCC in their interview. The 'educating' of stakeholders, or indeed as with the work with students from the University of Suffolk who might be considered future stakeholders, is not explicitly covered within academic writing on Relationship Marketing. For charities such as the RCC this aspect within relationship building emerges as an important and productive aspect of their work.

Maintaining the 'networks of relationships' described by Gummesson (2017, p. 16), and needed by charities like the RCC, requires time. Ann was very honest about the need to build and maintain relationships with a whole range of individuals, from the local council to philanthropist funders, as well as many different statutory bodies. Ann sees her role as investing considerable time into cultivating these relationships effectively to support the needs of the RCC. Whilst this work

FIGURE 9.1 The Rural Coffee Caravan at the University of Suffolk

and some of the stakeholder roles correspond with the Relationship Marketing work of individuals in the for-profit sector, such as with service users, employee and non-executive board members, listening to Ann describe her constant communications with all stakeholders gives useful examples of what putting this relational activity into practice entails for charitable organisations. For instance, Ann explained that 'out of the blue I will email the lady responsible for the lottery funding, just to see how she is' (Osborn, 2020). Indeed even for those 'obliged' to work with RCC as part of their professional role, Ann is intent on making this a positive and productive encounter. Describing when a council officer came to speak at an RCC event Ann said 'they have an outer shell... you can see their outer shell melt away over the two hours... once that's gone they manage to have a much better relationship with the people that they have come to talk to' (Osborn, 2020). Ann explained that, whilst 'I haven't got much to offer apart from my time over a coffee and a chat' (Osborn, 2020), when asking people for pro bono work, or to support the RCC with funding or grants, 'it isn't transactional... it's a warm relationship with, to be perfectly honest, the people you need' (ibid.).

Just as the work of the RCC in every village or community progresses differently, with one village taking the RCC coffee and meet up from the village green to a village hall, or another developing 'MeetUpMondays' with their local pub or setting up a regular quiz night, over time the RCC have found that relationships with all their other stakeholders will change and develop. Individuals supported by the RCC have gone forward to become community champions within their own villages, acting as catalysts of change in their immediate local areas (Osborn, 2020). Importantly Helen stressed that volunteers take pride in their work and she wanted to stress that a genuine enthusiasm exists to see the RCC succeed and to spread the word of the RCC's successes. Whilst this 'progression' of individuals bears some relation to the work of Dwyer et al. (1987) on relational stages, or work on loyalty by academics such as Christopher et al. (1991), or even the potential for individuals involved with organisations to progress forward to become influencers or advocates (Harridge-March & Quinton, 2009), the application of this theory to the work of the RCC and other nonprofits can be problematic.

Furthermore, nonprofits, and especially those such as the RCC who have a very locally based stakeholder network, can face a real challenge from relationship breakdown or dissolution (Christopher et al., 1991). The ending or exiting 'stage' of a relationship seems inherently more complex for charities and other nonprofit organisations (Pressey & Mathews, 2003). For the RCC it can be at these times that their deeply entrenched relationships within the communities of Suffolk can be a challenge to disentangle.

The exploration of the work of the RCC has shown that the interpersonal relationships and the examination of the depth and impact of the relational exchange underpinning so many of the RCC activities take place in 'real time' and without the use or meditation of digital techniques or platforms. Of course here it is important to note that for many charities, such as the RCC, digital platforms and customer relationship management software may simply be too expensive to consider, however the choice not to use such Relationship Marketing devices may also be intentional. The Relationship Marketing practice which seems to work for the RCC does not rely upon the direct and database marketing which characterises so much of the Relationship Marketing practice of the for-profit world (Payne & Frow, 2017). Here the RCC seems to be working in direct contrast to organisations in the for-profit sectors where the adoption of technology-enhanced Relationship Marketing practice has enabled a range of personalised communications with individuals across a variety of platforms to become part of everyday marketing practice. Furthermore, these developments have been widely attributed to a fall in costs and widespread availability and adoption of what is known as customer relationship management (CRM) techniques (Mitussis et al., 2006). Currently, for the RCC and many charities, it seems the work of a CRM system is undertaken by individuals such as Ann. Considering the trend of widespread adoption of digitally enhanced Relationship Marketing, O'Malley and Tynan (1998) identify and describe a certain 'euphoria' (p. 800) from marketing practitioners. Furthermore they see digital methods in Relationship Marketing, which have been developed without the need and importance of quality and relevance of interactions necessarily being considered, as a key driver causing a high volume of interactions with individuals (ibid.). At an extreme, the digitisation of Relationship Marketing could be suggested to have resulted in 'a misplaced or insincere desire for a relationship while exploiting information asymmetries and customers' goodwill' (Mitussis et al., 2006, p. 580). This contrasts very starkly with the personalised methods which have successfully underpinned the philosophy as well as the practices of the RCC for the last 17 years.

Implications for marketing practice

This examination of Relationship Marketing theory and the consideration of how this theory, developed within the for-profit sector, can be seen at work within the practices of the RCC has sought to highlight the unique and personalised nature of charity relationship building with a range of stakeholders. Networks have been built from face-to-face interactions through a regular physical presence in rural communities, over very genuine and sincere exchanges, many of which take place over coffee, rather than via social media.

Chapter discussion questions

1. The essence of the RCC relationships was shown in this chapter to be built on trust and commitment, and is heavily reliant on a core group of individuals led by Ann and supported by experts such as Helen. What are the risks to the RCC and other charities in this approach to Relationship Marketing?
2. A funder offers a large sum of money, but this is specifically to finance a CRM system as they want to help the RCC build a database, as well as build the capacity and expertise of the RCC to start using a more digital base for communicating with individuals. Should the RCC accept this funding?

3.   Revisit the suggestions of relational stages in Relationship Marketing theory, and by conducting some further research into this popular area of Relationship Marketing theory, adapt the existing modules to include what you see as the different relational stages for a range of charity stakeholders.

Note

1   http://ruralcoffeecaravan.org.uk/

Acknowledgements

The author would like to acknowledge the invaluable involvement and support of Anne and Helen for making the project for University of Suffolk students possible.

References

Bennett, R. & Barkensjo A. (2004). Relationship quality, relationship marketing, and client perceptions of the levels of service quality of charitable organisations. *International Journal of Service Industry Management*, 16(1), 81–105.

Berry, L. (1983). Relationship marketing. In L. Berry, L. Shostack & G. Upah (eds), *Emerging Perspectives on Services Marketing*. American Marketing Association.

Berry, L. (1995). Relationship marketing of services: Growing interest in emerging perspectives. *Journal of Academy of Marketing Sciences*, 23(4), 236–245.

CAMRA. (2018). Pub closures are making us all poorer, says CAMRA. Available at https://camra.org.uk/press_release/pub-closures-are-making-us-all-poorer-says-camra/ (accessed 5 August 2020).

Christopher, M., Payne, A. & Ballantyne, D. (1991). *Relationship Marketing*. Butterworth Heinneman.

Constantinides, C. (2006). The marketing mix revisited: Towards the 21st century marketing. *Journal of Marketing Management*, 22(3–4), 407–438.

Dwyer, F., Schurr, P. & Oh, S. (1987). Developing buyer–seller relationships. *Journal of Marketing*, 51(2), 11–27.

Gov.uk. (2018). A connected society: A strategy for tackling loneliness. Available at https://assets.publishing.service.gov.uk/government/uploads/system/uploads/attachment_data/file/750909/6.4882_DCMS_Loneliness_Strategy_web_Update.pdf (accessed 9 September 2020).

Gronross, C. (1996). Relationship marketing: Strategic and tactical implications. *Management Decision*, 34(3), 5–14.

Gummesson, E. (1983). *A new concept of marketing*. Proceedings from the European Marketing Academy (EMAC) Annual Conference, Institut d'Etudes Commerciales de Grenoble, April.

Gummesson, E. (2017). From relationship marketing to total relationship marketing and beyond. *Journal of Services Marketing*, 31(1), 16–19.

Harridge-March, S. & Quinton, S. (2009). Virtual snakes and ladders: Social networks and the relationship marketing loyalty ladder. *The Marketing Review*, 9(2), 171–181.

House of Commons. (2017). Loneliness and local communities. Available at https://hansard.parliament.uk/Commons/2017-11-15/debates/

D2106C26-6821-445C-8666-4F8D3445FFDA/LonelinessAndLocalCommunities (accessed 5 August 2020).

MacMillan, K., Money, K., Money, A. & Downing, S. (2005). Relationship marketing in the not-for-profit sector: An extension and application of the commitment-trust theory. *Journal of Business Research*, 58, 806–818.

Mitussis, D., O'Malley, L. & Patterson, M. (2006). Mapping the re-engagement of CRM with relationship marketing. *European Journal of Marketing*, 40(5/6), 572–589.

Morgan, R. & Hunt, S. (1994). The commitment-trust theory of relationship marketing. *Marketing Theory*, 58, 20–38.

Oldfield, H. (2020). *The Rural Coffee Caravan Interview*, online, 5 November.

O'Malley, L. & Tynan, C. (1998). Relationship marketing in consumer markets. *European Journal of Marketing*, 34(7), 797–815.

Osborn, A. (2019). *The Rural Coffee Caravan Interview*, University of Suffolk, 3 October.

Osborn, A. (2020). *The Rural Coffee Caravan Interview*, online, 5 November.

Payne, A. & Frow, P. (2017). Relationship marketing: Looking backwards towards the future. *Journal of Services Marketing*, 31(1), 11–15.

Pressey, A. & Mathews, B. (2003). Jumped, pushed or forgotten? Approaches to dissolution. *Journal of Marketing Management*, 19(1–2), 131–155.

Sargeant, A. & Lee, S. (2004). Trust and relationship commitment in the United Kingdom voluntary sector: Determinants of donor behavior. *Psychology and Marketing*, 21(8), 613–635.

Sheth, P. (2017). Revitalizing relationship marketing. *Journal of Services Marketing*, 31(1), 6–10.

Sweeney, J. & Webb, D. (2002). Relationship benefits. *Journal of Relationship Marketing*, 1(2), 77–79.

10

ASK NOT WHAT MARKETING PRACTICE CAN DO FOR NPOs; ASK WHAT NPOs CAN DO FOR MARKETING PRACTICE

Helen O'Sullivan

Overview

Veloutsou and Delgado-Ballester (2018, p. 256) define brand as 'an evolving mental collection of actual (offer related) and emotional (human-like) characteristics and associations which convey benefits of an offer identified through a symbol, or a collection of symbols, and differentiates this offer from the rest of the marketplace'.

Traditionally, marketing and branding have been associated with the commercial sector and products. They were seen as tools to increase profits, to differentiate products, and to improve market share – all very commercial aspirations.

Such activities were not generally seen as applicable to the nonprofit sector, because 'competition' was not seen in the same way. However, as funding was reduced dramatically, organisations within the nonprofit sector began to identify that they needed to become more competitive in order to engage potential donors. By beginning to compete with other organisations, the sector propelled itself into adopting sophisticated and sleek business practices including marketing and branding (Hemsley-Brown & Goonawardana, 2007; Melewar & Akel, 2005). Studies by Temporal explain how branding a public sector company now is 'no longer a "nice to have" but a "must have"' (Temporal, 2015).

This would explain the speed with which branding in the nonprofit sector has grown. While branding is arguably a relatively new development in the sector, as highlighted by (Dholakia & Acciardo, 2014), it has quickly become a consideration for all nonprofits, including charities. Brands now have a fundamental role to play for private and public organisations alike (Dholakia & Acciardo, 2014; Gromark & Melin, 2013).

The brand represents a valuable strategic resource. In private companies it can play a crucial role in creating a competitive advantage, generating and sustaining financial performance (Aaker, 1996). However, this is also the same for the

DOI: 10.4324/9781003134169-13

nonprofit sector – indeed, it is the driver behind the increased use of branding within the sector. As revenue streams became increasingly scarce, organisations like charities found themselves competing with each other for the same donations. Money being donated to charity A was viewed by charity B as potential revenue lost. Competitor sets were defined, unique selling points were identified, and the same terms of engagement that had been so prevalent in the private sector became second nature in the nonprofit arena.

Another important area of overlap in the role branding and marketing plays can be seen in the establishment of increased legitimacy, trust (Gromark & Melin, 2013; Sataøen & Wæraas, 2015) and visibility (Gromark & Melin, 2013). Larger nonprofit organisations and charities will deliberately play on their heritage, emphasising the role they have played in their particular arena for many years. Their long-term commitment to their causes becomes a key part of their brand, and helps prevent newer, smaller organisations operating in the same space. Longevity and trust can give the impression to the consumer that their money will definitely be going to the cause they want it to and that they are contributing to substantial differences.

With the difficulties involved in differentiating products with no tangible characteristics or products, Berry (2000) underlines that brand development is crucial for nonprofits. As Temporal asserts, products and services can be copied; the only thing a public sector company has that cannot be replicated is a powerful brand image (Temporal, 2015).

However, charities have their own complexities, and numerous studies suggest that existing brand management theories and marketing models may not be fully transferable to this context (Chapleo, 2010; Dean et al., 2016; Hytti et al., 2015; Wæraas & Solbakk, 2009). Choosing to donate to a charity, which one to support, and how much to give involves an entirely different set of motivations and influences to deciding which brand of soft drink to buy, or what type of car to purchase. While it can certainly be argued that the nonprofit sector has much to gain from the benefits of branding, more research is needed that relates to the branding efforts of public organisations (Watkins & Gonzenbach, 2013).

It is not just more research that is needed, however. Education has historically been lacking in considering the ways that marketing practices could be applied to nonprofit organisations too. A university education in marketing traditionally prepares graduates for a wide range of potential careers in almost any sector. Wherever you are, and whatever line of business you are in, someone in your organisation will need to understand how to market and sell your product or service to interested parties, how to find them, how to keep them, how to follow and understand cashflow, when to invest in new areas, when to disinvest in fading markets and how to make an organisation successful.

However, the principles that are usually taught at universities are those that have been tried and tested in the commercial world. Charities, nonprofit organisations and the public sector are very much the poor relation, with little consideration given to the application of marketing theory within the sector – despite more and more marketing roles becoming available in them.

This chapter explores the ways that theory and practice can combine to deliver a better understanding of how contemporary issues in marketing and branding can be best applied to nonprofit organisations. A case study based on a collaboration between Bournemouth University and Anthony Nolan is presented which demonstrates the added value higher education institutions and the wider nonprofit sector can realise when they engage in co-creation surrounding knowledge transfer. Specifically, this chapter demonstrates the activities undertaken which helped facilitate positive societal impact by saving lives and inspiring young people's future involvement in the nonprofit sector.

Bournemouth University undergraduate marketing students and Anthony Nolan worked together to bring contemporary professional nonprofit organisation practice into the curriculum with a live assignment brief. The assignment brief was jointly set by Anthony Nolan and the teaching team.

The value of aligning the study of theory with a real-life case study is a well-versed pedagogy for universities across the world. While it is impractical to factor in case studies from each of the myriad industries in which a university student might find themselves practising in the future, there are many concepts that translate well across the spectrum – the product or service might change, but the fundamental principles behind its success remain the same. This cannot be said for the nonprofit organisation (NPO) sector; there are subtleties and differences that make this arena truly unique, and at present this gap is not being addressed in traditional marketing degrees at undergraduate level.

This begs the question of whether universities are doing enough to ensure marketing graduates leave with an understanding of what makes an NPO different, and how they can play a successful leadership role in one. Many universities talk about the purpose of their courses being to develop the thought leaders of the future – but if the NPO sector is not being thought about by those same universities, how can the sector grow? It is an arena crying out for further investigation, for better understanding, for a more-rounded education, and for the development of true leaders steeped in the accepted principles of practices specific to the industry – rather than the shoehorning of techniques from elsewhere into situations that might not suit them.

As this chapter has already suggested, NPOs have much to gain from understanding which elements of marketing practice can be taken directly from the private sector, which need to be modified in order to have the desired impact, and which are not appropriate or are unlikely to succeed.

However, what is also clear is that further insights into how to achieve successful, efficient partnerships with universities are needed. Thus, this research also contributes an understanding of how universities should prepare students with an appropriate toolkit for all contexts. Judging a student's theoretical mastery by grades is no longer sufficient (Caspersen & Smeby, 2018) as we also require complementary practical experience to ensure competency in a chosen discipline (Polkinghorne et al., 2019).

Theoretical background: marketing in the nonprofit sector

Nonprofit organisations contribute significant value to society (Bradford & Boyd, 2020), delivering services to their clients through donations from individuals (Winterich et al., 2017), but also serving the public interest by providing a wide array of crucial services, goods, and resources – from food and shelter to body parts (Bradford & Boyd, 2020). Donations are most often provided by individuals who intentionally offer their support without receiving tangible rewards (Gershon & Cryder, 2018).

Branding in the NPO sector is emerging as an interesting area of research, as 'diverse organisations find themselves using branding principles to promote a consistent and clear brand' (Leijerholt et al., 2019, p. 277). Nonprofit organisations invest in developing their brand to establish their point of differentiation (Temporal, 2015). This is supported by the findings of Sataoen & Wæraas, who identify that public sector organisations must use their branding to focus on uniqueness and differentiation while at the same time providing equal services in order to gain legitimacy (Sataøen & Wæraas, 2015). Studies by Kirovska also suggest that a corporate brand is a comprehensive and integrated approach to strategic planning, marketing communications and design (Kirovska & Simonovska, 2013).

In Leijerholt et al. (2019), it was suggested that traditional brand management approaches may not always be suitable in an NPO sector context, and that rather public organisations may need to adapt brand practices to suit the complex nature of the sector. A gap also exists in identifying and evaluating latest marketing theory and best practice specifically within the NPO sector. Simply adopting the principles and approaches of the market may be theoretically and practically uncomfortable, and bespoke approaches are needed (Chapleo, 2011). The complex nature of the sector makes the activity of branding an even more difficult task than in traditional, commercial contexts (Dholakia & Acciardo, 2014).

Chapleo and O'Sullivan (2017) assert that the issues and challenges of twenty-first century higher education are significant. They propose that universities operate in an increasingly uncertain environment, with the value of a degree programme having increased focus and challenge (Chapleo & O'Sullivan, 2017; Roohr et al., 2017). However, it is accurate to state that the wider NPO sector, including charities, are also dealing with macro forces moving with increasing speed, complexity and risk (Chapleo & O'Sullivan, 2017).

Equally, charities continue to face increasing cost pressure and investment is needed if they are to continue delivering the same standard of care. Clearly, the importance of a customer value proposition has never been so great, and the value and success of NPO brands is under great scrutiny and has raised many concerns within the general public.

Legislative, social and technological changes, and the need to reconcile the interests of different stakeholders, have required a more professional and business-like management approach. Furthermore, in this increasingly competitive and turbulent environment, brands are concerned with differentiation, enhancing images and improved communications. Therefore, branding has become a strategic priority for many charities in order to develop a meaningfully differentiated brand which enables them to communicate their strengths.

It seems apparent that in an increasingly competitive and uncertain environment, charities have moved towards adopting a corporate brand. Roper and Davies (2007) reinforced this suggestion, identifying that corporate branding is a more suitable brand categorisation than product branding for nonprofit organisations, charities, healthcare and universities specifically.

Co-creation between higher education institution and NPO

Anthony Nolan is a charity that saves the lives of people with blood cancer and blood disorders. It matches people in need of bone marrow transplants with suitable donors, arranging over 1,400 transplants a year as well as conducting research into stem cell matching and transplants, and providing a patient information and support system (anthonynolan.org).

However, even with over 800,000 registered donors, there are still people who cannot find a suitable match. For that reason, one of the key goals of Anthony Nolan's organisational strategy is to reach recruitment levels of 100,000 new potential donors per year by 2022. Therefore Anthony Nolan is looking for more people, particularly university-aged donors, to join the register.

Nonprofit organisations such as Anthony Nolan are appreciating the importance and value of utilising their brands. The same can be said for Bournemouth University who recognise the value students will gain from working with a live brief from the charity sector. Raising awareness and inspiring students to be involved in charitable organisations was a joint objective for both Anthony Nolan and Bournemouth University as the mutual benefit of the co-creation was clear.

In 2018 a new teaching team took over the responsibility for leadership of this newly Chartered Institute of Marketing accredited unit; level 4 Marketing – a unit on BA (Hons) Business Studies (BABS). BABS is a capstone programme within The Business School. The largest undergraduate programme at Bournemouth University, it currently has a cohort of over 1,100 students. This unit is a core level 4 unit with a cohort number of 420 approx.

The unit has suffered from consecutive years of poor student feedback due to a lack of an application of real-life marketing issues in a variety of sectors as opposed to traditional product marketing contexts. To tackle this, the unit was rewritten, working closely with Anthony Nolan, to bring contemporary professional NPO practice into the curriculum. A live brief with Anthony Nolan was born.

The brief

On average, people have around a 1 in 800 chance of being asked to donate stem cells or bone marrow. However, men aged 16–30 have a 1 in 200 chance of being chosen to donate because Anthony Nolan's research confirms that the use of donors under 30 is associated with a trend towards better survival rates. Today young men make up only 16% of the register; therefore, there is a need to get more young men to register as donors.

Responding to Anthony Nolan's key strategic objective to increase university-aged donors to join the register, the aim of the unit assessment was to create an integrated marketing campaign to specifically target and raise awareness of stem cell donation, with the overarching aim being to increase the number of stem cell donors from younger donors.

Working in groups of five, students created a marketing campaign targeting 18–24-year-old men in order to increase awareness of the Anthony Nolan charity, and to increase the number of stem cell donors from the target demographic.

Anthony Nolan worked with the teaching team and students to provide the main idea for this project and share insights about the charity, and at the end of the semester Anthony Nolan selected the best campaign and put it into practice.

Various pedagogical instruments were deployed in this unit which included working with the marketing team from Anthony Nolan to build insights and experience of real-world marketing in the nonprofit environment.

Students were encouraged to consider their future roles as marketers and to enhance a wide range of skills, competencies, attitudes and attributes, which are known to be characteristics of effective and successful marketing professionals. Students needed to demonstrate clear and competent communication, cohesion and logical links between the research, creative inputs and decisions made.

Implications for theory and practice

The prompt for this case study focus was the need to provide undergraduate students with an understanding of the fundamentals of marketing theories to enable them to develop marketing approaches for a range of marketing scenarios within the NPO context. Demand for this had been articulated from NPOs who had identified graduates predominantly having learned marketing from a product/commercial context. However, demand for greater focus on a career in the nonprofit arena was also popular from the student body.

Using a live brief from an NPO proved to be a successful initiative from every perspective. Anthony Nolan gained valuable insights into their brand from a variety of different viewpoints, and the quality of the submissions was so high that the organisation was able to put the winning concept into operation.

> Working with universities is an excellent way for a charity like Anthony Nolan to engage directly with people who can really make a difference for the patients we support. Working in partnership with young people and Bournemouth University has allowed us to co-create exciting projects such as this to reach this important audience, as well as to offer BU students the chance to make a lifesaving difference while learning.
>
> *(O'Leary, 2021)*

Meanwhile, the academic team delivering the unit grew and developed their knowledge of the NPO sector and the ways in which marketing practices could be adapted to work within it. The exercise provided them with further areas to explore in more detail, and also increased their experience of dealing with an NPO in running a live brief activity.

Perhaps most importantly, the students themselves benefitted by adding a genuinely different experience to their education. They adapted and applied the principles they had studied in their lectures and seminars to a real-life NPO, learning along the way that the skills they were developing could be used to deliver societal good as well as helping commercial organisations improve their bottom line. A self-reflective survey showed that students increased their understanding of the importance of social enterprises and the NPO sector in general, and that they had thoroughly enjoyed the experience.

In addition, their formal results – as judged by the academic team and Anthony Nolan – showed that they had met the key learning outcomes intended for the exercise, namely:

1. Demonstrate a clear understanding of marketing principles and practice.
2. Describe marketing environment and specific marketing problems. This allows students to demonstrate both intellectual/cognitive and transferable skills.
3. Demonstrate an ability to develop appropriate marketing solutions to marketing problems, allowing demonstration of both intellectual/cognitive and transferable skills.
4. Demonstrate an ability to apply appropriate marketing techniques across a range of market sectors.

Through networking with Anthony Nolan, strong contacts have been passed to students, as well as leveraging them to add value to our undergraduate and postgraduate portfolio so that initiatives will build and create good education and professional practice. This unit has provided students with excellent skill-building opportunities which will benefit their entire student journey including placements and employment opportunities.

Using practical examples and focusing on a real-life case study, this unit demonstrated the exciting world of marketing in the real world and the challenges it brings. This unit enabled students to identify marketing problems effectively, understand the range of marketing solutions available and then identify the appropriate marketing solutions. Students learnt the cause and effect of their marketing decisions.

Working with a live brief in a nonprofit context has allowed the students to gain a real-life understanding of the key concepts underpinning marketing practice, while also offering the opportunity to make a positive impact on wider society.

The primary objective of the campaign was to raise awareness and increase the number of younger people joining the stem cell donor registration list. Through this campaign not only was awareness of Anthony Nolan built significantly with their target audience of young people, but also by hosting donor recruitment events on campus at BU, more young men become donors. In addition, this study offers practical applications to Anthony Nolan by providing valuable insights from their key target audience.

Conclusion

In conclusion, it is clear that co-creation between higher education institutions and charities is an important activity to ensure the next generation of marketers are provided with a diverse toolkit to allow them to flourish in the nonprofit as well as commercial world.

The co-creation has enabled students to understand the contemporary picture of marketing and branding practices within the wider NPO landscape. Working alongside our students, the charity considerably helped students develop their experience of marketing in the nonprofit sector, giving them valuable insight that will make them more attractive to employers on graduation.

Through providing students with an understanding of the bespoke requirements of NPO marketing efforts, BU is helping to develop graduates who leave with a solid understanding of the sector. This will not only help those who choose to enter the NPO sector directly, but also builds an understanding of the importance of the pillars that NPOs are built on – the importance of a mission and values, collaboration and the ability to deal with multiple stakeholders.

In providing students with direct hands-on experience of working on a case study that focuses on an NPO which features all of these challenges, our graduates are also prepared to enter the world of work with an understanding of how to work alongside NPOs.

Crucially, they are also equipped with the skills to see how those cornerstones of NPOs can help to develop the brand, identity and marketing of any organisation, where appropriate. Embedding a mission and principles into the heartbeat of an organisation, understanding how and when to collaborate and with whom, and being able to develop strategic and tactical plans to manage multiple stakeholders are skills that NPO practice can help the marketing industry to strengthen.

The teaching team was awarded Bournemouth University's 'Excellence in Sustainable Teaching' award. The award, which was presented during the BU Service Excellence Conference in April 2019, recognises their efforts in embedding UN Sustainable Development Goals into their unit and their teaching.

Chapter discussion questions

Reflecting on what has been outlined in this chapter, consider the following questions:

1. Nonprofit organisations often have diverse and varied stakeholders. How might that impact the development of a marketing strategy for a nonprofit organisation?

2. What do you think the benefits are for students when using a live brief as an assessment rather than a theoretical exercise?
3. Do you think there is room in the HE sector for degrees focusing exclusively on working in the nonprofit sector? Explain your answer and give examples.

Acknowledgements

The author appreciates the valuable comments on this research from Anthony Nolan. During the assignment, the organisation invested a considerable amount of time and energy into the partnership, at all levels. Every interaction with our students was considered, insightful and supportive, and we thank everyone at Anthony Nolan for approaching the project with the same passion and commitment they put into the vital work they do every day. In particular, the author would like to thank Ann O'Leary, Director of Donor & Transplantation Services, Anthony Nolan, without whom the idea would never have progressed beyond being a pipe dream.

For more information on Anthony Nolan and the lifesaving work they undertake please visit www.anthonynolan.org.

If you've enjoyed reading this chapter, why not see if you are a compatible donor yourself? You might save someone's life too…

References

Aaker, D. (1996). Measuring brand equity across products and markets. *California Management Review*, 38(3), 102–120.

Berry, L.L. (2000). Cultivating service brand equity. *Journal of Academy of Marketing Science*, 28(1), 128.

Bradford, T.W. & Boyd, N.W. (2020). Help me help you! Employing the marketing mix to alleviate experiences of donor sacrifice. *Journal of Marketing*, 84(3), 68–85.

Caspersen, J. & Smeby, J. (2018). The relationship among learning outcome measures used in higher education. *Quality in Higher Education*, 24(2), 117–135. doi:10.1080/13538322.2018.1484411.

Chapleo, C. (2010). What defines 'successful' university brands? *International Journal of Public Sector Management*, 23(2), 169–183.

Chapleo, C. (2011). Exploring rationales for branding a university: Should we be seeking to measure branding in UK universities? *Journal of Brand Management*, 18(6), 411–422.

Chapleo, C. & O'Sullivan, H. (2017). Contemporary thought in higher education marketing. *Journal of Marketing for Higher Education*, 27(2), 159–161. doi:10.1080/08841241.2017.1406255.

Dean, D., Arroyo-Gamez, R.E., Punjaisri, K. & Pich, C. (2016). Internal brand co-creation: The experiential brand meaning cycle in higher education. *Journal of Business Research*, 69(8), 3041–3048.

Dholakia, R.R. & Acciardo, L.A. (2014). Branding a state university: Doing it right. *Journal of Marketing for Higher Education*, 24(1), 144–163.

Gershon, R. & Cryder, C. (2018). Goods donations increase charitable credit for low-warmth donors. *Journal of Consumer Research*, 45(2), 451–469.

Gromark, J. & Melin, F. (2013). From market orientation to brand orientation in the public sector. *Journal of Marketing Management*, 29(9–10), 1099–1123.

Hemsley-Brown, J. & Goonawardana, S. (2007). Brand harmonization in the international higher education market. *Journal of Business Research*, 60, 942–948.

Hytti, U., Kuoppakangas, P., Suomi, K., Chapleo, C. & Giovanardi, M. (2015). Challenges in delivering brand promise: Focusing on municipal healthcare organisations. *International Journal of Public Sector Management*, 28(3), 254–272.

Kirovska, Z. & Simonovska, K. (2013). Branding and its sustainability in the public sector. *Journal of Sustainable Development*, 4(7), 55–70.

Leijerholt, U., Chapleo, C. & O'Sullivan, H. (2019). A brand within a brand: An integrated understanding of internal brand management and brand architecture in the public sector. *Journal of Brand Management*, 26(3), 277–290.

Melewar, T.C. & Akel, S. (2005). The role of corporate identity in the higher education sector: A case study. *Corporate Communications*, 10(1), 41–57.

O'Leary, A. (2021) Email correspondence with Helen O'Sullivan. 7 April 2021.

Polkinghorne, M., O'Sullivan, H., Taylor, J. & Roushan, G. (2019). An innovative framework for higher education to evaluate learning gain: A case study based upon the discipline of marketing. *Studies in Higher Education*, 46(9), 1740–1755.

Roohr, K., Liu, H. & Liu, O. (2017). Investigating student learning gains in college: A longitudinal study. *Studies in Higher Education*, 42(12), 2284–2300. doi:10.1080/03075079.2016.1143925.

Roper, S. & Davies, G. (2007). The corporate brand: Dealing with multiple stakeholders. *Journal of Marketing Management*, 23(1–2), 75–90.

Satøen, L. & Wæraas, A. (2015). Branding without unique brands. *Public Management Review*, 17(3), 443–461.

Temporal, P. (2015). *Branding for the Public Sector: Creating, Building and Managing Brands People Will Value*. John Wiley & Sons.

Veloutsou, C. & Delgado-Ballester, E. (2018). New challenges in brand management. *Spanish Journal of Marketing*, 22(3), 254–271.

Watkins, B.A. & Gonzenbach, W.J. (2013). Assessing university brand personality through logos: An analysis of the use of academics and athletics in university branding. *Journal of Marketing for Higher Education*, 23(1), 15–33.

Wæraas, A. & Solbakk, M.N. (2009). Defining the essence of a university: Lessons from higher education branding, *Higher Education*, 57, 449–462.

Winterich, K.P., Reczek, R.W. & Irwin, J.R. (2017). Keeping the memory but not the possession: Memory preservation mitigates identity loss from product disposition. *Journal of Marketing*, 81(5), 104–120.

11

STAKEHOLDERS IN THE PALLIATIVE AND END OF LIFE CARE SERVICE ECOSYSTEM

A study of the hospice sector

Ahmed Al-Abdin, Philippa Hunter-Jones, Lynn Sudbury-Riley, Andrew Ryde and Lucy Smith

Introduction

This chapter seeks to provide a more nuanced understanding of the role of the nonprofit sector in the current palliative and end of life care landscape. It has a particular focus upon exploring the role of different stakeholders in this landscape. It does this by reviewing a research-driven collaboration with Oakhaven Hospice, a nonprofit provider serving a particular geographical footprint, the New Forest, Waterside and Totton areas of the UK. The aim of this collaboration was to deploy a stakeholder engagement and service ecosystem lens to better understand the needs of current and future service users. Oakhaven provides palliative and end of life care both onsite (inpatient and day patient facilities) and through a community nursing service that includes hospice at home services. It is one of over 200 nonprofit hospices in the UK, supporting around 200,000 palliative care patients annually and receiving an average of 32% of their funding from the government, with the rest coming from fundraising (Hospice UK, 2013). Hospices deliver multiple services through inpatient units, outpatient and day care centres, programmes (e.g. Living Well) and clinics (e.g. Breathlessness Clinic and Lymphoedema Clinic). The combination is specific to the unit in question.

The demand for hospice care is rising. Advances in medical care have prompted a transition in the nature of deaths today. Non-communicable diseases – cancer and coronary heart disease for instance – now account for over two-thirds of all global deaths and are set to rise (WHO, 2012). Enhanced treatment regimes have extended the lifespan of patients, increasing numbers now living with the long-term consequences of treatment and chronic conditions. Indeed globally, life expectancy has increased by almost 20 years over the last five decades (UN, 2015). Overall morbidity rates have not changed (Davies, 2015). With the post-war baby boom and consequential ageing population, the number of deaths in England and

DOI: 10.4324/9781003134169-14

Wales is projected to increase by 27% in the next 2 decades (Bone et al., 2017). These trends become all the more important when set against a backdrop of changing society structures. Greater employment opportunities, alongside smaller and more fragmented families, are placing increasing demand upon palliative care services (Hospice UK, 2013).

The healthcare sector response to terminal illness involves a journey, a move into a liminal state of healthcare delivery. In this state, conversations shift beyond curative and treatable healthcare dialogues into palliative care where holistic care, psychosocial and spiritual support for patients and their families is prioritised (Cloyes et al., 2014; WHO, 2012). It is a transitional stage haunted by many mis-perceptions, a key one being associations with imminent death (Giovanni, 2012; NHPCO, 2015). This is not always the case; every disease trajectory is unique. 'Dying well' is championed within policy rhetoric in the UK and all mechanisms for managing pain, symptoms and medicines are keenly sought (Department of Health, 2008; Department of Health, 2016; National Palliative and EOLC Partnership, 2015; The Choice in End of Life Care Programme Board, 2015).

By adopting a stakeholder engagement and service ecosystems lens, this chapter adds to our understanding of the relationship between hospices and nonprofit marketing. First, the theoretical arguments apparent in the stakeholder engagement literature are reviewed, followed by a brief review of the service ecosystems literature.

The chapter then progresses to explain the research with Oakhaven Hospice, the provider at the heart of this case study. Methods of data collection are then outlined followed by a discussion of the primary data collected from multiple stakeholder groups: general practitioners (n=5); district nurses (n=5); hospital staff (n=7); care home managers (n=5); hospice service users (n=31); and non-service users (n=100). Implications for practice are then presented.

Stakeholder engagement

Stakeholder theory advocates that the main purpose of an organisation is to create maximum value for its stakeholders (see e.g. Voyer et al., 2017). Within this theory, idea, metaphors and expressions are brought together to achieve a 'common purpose' (Strand & Freeman, 2015). In his seminal work on stakeholders, Freeman (1984) discusses how there are two main types of stakeholder groups. These are primary and secondary stakeholders. Primary stakeholders could be employees, suppliers, the local community, shareholders and customers, and secondary stakeholders could include government, competitors, consumer advocates and activists, media and social networks.

One of the central dilemmas of stakeholder theory is knowing who to prioritise and how, as there are usually a plethora of stakeholder groups involved. In the context of nonprofit organisations, identifying to whom these stakeholder groups are responsible and their remit (i.e. how far their power and influence extends) is key (O'Riordan & Fairbrass, 2014). For example, hospices serve multiple stakeholders. Externally, these might be patients, governing health bodies, e.g. the

National Health Service (NHS), community groups, specialist community groups (e.g. Marie Curie), quality assurance bodies such as the Care Quality Commission (CQC), Clinical Commissioning Groups overseeing GP networks, other hospitals in a particular geographical patch and many more. Internally, key stakeholders might include the board of trustees, clinicians, nurses and volunteers. Crucially, while a holistic understanding of who 'exactly qualifies as a stakeholder' is somewhat fragmented in the literature, the identification of what counts as a stakeholder claim is significant (Mitchell et al., 1997).

Emanating from stakeholder theory, stakeholder priorities and choices can come down to what is known as stakeholder prioritisation (Hill & Jones, 2007). Here, decisions are made about how to engage with a range of stakeholders. This leads onto a discussion of 'stakeholder engagement', which is broadly defined as the organisational practices undertaken to engage stakeholders in a positive vein with organisational activities (Greenwood, 2007). Process wise, this involves obtaining, developing and building up stakeholder relations via stakeholder identification, consultation, communication, dialogue and exchange (Burchell & Cook, 2006). Stakeholder engagement can take years, if not decades in some cases, and it rests on the fundamental belief that interaction with fellow stakeholders is a logical prerequisite for organisations. By engaging with stakeholders, engagement is viewed as the key driver in achieving organisational objectives and priorities including (but not limited to) aspects of consent, control, co-operation, accountability and involvement, mechanisms of fairness and trust. For example, consider how hospices proceed in terms of referral criteria and who gets access to one and how. The answer here cuts across multiple stakeholders and might entail evaluating aspects like the patient's place of residence in proximity to the hospice, hospice capacity and prioritisation based on the type of illness. The key point here is that stakeholder engagement needs to be as mutually beneficial as possible for all parties. The ultimate goal of stakeholder engagement is to promote virtue and morally responsible decisions and organisational behaviour (Greenwood, 2007). Noland and Phillips (2010), for instance, take an ethical strategist view to stakeholder engagement and propose that for it to work in practice, the honest, open and respectful engagement of stakeholders as part of an overall organisation's strategy is paramount. Noland and Phillips's view here would seem to echo that of business's role in society and the pursuit for a better life. There are obvious parallel's here with hospices striving to improve quality of life for patients, their families and the bereaved.

In a recent paper by Mitchell and Clark (2019), the authors reconceptualise the Product Life Cycle theory (PLC – developed over 50 years ago) and anchor their theorisations based on stakeholder engagement for nonprofit organisations. In its most basic form, the original PLC model advocates four main stages that a 'product' takes over its lifecycle. These are introduction, growth, maturity and decline. Mitchell and Clark re-imagine the PLC through the lens of market orientation and discuss how stakeholder engagement forces a revised and fresh perspective on the original PLC. In this regard, they developed an 'Engagement Life Cycle' (see Figure 11.1).

FIGURE 11.1 Engagement Life Cycle (Source: Mitchell & Clark, 2019)

At the incubation stage, it is argued that stakeholder engagement is minimal and the nonprofit organisation operates without external influence. This might be because the organisation is new or because it does not require external engagement to exist. Consider for example a new hospice launch. The hospice is new so will embryonically grow. It might lack the necessary resources in the inauguration phase to establish a presence such as a dedicated marketing team for instance. At the interaction stage, this is where social exchanges start to proliferate. Think about a new hospice trying to accrue multiple donations via trustees, private groups, the NHS and the establishment of a volunteer network. Here, customers are key resources to getting the hospice off the ground. At the involvement stage, an active affinity develops between key stakeholder groups and the organisation. Value is assessed in the form of outcomes of funding or volunteering time for example. Stakeholders will be interested in how the organisation is furthering its ambition. This might also involve reach and significance and what progress the 'new hospice' has made on a particular geographical patch.

Unlike at the incubation and involvement phase, stakeholder engagement is usually steady at the interactive phase, meaning that they may not be as aggressively involved and, rather, intermittently scan relevant communications such as news and emails, and they will be invited to for example hospice strategy away days (which for most hospices take place once or twice a year). At the fourth stage (immersion), it involves the key stakeholders being committed to the organisation for the long haul. For example, a hospice might encourage stakeholders to support their mission and vision online via actively engaging with social media, the wider community, other charities such as Marie Curie or Macmillan, hospitals in close proximity to the hospice and so on. The key emphasis at this stage is on intensifying stakeholder commitment and encouraging feedback from key stakeholders in decision-making and the future trajectory of said hospice. The final stage (incapacitation) is where the engagement between stakeholders and the organisation is said to become obsolete. In this worst-case scenario, a hospice for example might seek to merge with another hospice on a similar geographical patch or cease to exist (though this is very rare).

Overall, the stages of Mitchell and Clark's (2019) Engagement Life Cycle are fluid with no expectation that each stage must be fulfilled sequentially and some stages may be skipped with the exception of the incubation stage.

Service ecosystems

Service ecosystems are broadly defined as a 'relatively self-contained, self-adjusting system of resource-integrating actors connected by shared institutional arrangements and mutual value creation through service exchange' (Vargo & Lusch, 2016,

p. 10). In simple terms, it involves the institutional arrangement of actors at multiple levels (Finsterwalder & Kuppelwieser, 2020). These levels are more commonly known as macro, meso and micro. Let us contextualise these levels via an example of a hospice. At the macro level, these 'actors' or stakeholders might be the government, NHS, CQC and so on. At the meso level, this might include the hospice itself, neighbouring hospices on a similar geographical patch, GP surgeries, nearby hospitals, etc. At the micro level, this entails patients, families and communities.

The main strand that links service ecosystems and stakeholder engagement together is the 'engagement side'. Both concepts find common accord in engaging with service exchanges, co-creation processes and/or solution development. The common thread here being that within a service ecosystem, value must be added amongst key stakeholders (Loureiro et al., 2020). The co-creation of value is predicated on the interaction between stakeholders and organisations who are said to create value via collaborative exchanges that take place (see for example Prahalad & Ramaswamy, 2004). What this collaborative exchange means in a stakeholder context is that the key stakeholders join forces to co-construct an experience via active dialogue and mutual learning. In the hospice context, for example, consider the service experience that one provides, the types of facilities on offer, clinical comfort and support, shared spaces, little extras and so on. More recently, theorisations on co-creation have advanced to include customers (Letaifa & Reynoso, 2015), or in the context of healthcare and hospices patients, their families and the bereaved in the co-design and co-production of the service being offered (Brodie et al., 2021). Thus, a service ecosystem approach supports the mapping of direct and indirect stakeholders and influencers of a nonprofit organisation.

The importance of sharing goals and priorities amongst stakeholders gives rise to interpersonal relationships, which in turn contributes co-creation opportunities within the service ecosystem. As Loureiro et al. (2020) contend, certain factors can impact stakeholder engagement – for example company size: smaller nonprofit organisations might prefer closer interpersonal relationships. Strong personal relationships, high-quality information exchange, affinity and transparency in sharing information can all contribute to reinforcing improved stakeholder engagement and input into the co-creation process. Referring back to the previous example on hospice admissions criteria, for example, the aforementioned factors play a key role in the advancement of co-creation and the management of the service ecosystem within which the nonprofit organisation operates.

The research team collaborated with Oakhaven Hospice and looked at scoping the current ecosystem in and around Oakhaven's geographical patch. The key headline findings are detailed via a case study, presented next.

Case study: Oakhaven Hospice

Background: Oakhaven Hospice provides palliative and end of life care both onsite (inpatient and day patient facilities) and through a hospice at home service. It began as a charitable trust in the 1980s and today covers a geographical patch (see Figure 11.2) which includes 15 primary care practices that are grouped into 10 Public Health England Profiles. This area has a total population of 114,000 registered patients. The services offered at Oakhaven are free to patients and their families. Fundraising is a pivotal means of raising the monies needed to support these services.

Research questions

In 2016, recognising the end of life care future projections, the hospice management embarked upon a project to plan for future service needs. They commissioned a research project with two research questions: What is happening in the Oakhaven geographical patch? And what explains these trends? A mixed-methods approach was adopted. Scoping out the end of life care landscape (research question 1) utilised desk-based research. The second part of the study (research question 2), aiming to understand factors contributing to the end of life care landscape, utilised semi-structured interviews to collect data.

Research methods

Routinely collected data was utilised for research question 1. Two sets of data were valuable here: mortality statistics and Oakhaven daily statistics. This information

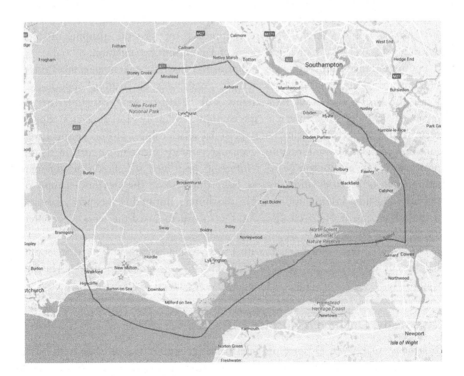

FIGURE 11.2 Oakhaven's geographical patch

was valuable in profiling patients who were referred to the hospice. Profiling was possible by five variables: diagnosis; who referred the patient; services accessed; the patient's own GP practice; and place of death. Once the emergent trends were identified, primary data was collected with multiple stakeholders in order to explain these trends (research question 2). In-depth interviews, some lasting an hour, were utilised for this purpose. Fifty-three stakeholders were interviewed. These included: general practitioners (n=5); community nurses (n=5); hospital staff (n=7); care home managers (n=5); and hospice service users (day patient; inpatient; family; friends; carer; bereaved) (n=31), and a questionnaire with 100 non-users at Lymington Hospital (Hampshire).

Each stakeholder was asked to identify and explain the key issues facing end of life care provision and what could be done to improve care provision in the area. Each interview was audio recorded with permission, transcribed verbatim and then subjected to rigorous in-depth thematic analysis in order to identify common themes. Full ethical approval was granted by the university ethics committee prior to data collection.

Findings

In this section, we present the product of our findings. An overview of the main emergent themes is available in Table 11.1.

Communication and integration

A dominant theme within most stakeholder interviews was the lack of integration and communication between the different stakeholders providing end of life care in the area. One GP commented: 'we are really poor at… sharing experience', going on to explain the 'we' in end of life care to be: 'about what the primary care

TABLE 11.1 Emergent Themes

Common themes	General practitioner (GP)	Commu- nity nurses (CNS)	Lymington New Forest Hospital (LNFH)	Care home managers (CHM)	Service users (SU)
1. Lack of communication and integration in end of life care provision	✓	✓	✓		✓
2. Referral criteria issues	✓		✓		✓
3. Community role for Oakhaven	✓	✓	✓		✓
4. Training	✓	✓	✓	✓	
5. Lack of resources in community and social services	✓	✓	✓	✓	

team do, what Oakhaven do, what social services do'. For this GP, realising the opportunities integrated thinking offered was the key to moving forward. Oakhaven is pivotal in this relationship: 'so there are a lot of things that goes on, sharing best practice is something we don't do as a health environment. I think we could learn from each other and it could be facilitated by Oakhaven' (GP).

Poor communication and integration between different services was identified as a key issue for community nurses who spoke of arriving at a patients' home unaware if the patient had an advanced care plan:

> What does the patient know about it, it isn't for us, we might have a little bit of information about their diagnosis and prognosis, but it isn't for us to share that with them if it hasn't been shared with them already. So it can be very tricky and you have to really fish around to get the information.
>
> *(CNS)*

Uniting all feedback was the need for increased integration and improved communication between different services:

> If we could have someone who could liaise or coordinate within the hospital. The only times I feel less comfortable is not when we are palliating here, but when we are sending people home for palliation… what makes me anxious is I'm not so sure of what will be going on with the people we are sending out for care or palliation.
>
> *(LNFH)*

Again, in common with GPs and CNS feedback, it was also suggested that Oakhaven could play a pivotal role in bringing end of life care services together:

> I think that it is to get, whether it is run out of Oakhaven or whatever, is to get some kind of broader palliative team, because the team that run out of Oakhaven is really their patients first isn't it. We can go to them, and I think that our health needs probably contribute towards them.
>
> *(LNFH)*

An appetite was also voiced for Oakhaven to establish an end of life care team or an end of life care ward within LNFH itself, although the resource issues were readily recognised too:

> What we have is we have a ward that is abandoned, that isn't used because they ran out of funding for it, so basically Oakhaven each year have put forward Southern Health to have an inpatient Hospice, which would be amazing, and I know a lot of our nurses here would really enjoy that opportunity and it would give us just all that we would need, it would give us the training, and the rooms for relatives to stay in. That would be amazing, so when we win the lottery!
>
> *(LNFH)*

Referral criteria

A significant issue identified by stakeholders such as GPs, LNFH nurses and service users in particular were problems with defining end of life care and confusion over referral criteria. This was particularly problematic given the population characteristics on the patch. For example, one GP remarked:

> Our population has double the amount of over 85s, 5.2% of our population is over 85…, as you age you are going to get disease everyone will have a bit of cancer somewhere when you reach 95, it is astounding if you don't.
>
> *(GP)*

The consequences of this ambiguity were felt particularly in relation to decisions linked to referral criteria. GPs expressed concern over the timing of referrals:

> There is no clear defined way of when you refer to palliative care, and my opinion is that, and I think it's true in all areas, some GPs have the default and will refer everybody whereas I only refer at the point at which I can think of something that they can provide that I can't.
>
> *(GP)*

And indeed what to refer patients for:

> Referral criteria was quite tight at the beginning, it was really only cancers, now it is motor neurone disease, coronary respiratory disease, some of the other stuff, so it is a broader category. I think there is some confusion amongst GPs.
>
> *(GP)*

There was a clear link between this confusion over referral criteria and the increased propensity for GPs to refer cancer patients to Oakhaven. For example, one GP explained he was more likely to refer cancer patients than those suffering with dementia and heart failure:

> The cancer patients are always easy to do because they do usually require a palliative care input, the more difficult ones… conditions like dementia and heart failure are always tricky… Oakhaven are happy to take them but I guess I am reluctant to refer them.
>
> *(GP)*

Community role

In helping the wider community to appreciate the value of Oakhaven's work and select them as their preferred charity to support, several stakeholders identified the importance of the community role on the New Forest patch. For example, one service user noted:

> To be honest I think it would help with their fundraising as well, it sounds awful but, we used to take stuff into the charity shop, but if one understood how much they offer the community one may have been a bit more enthusiastic about that, you know. We used to spread ourselves amongst several charity shops but now it is going all to Oakhaven because we think this is a great local facility you know.
>
> *(Family Carer)*

Overall, it was suggested Oakhaven was well placed to play a pivotal role encouraging shared practice in the area. This role was considered particularly necessary given the changing relationships between community care and GPs, and the ambiguity which could arise:

> I think sometimes it is a bit ad-hoc and sometimes it feels like, we will ring the patient or we will text them, it feels like we are working on two parallel tracks rather than as a team.
>
> *(GP)*

Key stakeholders such GPs, district nurses, staff at Lymington New Forest Hospital and service users collectively suggested the need for one organisation to act as a facilitator, an enabler, even a point of contact in end of life care in the area. Oakhaven was considered well placed to play a pivotal role as a central point of contact for local end of life care services. Clearly there are resources implications attached to this. Nevertheless, support in the community is high for Oakhaven.

Training

Training was another key theme that emerged from the findings. In particular, GPs spoke of a lack of specific training in end of life care and an appetite for more training programmes in this area. District nurses, care home managers and hospital staff requested further training (e.g. through observation) to perform end of life care, especially in the areas of having difficult conversations, symptom management and medicine management. For example, one nurse remarked how many patients were reluctant to talk about death. Some were reluctant to go to Oakhaven:

> Yes, but as a country we still don't like to talk about death, we don't at all, but yet we should and getting people to think about advanced care planning, but they are difficult conversations to have which is why the workforce has to have training so they can develop the skills.
>
> *(LNFH)*

The need for training to help them cope with these conversations was also cited by district nurses as a central theme. For instance, one told how:

> It is sometimes hard to know who will be having those conversations with them… about where they want to die and those kinds of conversations would fall to, other than us, which we can do but it is not always appropriate as we are not experts.
>
> *(CNS)*

This was particularly important for those in the early years of their career development:

> I knew in this community a large part of the service we provide is end of life care but I was not prepared for it in my training, nothing… it is hard, being newly qualified having those conversations, but I would feel so much more prepared if I knew what they knew and the conversations they had had.
>
> *(CNS)*

A common theme within interviews was the opportunity for Oakhaven to play a central role in wider training for those involved in palliative and end of life care. Multiple suggestions were offered, including the need for different levels of training:

> Yes and I think the practical things of symptom management, I think it is hard to be taught that and it comes with experience. The training courses that Oakhaven provide, whilst they are good I think that they miss the mark for people at our level, we need a bit more than that.
>
> *(CNS)*

Resources shortfall

Under the theme of resource shortfall, two key headline findings emerge. First, a lack of resources in the community and social services and second, for Oakhaven to sustain a pivotal role in the community, greater resources are required. GPs for example believed that Oakhaven would benefit from being better resourced, which in turn would support the wider palliative and end of life care community:

> I suppose more beds at Oakhaven, more hospice at home staff… and an enhanced educational role. It would be nice for us to have education as GPs on a regular basis, to discuss case scenarios, I think that is always helpful. So I think increased beds, increased services, just more of them.
>
> *(GP)*

The importance of Oakhaven's work led to a question over funding and whether more statutory funding should be made available:

> I think just better resources for palliative care services, I think they rely a lot on charitable donations and perhaps that should be centrally funded. I think there is a very strong argument for that, especially with an aging population and more people dying at home.
>
> *(GP)*

Nurses also welcome more resources to help cope with demand. For instance, one nurse remarked:

> I do find 80%, 90% of the time it's the nurses that are actually looking after the patients that are the ones that recognise the signs. I think what would be good in a lovely, ideal world is that we've said about- I've spoken to our management team about having, whether or not it's one CNS or having some more trained staff within the hospital, because Oakhaven are limited and obviously they can only provide a certain amount of support to us. It would be great if we had some resources here actually within the hospital.
>
> *(LNFH)*

In summary, the findings regarding resource shortfall point in the direction of Oakhaven considering the implications for the wider end of life care community network on their own geographical patch. Yet from a stakeholder engagement perspective, how should Oakhaven proceed? Is it their sole responsibility? The answers to these complex questions are multifaceted. To gain a better idea of potential solutions, the conclusion/recommendation sections that follow draw together the main implications for theory and practice.

Conclusion

This chapter set out to provide a more nuanced understanding of the role of the nonprofit sector in the current palliative and end of life care landscape. It was particularly interested in listening to the voices of different stakeholders operating in this landscape and utilised a research-driven collaboration with Oakhaven Hospice, a nonprofit provider serving a particular geographical footprint in the UK to achieve this. In this conclusion we reflect back upon the learnings from this work, particularly in relation to stakeholder engagement as seen through a service ecosystem lens.

In relation to theory and as documented in this chapter, one of the central dilemmas of stakeholder theory is knowing exactly who to prioritise and how, especially when there are multiple stakeholders involved with potentially competing interests. Who has responsibility and how far does this responsibility and influence extend (O'Riordan & Fairbrass, 2014) within a service ecosystem can be a grey area (Vargo & Lusch, 2016). In this case study, for instance, questions regarding whether training should be led by Oakhaven, should it be led by other stakeholders like Lymington Hospital or by the GPs, illustrate well the complexity of the wider ecosystem There is no textbook answer here because it relies on key stakeholders consistently communicating and liaising with each other in an attempt to co-create value (Prahalad & Ramaswamy, 2004).

Often within stakeholder engagement, stakeholder prioritisation (Hill & Jones, 2007) is key. Sometimes, this means, as in the case of Oakhaven, that priorities have to be made in terms of designated patient need, yet other stakeholders such as GPs welcome greater clarity on aspects such as referral criteria. Thus, it is only through obtaining, developing and building up stakeholder relations via stakeholder identification, consultation, communication, dialogue and exchange (Burchell & Cook, 2006) that such issues can be remedied. Similarly, stakeholder engagement needs to be as mutually beneficial as possible for all parties. As Noland and Phillips (2010) suggest, for it to work in practice, it relies on the honest, open and respectful engagement of stakeholders. For a hospice like Oakhaven, it is likely to operate at the 'immersion' stage of Mitchell and Clark's Engagement Life Cycle. This is because it has developed a positive reputation over a long period and is influential on other stakeholders within the service ecosystem including hospitals, GPs, care homes and indeed the wider community. Given Oakhaven's potent stakeholder power, it has the ability to implement key changes related to the key themes from this research. Namely, communication and integration in end of life care provision, referral criteria issues, energising the community role, supporting further training initiatives and working with other key stakeholders on their geographical patch to improve resources in the community. Each of these themes will likely resonate with other nonprofit providers similarly embedded in a complex service ecosystem. Future research would benefit from exploring this in other service contexts.

Chapter discussion questions

1. How have Oakhaven Hospice deployed stakeholder engagement in their organisation?
2. What key recommendations might you suggest for Oakhaven moving forward?
3. Prepare a short proposal for a nonprofit organisation of your choice and consider the following questions. What key considerations need to be made for stakeholder engagement and why? What is their geographical patch? Where does your chosen organisation sit on Mitchell and Clark's (2019) Engagement Life Cycle?

References

Bone, A.E., Gomes, B., Etkind, S.N., Verne, J., Murtagh, F.E.M., Evans, C.J. & Higginson, I.J. (2017). What is the impact of population ageing on the future provision of end of life care? Population-based projections of place of death. *Palliative Medicine*, 32(2), 329–336.

Brodie, R.J., Ranjan, K.R., Verreynne, M.L., Jiang, Y. & Previte, J. (2021). Coronavirus crisis and health care: Learning from a service ecosystem perspective. *Journal of Service Theory and Practice*, 31(2), 225–246.

Burchell, J. & Cook, J. (2006). It's good to talk? Examining attitudes towards corporate social responsibility dialogue and engagement processes. *Business Ethics: A European Review*, 15(2), 154–170.

Cloyes, K.G., Carpenter, J.G., Berry, P.H., Reblin, M., Clayton, M. & Ellington, L. (2014). 'A true human interaction': Comparison of family caregiver and hospice nurse perspectives on needs of family hospice caregivers. *Journal of Hospice and Palliative Nursing: The Official Journal of the Hospice and Palliative Nurses Association*, 16(5), 282.

Davies, S.C. (2015). Annual report of the Chief Medical Officer 2015, on the state of the public's health, baby boomers: Fit for the future. Available at: https://assets.publishing. service.gov.uk/government/uploads/system/uploads/attachment_data/file/654806/ CMO_baby_boomers_annual_report_2015.pdf (accessed 7 September 2021).

Department of Health. (2008). *End of Life Care Strategy*. HMSO.

Department of Health. (2016). Commissioning person centred end of life care. Available at: www.england.nhs.uk/wp-content/uploads/2016/04/nhsiq-comms-eolc-tlkit-.pdf (accessed 7 September 2021).

Finsterwalder, J. & Kuppelwieser, V.G. (2020). Equilibrating resources and challenges during crises: A framework for service ecosystem well-being. *Journal of Service Management*, 31(6), 1107–1129.

Freeman, R. (1984). *Strategic Management: A Stakeholder Approach*. Pitman.

Giovanni, L.A. (2012). End-of-life care in the United States: Current reality and future promise-a policy review. *Nursing Economics*, 30(3), 127.

Greenwood, M. (2007). Stakeholder engagement beyond the myth of corporate responsibility. *Journal of Business Ethics*, 74, 315–327.

Hill, C.W.L. & Jones, G.R. (2007). *Strategic Management: An Integrated Approach* (7th edn). Houghton Mifflin.

Hospice UK. (2013). *Future Needs and Preferences for Hospice Care: Challenges and Opportunities for Hospices*. Hospice UK.

Letaifa, S.B. & Reynoso, J. (2015). Toward a service ecosystem perspective at the base of the pyramid. *Journal of Service Management*, 26(5), 684.

Loureiro, S.M.C., Romero, J. & Bilro, R.G. (2020). Stakeholder engagement in co-creation processes for innovation: A systematic literature review and case study. *Journal of Business Research*, 119, 388–409.

Mitchell, R.K., Agle, B.R. & Wood, D.J. (1997). Toward a theory of stakeholder identification and salience: Defining the principle of who and what really counts. *Academy of Management Review*, 22(4), 853–886.

Mitchell, S.L. & Clark, M. (2019). Reconceptualising product life-cycle theory as stakeholder engagement with non-profit organisations. *Journal of Marketing Management*, 35(1–2), 13–39.

National Palliative and End of Life Care Partnership. (2015). Ambitions for palliative and end of life care: A national framework for local action 2015–2020. Available at www. eolc.co.uk/educational/ambitions-for-palliative-and-end-of-life-care-a-national-fram ework-for-local-action-2015-2020/ (accessed 17 August 2021).

NHPCO. (2015). NHPCO's facts and figures: Pediatric palliative & hospice care in America. Available at: www.nhpco.org/wp-content/uploads/2019/04/Pediatric_Facts-Figures. pdf (accessed 7 September 2021).

Noland, J. & Phillips, R. (2010). Stakeholder engagement, discourse ethics and strategic management. *International Journal of Management Reviews: Corporate Social Responsibility* (Special Issue), 12(1), 39–49.

O'Riordan, L. & Fairbrass, J. (2014). Managing CSR stakeholder engagement: A new conceptual framework. *Journal of Business Ethics*, 125(1), 121–145.

Prahalad, C.K. & Ramaswamy, V. (2004). Co-creating unique value with customers. *Strategy & Leadership*, 32(3), 4.

Strand, R. & Freeman, R.E. (2015). Scandinavian cooperative advantage: The theory and practice of stakeholder engagement in Scandinavia. *Journal of Business Ethics*, 127(1), 65–85.

The Choice in End of Life Care Programme Board. (2015). What's important to me: A review of choice in end of life care. www.gov.uk/government/publications/choice-i n-end-of-life-care (accessed 7 September 2021).

United Nations. (2015). World population prospects. Available at http://esa.un.org/unpd/ wpp/Publications/Files/Key_Findings_WPP_2015.pdf (accessed 4 August 2017).

Vargo, S.L. & Lusch, R.F. (2016). Institutions and axioms: An extension and update of service-dominant logic. *Journal of the Academy of marketing Science*, 44(1), 5–23.

Voyer, B.G., Kastanakis, M.N. & Rhode, A.K. (2017). Co-creating stakeholder and brand identities: A cross-cultural consumer perspective. *Journal of Business Research*, 70, 399–410.

WHO. (2012) WHO definition of palliative care. Available at www.who.int/cancer/pallia tive/definition/en/ (accessed 23 November 2017).

12

INTERNAL MARKETING AND BRANDING

Nonprofit marketing starts from the inside

Chris Chapleo and Kati Suomi

Why it matters

There is no doubt that as charities have embraced the ethos and practice of marketing they have become increasingly sophisticated in their approaches. Nevertheless, there are several areas where cutting-edge research can help inform better and more effective practice. The internal marketing infrastructure is one such area of theory, where a better understanding of the best way to organise resources for marketing, execute brand management, manage the internal brand and build a culture that underpins marketing orientation is both important and challenging. Therefore, this chapter focuses on contemporary thinking on the issues around internal marketing and branding in nonprofits and brings together theory and practice to deliver impact. An example based in the Finnish nonprofit festival market is explored.

Internal marketing

Internal marketing as a concept has been researched for 40 years (Yildiz & Kara, 2017). For example, Berry (1981, p. 34) defined it as 'viewing employees as internal customers, and viewing jobs as internal products that satisfy the needs and wants of these internal customers while addressing the objectives of the organization'. Most research has focused on how to implement internal marketing and the outcomes (Huang, 2020), but recently this has widened to understanding underlying concepts in sectors beyond traditional consumer marketing, such as nonprofit marketing.

Marketing has a close relationship with branding, the two terms overlapping in general usage, and this is true in terms of the internal marketing concept in the nonprofit sector.

DOI: 10.4324/9781003134169-15

Internal branding

In Clark et al. (2020) it was argued that marketing needs to start from the inside out. Internal branding has its roots in internal marketing, which builds on the idea of the employee as a customer. Accordingly, Liu et al. (2015, p. 319) outline internal branding as 'an organization's attempts to persuade its staff to buy in to the organization's brand value and transform it into a reality'.

Internal branding therefore refers to brand-building efforts that focus on promoting a brand inside an organisation to motivate the employees to transform the brand promise into reality. Increasingly, organisations worldwide are investing significant resources in internal branding and it is evident that internal branding has become an important topic in nonprofit brand research in the UK (e.g. Hankinson, 2004; Liu et al., 2015).

Internal branding is important to understand in its fullest sense, as the literature suggests that too often brand-building efforts have been limited to superficial and quick solutions, such as logo redesigns and catchy slogans. However, designing visible elements of the brand (e.g. logos, slogans and colours) is only a part of successful brand building. Internal branding, it is suggested, should precede design of any tangible brand elements and certainly any external branding (the goal of which is to communicate a compelling brand image and value proposition to often diverse stakeholders).

Internal branding is therefore critical in enhancing employees' attachment and identification with the brand, as well as in managing employees' awareness and perceptions of the brand. Ind (2001) suggests that employers should make efforts to engage employees so that they can identify with the organisation and thus become brand champions who embrace the brand. In turn, managers need to promote a shared understanding of organisational brand values by implementing 'brand-supportive behaviour'. The concept of internal branding is therefore related to, yet distinct from, that of employer branding (Hytti et al., 2015; Saleem & Iglesias, 2016).

Challenges of internal branding

However, charities face significant challenges when implementing the internal branding concept. Some of these are external, exemplified in work by the authors where a marketing manager from a nonprofit argued that 'unlike commercial businesses, the public will question the charitable nature of our business, if we spend too much on [external] marketing activities to build the reputation of our brand'. Despite this, they felt that 'internal branding can help us to communicate about our brand in a cost-efficient manner, so we can devote more resources toward our charitable activities' (Liu et al., 2017, p. 4).

Challenges are also internal, however, and it has been suggested:

> For most people employed by charities, branding is 'not my business' even if I realise it's important. However, for a brand to really live and grow, it has to be owned at some level by everyone who represents it. The challenge is to turn

brand strategy into something meaningful for the majority of a charity's own people. It can be done.

(Grounds, 2005, p. 65)

Despite challenges, the branding of nonprofit organisations enables them to succeed in a competitive environment, and it seems that the difficulty of branding in this sector compels these organisations to develop different, creative strategies and solutions (Stuart, 2016). This emphasises the potential importance of appropriate internal branding strategies and models, and a number of areas of theory and their application are explored in the rest of this chapter.

Brand orientation

Brand orientation can logically be argued to be a necessary precursor for internal branding to be effectively implemented in charities. The concept of brand orientation refers to an organisation's focus on building and sustaining their brand promise (Ewing & Napoli, 2005) and is key to internal branding strategies and approaches.

Therefore, to implement internal branding, charities must build employees' knowledge of the brand promise, and also the important role that brand orientation and internal branding techniques fulfil (Urde et al., 2013).

In Liu et al. (2017), a positive and linear relationship between internal branding mechanisms (IBM) and employee brand-building behaviours (EBBB) was identified and assessed. EBBB refers to the concept of employees' actions determining a target audience's perceptions of the brand promise, which in turn enhances brand-building outcomes (King et al., 2013).

In this paper, interviews with senior managers in nonprofit organisations demonstrated this. One such interviewee argued that:

> We constantly communicate our values [reflected in our brand] through our newsletter and meetings..., as well as our training programs.... I think that is why the people [staff and volunteers] in our organization accept and act consistently with our [brand] values.

(Liu et al., 2017, p. 8)

This supports the argument that internal brand communication activities enable organisations to build their employees' understanding of their brand promise, which in turn motivates employees to behave consistently (in terms of the brand promise) when interacting with others.

This therefore endorses the positive relationship between IBM and EBBB. However, a communication director from an arts nonprofit argued that an excessive focus on brand communication can be detrimental to ensuring EBBB, because 'the staff may feel that they should not do anything beyond what we've asked them to do'.

A care charity expressed a different view that 'our [brand] messages are consistent across every communication channel we use.... For internal [brand] communication, we work with HR to integrate these [brand] messages into the staff training manuals and orientation package' (Liu et al., 2017, p. 8).

In summary, therefore, the authors in this work found that:

> The development of effective internal communication tools and training programs requires: 1) the organisations' brand promise information is consistent across the various communication channels during dissemination; and 2) the organisations' development of the brand promise must incorporate the different stakeholders' (including the employees') points of view and feelings about the organisation. These findings are in line with theoretical logic regarding the relationship between brand orientation and internal brand mechanisms.
>
> *(Liu et al., 2017, p. 8)*

This work clarified that organisations' investment in establishing brand orientation can underpin the development of structured external communication to help employees to articulate the organisational values and understand their roles within the organisation.

Internal structure and its relationship to internal branding

Charities vary greatly in size, but also in how they are structured. Some are highly centralised, others have multiple and highly autonomous centres. This has its own implications for the approach to and effectiveness of internal branding. Interfunctional communication needs to be carefully considered.

Liu et al. (2017, p. 8) explored and suggested a significant outcome regarding this; specifically, that 'too much communication between staff from different functional departments within the organization can sometime undermine internal branding efforts', especially when staff are unfamiliar with the branding theory and practice. Interviewees in this paper stated that they 'must always ensure that our new brand is not being misinterpreted or miscommunicated by our staff'.

This comment implies that greater interfunctional communication creates a work environment in which employees can express and share their personal views about the brand promise. This in turn can create inconsistent information about the brand promise within the organisation.

So what can be done to mitigate this? In Liu et al. (2017, p. 9), results suggested that efforts to engage in internal communication and encourage:

> Staff to share what they learn about the brand may not yield a great benefit initially. However, beyond a certain point, staff may start to come up with creative ideas regarding what they can do to help to build a strong nonprofit brand and communicate the brand promise to stakeholders. Greater interfunctional communication creates a work environment in which employees

exchange their personal ideas about how to participate in the organisations' brand-building efforts in their own way.

On the other hand, when well-established IBM and greater interfunctional communication are both present, organisations become highly effective at communicating the brand promise to their employees. Therefore, IBM can facilitate EBBB at an accelerating rate. This paper, in summary, contributed to the internal branding literature by enriching understanding of the extent to which the nature of the work environment affects internal branding (e.g. Punjaisri & Wilson, 2011; Vallaster & de Chernatony, 2006).

The above naturally leads to the question of whether a centralised or decentralised organisation is better placed to manage internal branding. This was explored in Leijerholt et al. (2019) in the context of public sector organisations. They found that in nonprofits where there are related but fairly independent departments or units, internal stakeholders need to understand how the organisational and departmental brands are linked. The organisation also needs to work towards alignment in branding. Therefore, supporting efforts such as style guides, marketing support and integrating the brand into internal systems can support a level of consistency of the brand while also providing departmental autonomy. Of course, the challenge is to find a balance between departmental autonomy and brand consistency, as complete consistency may not be wholly desirable in nonprofits. Instead, departments may need some flexibility in managing their brands, although such practices may contradict traditional branding practice and theory. However, results in this work suggested that greater freedom for individual departments to interpret the overarching brand may, perhaps surprisingly, not only ensure greater employee commitment but also improved external brand perception. There are, however, certain connection points that seem to have a positive influence on the department–organisational brand relationship. These include the core value statement, organisational branding structures and connections, and overall charity/public sector values. Combined, these connection points, and the general nature of the brand, may, if managed well, support a strong and positive brand for the organisation. Compared to branding in the private sector, branding seemingly warrants a somewhat different approach in nonprofits. Thus, this study suggests that individual departmental branding may be a fruitful path to building a positive brand for the overall organisation.

If departmental brands support a positive, and sector-relevant, organisational brand, the two brands may in fact align. This work therefore concluded that 'such alignment can be supported through some supporting factors linking the departmental brand efforts to the organisation' (Leijerholt et al., 2019, p. 287).

In terms of facilitating that discussed so far, internal brand management approaches need to be employed. The stakeholder environment of charities may make this particularly challenging. However Kuoppakangas et al. (2019) employed change management theory from elsewhere to increase the effectiveness of brand management in the higher education sector, in particular that of dilemma theory (see also Suomi et al., 2014).

This paper revealed that involving and empowering employees in dilemma reconciliation helped in consistent internal branding. The reconciliation of brand-related dilemmas with and by employees can be attained by engaging employees in the process of rebranding from the beginning. Indeed, this paper suggested the preparedness to detect and address dilemmas is central to successful branding. In summary, traditional change management approaches were found to produce unreconciled dilemmas that obstruct the implementation of a brand; efforts to build employee engagement in rebranding do not build employee supportiveness towards the new brand if core dilemmas are not reconciled.

Uniqueness of message

Another challenge that has its basis in internal marketing is that of nonprofit organisations finding and articulating a unique message (or USP) that all employees can relate to.

Research conducted by Leijerholt et al. (2019) suggests that struggling to identify a USP may not necessarily be as negative an issue as traditional branding theory suggests. This may be because nonprofits can benefit from a general positive perception of the organisation rather than achieving a differentiated and unique brand. This aligns with the findings by Sataøen and Wæraas (2015) who argue that public organisations have pressure to be perceived as 'normal' and to conform to institutional expectations. Therefore, departmental brands should not compete with but rather support the organisational brand.

> The differentiated and fragmented service offering of the organisation means that while the brand is meant to provide consistency and focus, externally and internally, the complexity of the organisation is argued to make traditional, fully consistent brand management efforts difficult. By having sector-relevant, and thus rather general, brand values as an overarching focus of the organisation, departments are able to connect to brand values that are founded in their reason for existing, ensuring societal values.
>
> *(Leijerholt et al., 2019, p. 287)*

A second conclusion of this research was that in branding nonprofit organisations the values and purpose of the sector may need to be integrated into the organisational brand values.

> Within such an environment, departments can be allowed to take greater responsibility of interpreting the brand according to their role in the organisation while staying aligned to the meaning of the brand values. With such an approach the brand value becomes a common denominator, providing a focus and direction that departments are encouraged to dock into; a compass in employees' everyday work life.
>
> *(Leijerholt et al., 2019, p. 287)*

Real-life case study: the role of a strong brand in recruiting volunteers and attracting stakeholders for a nonprofit organisation

Many nonprofit organisations face challenges in recruiting enough suitable volunteers (who the authors perceive as internal stakeholders and therefore important in the internal branding process). However, research has found that like profit-oriented organisations, nonprofit organisations' brand image is an important variable influencing the outcome of any recruitment process (Febriani & Selamet, 2020).

This is illustrated through the example of the nonprofit festival market in Finland, highlighting the significance of a strong brand image. In addition to other benefits of a strong brand, such as attracting festival attendees, sponsors and positive media coverage, festival managers need to pay attention to building strong brands in order to ensure adequate enrolment of volunteer workers, to therefore ensure the resourcing of production (see also Luonila, 2016).

Pori Jazz is a nonprofit festival arranged in the city of Pori in south-west Finland about 240 kilometres from Helsinki. In Finland hundreds of nonprofit and for-profit festival productions produced over two million festival visits in 2019. Relative to the size of the country, Finland is a 'land of festivals', as Finns make the most of the short, but light, summer months to enjoy outside activities.

Pori Jazz is one of the oldest and most notable jazz and rhythm music festivals in Europe, and within Finland it is very high profile and well known (Lemmetyinen et al., 2013). It has been running since 1966, initially growing from enthusiasm for jazz music among its founders; in fact, in the early years, it was to some extent the organisers' hobby. The history of the festival is therefore an important part of its brand story today (Pori Jazz, 2021).

Over the decades, there have been thousands of musicians performing at Pori Jazz, including international names such as B.B. King, Dizzy Gillespie, Miles Davis, Björk, Sting, Phil Collins and Elton John (Pori Jazz, 2021). In its founding year, the festival attracted about 600 'friends of jazz music', whereas in 2019 there were over 340,000 attendees (Pori Jazz, 2021). This made it the biggest festival in Finland in 2019 (Finland Festivals, 2021).

Throughout its history, the festival has developed a unique message with its own style, and this can be linked to its strong reputation (which of course underpins the brand). The festival organisers work hard to create media coverage and a 'buzz' around the festival to keep it vital beyond the actual festival dates (Luonila et al., 2016). As discussed, the festival has taken place annually since 1966 (with the exception of 2020 because of the Covid-19 pandemic). The long heritage of the festival has developed a positive relationship with the Pori city brand. This is particularly notable, as industry in the region was historically associated with manufacturing, but the city has renewed itself and built its brand as one of the leading event cities in Finland, based largely on Pori Jazz (Lemmetyinen et al., 2013; Pori, 2021). Among both Finns and foreigners, Pori is therefore now probably best known for its festival. Accordingly, Pori Jazz is an important brand for the city (see also Mäkelä, 2019). Whilst this can be mutually advantageous for the city and the festival itself, it also adds to challenges in consistent brand messaging that must incorporate the different stakeholders' (including the employees') points of view and feelings about the organisation. Internal marketing and training are key to managing this.

The organisational structure of the festival is important in understanding their internal marketing. The festival is a professional organisation, but surprisingly it has only six full-time paid employees and one freelancer employed. This obviously raises the question of how is it possible to arrange an event with over 340,000 attendees with so few employees?

The answer largely lies (in common with many charities) in the volunteer strategy. In addition to the employees, each year Pori Jazz has about 600 extra pairs of hands who have roles before, during and after the festival. Of these 600 people, about 300 are Pori Jazz's own volunteers, and 300 further volunteers come from Pori Jazz's partner organisations, for example sport clubs. Volunteers' work is mainly concentrated on actual festival days, as well as days just before and after the festival, when the festival infrastructure is being built and removed. Volunteers work in a number of different tasks which are vital for the festival, such as cleaning up litter, ticket sales, first aid, driving, assisting performers or attendees.

According to management, the programme of internal marketing activities aimed at the team-leaders is an organised and systematic process, and it comprises two-level training. All the team leaders who work for Pori Jazz participate in the initial training. This is important in establishing consistency and understanding in brand terms, and covers the history, ethos and values of Pori Jazz (particularly with regard to the environment, and which environmental management tools and certificates it employs). After this more general part of the training, each group of team leaders undergo specific training (focused on the festival sector) concentrating on how Pori Jazz wishes the team leaders to act in customer service situations to deliver consistent messages. This resonates with theory discussed in the earlier part of this chapter on the identified importance of the organisation's brand promise information being consistent across communication channels.

Typically, volunteers (other than team leaders) work in tasks that are not direct customer service situations. However, if the volunteers have a customer-facing role, they will be trained for the task. Motivation is also key as the volunteers are highly engaged, and often work in the same roles from year to year. This allows them to become highly familiar with their tasks and their requirements, and ultimately to become what may be termed 'brand ambassadors'. Before the volunteers start their work, they become members of a volunteer association. They all receive a merchandise package from Pori Jazz. The package slightly differs depending on the year in question, but typically it contains a bag, the festival t-shirt of the year and a jacket. The volunteers use these branded clothes during the festival (and they do not return them afterwards). Further, materials to underpin internal marketing are produced: all the extra pairs of hands receive a leaflet containing important information about policies and procedures in different situations. This ensures that processes are clear not only for the core team at the office but also for all the team leaders and other volunteers working in various tasks in festival production in different locations in Pori. This activity is therefore the underpinning of internal branding and is important to external perceptions and brand experience. It is an example of the discussed theoretical finding that when well-established internal brand management and interfunctional communication are both present, organisations become effective at communicating the brand promise to their employees and therefore volunteers. According to the festival management, materials that are handed out for the volunteers and their team leaders are in line with Pori Jazz's brand communication strategy, which supports the festival's vision, grasps its mission, and puts the business strategy in practice. The mission of Pori Jazz is: 'One feels good at Pori Jazz. The festival connects people via holistic experiences that will be remembered for a long time'. (Pori Jazz, n.d.). The brand communication strategy crystallises the way in which the business strategy should be visible in all communication. This brand strategy is aimed at all internal stakeholders (be they full-time employees or volunteers), gives mutual direction and describes what kind of communication Pori Jazz needs and how this communication is integrated in the broader societal context. Thus, the brand communication strategy is important in making sure that all communication, whether directed towards internal or external stakeholders (such as consumers and sponsors), is consistent both in the Pori Jazz's own media channels and in media collaboration, and at the levels of local, national and international communication. (Pori Jazz, n.d.).

The aim of Pori Jazz's internal communication targeted at the employees and internal stakeholders is to make sure that: 'we build and cherish our internal community with active communication. We encourage and support each other and respect one another's expertise. We build Pori Jazz's reputation by open communication and by paying attention to social responsibility in all actions'. Consequently, the core message of this internal communication is emphasising that: 'we are bridge builders between culture, music and people. We guarantee a successful festival experience: we want the visitor to feel comfortable, we make people happy. We want to surprise people positively' (Pori Jazz, n.d.).

In relation to the volunteers, the aim of Pori Jazz's internal communication targeted to this group is to underline that:

> We value the contribution of the volunteers and their skills and make sure that everyone has the necessary knowledge to carry out the festival successfully. We encourage creativity, solution-focused customer service and positive interaction with our teams. We communicate openly and create community, we engage – without volunteers Pori Jazz would not be Pori Jazz.
>
> *(Pori Jazz, n.d.)*

The core message related to this aim and targeted for the group of volunteers is: 'we are an equal and community builder and a partner who it is easy to work with. We wish that joy and easiness grasp our volunteers' (Pori Jazz, n.d.).

It is clear that, as in many nonprofit organisations, volunteers are critical to ongoing success. What then motivates these volunteers, some of them working year after year (some have a 30-year volunteer career at the festival!), to engage with the brand so deeply (Yle, 2015)?

The answer has its basis in the fact that, with over 50 years' history, Pori Jazz has a leading position in Finland's music festival scene, and a strong international reputation. Indeed, a long-serving former CEO believed that many volunteers appreciate the work experience gained as a volunteer at Pori Jazz, and are very proud to add it to their CVs; in short it is a brand that they wish to be associated with, and this is testament to ongoing internal branding. The festival's brand awareness is strong in Finland; volunteers find it attractive and wish to maintain ongoing links (see also Febriani & Selamet, 2020). Further, they feel important as part of a team producing a national festival and are motivated to ensure that everything works well at the festival.

The festival has a strong brand experience element which underpins internal branding; the event itself, its social context, shared memories and belongingness can form an unforgettable and holistic experience for a volunteer, and positive word-of-mouth received from past and current volunteers therefore attracts new volunteers (see also Luonila et al., 2016). During the festival days, the whole city starts to bustle, as local stores, cafes and restaurants are full of customers. Indeed, many local people are engaged in supporting the festival and its successful production in many ways; all this helps enhance the brand experience.

In addition to recruiting volunteers, a consistent and clear brand message is vital to obtaining sponsors and building collaboration with companies, as well as building relationships with other relevant stakeholders, such as festival attendees, media and the local community (see also Luonila et al., 2016). A strong brand is obviously also important in attracting world-famous performers to this Finnish city far away from the capital (a location that some might consider remote).

The brand also protects a nonprofit organisation in the event of any unforeseen crisis (for example in 2018 when earlier comments of Pori Jazz's new CEO on homosexuality became public and led to negative publicity). Some of the performers began to cancel their shows at the festival and the sensation was covered in national news. The association behind Pori Jazz fired the CEO in less than 24 hours to save its reputation (and therefore save support from festival attendees, performers and other stakeholders). However, without such a strong brand, the harm could have been more severe for the festival, despite the organisation's prompt action (see also Mäkelä, 2019).

In conclusion, a strong brand is important for nonprofit organisations (such as festivals) in attracting and engaging both internal and external stakeholders; in this case the primary internal branding focus is on both employees and volunteers. Innovative marketing strategies and a coherent message, which is relevant to festival attendees and stakeholders, are crucial in ensuring the viability and permanence of the festival in a competitive environment (Luonila et al., 2019; Suomi et al., 2020). Further, the strong brand of such a nonprofit organisation may have a significant

TABLE 12.1 Pori Jazz Festival internal marketing best practice lessons; what they got right!

The festival's brand communication strategy was vital in making sure that all communication, whether directed towards internal or external stakeholders, was consistent (in Pori Jazz's own media channels, in media collaboration and at local, national and international levels)
The organisers built and cherished their internal community with active communication (valuing the contribution of the volunteers, employees and partners)
There was a volunteer association to embed belonging. All received a merchandise package from Pori Jazz.
All the team leaders who work for Pori Jazz participated in initial training. This was important in establishing consistency
Consistent materials to underpin internal marketing were produced
Many local people were engaged in supporting the festival and its successful production; community links helped enhance the brand experience
Many volunteers valued the work experience gained as a volunteer at Pori Jazz, and were proud to add it to their CVs; in short it is a brand that they wish to be associated with

impact on the brand of its hosting city (e.g. Lemmetyinen et al., 2013). A number of the findings and conclusions of the research outlined in this chapter are therefore applicable and demonstrable through the example of the Pori Jazz festival (see Table 12.1).

Chapter discussion questions

1. We are taught at an early stage in marketing education to seek a unique selling point – why might this not always be as essential for NPOs?
2. NPOs generally have a complex stakeholder network. What are the implications for internal branding?
3. How can brand strategy be made into something meaningful for the majority of people working for and with a charity?

References

Berry, L.L. (1981). The employee as customer, *Journal of Retail Banking*, 3(1), 33–40.

Clark, P., Chapleo, C. & Suomi, K. (2020). Branding higher education: An exploration of the role of internal branding on middle management in a university rebrand. *Tertiary Education and Management*, 26(2), 131149.

Ewing, M.T. & Napoli, J. (2005). Developing and validating a multidimensional nonprofit brand orientation scale. *Journal of Business Research*, 58(6), 841–853.

Febriani, D.M. & Selamet, J. (2020). College students' intention to volunteer for non-profit organizations: Does brand image make a difference? *Journal of Nonprofit & Public Sector Marketing*, 32(2), 166–188.

Finland Festivals. (2021). Festivaalien käyntimäärät 2019 [Festival visits in 2019]. Available at www.festivals.fi/tilastot/festivaalien-kayntimaarat-2019/#.ydusrugzy2w (accessed 23 February 2021).

Grounds, J. (2005). Charity branding. *International Journal of Nonprofit and Voluntary Sector Marketing*, 10(2), 65.

Hankinson, P. (2004). The internal brand in leading UK charities. *Journal of Product & Brand Management*, 13(2), 84–93.

Huang, Y.T. (2020). Internal marketing and internal customer: A review, reconceptualization, and extension. *Journal of Relationship Marketing*, 19(3), 165–181.

Hytti, U., Kuoppakangas, P., Suomi, K., Chapleo, C. & Giovanardi, M. (2015). Challenges in delivering brand promise: Focusing on municipal healthcare organisations. *International Journal of Public Sector Management*, 28(3), 254–272.

Ind, N. (2001). *Living the Brand. How to Transform Every Member of Your Organization into a Brand Champion* (3rd edn). Kogan Page.

King, C., So, K.K.F. & Grace, D. (2013). The influence of service brand orientation on hotel employees' attitude and behaviors in China. *International Journal of Hospitality Management*, 34 (1), 172180.

Kuoppakangas, P., Suomi, K., Clark, P., Chapleo, C. & Stenvall, J. (2019). Dilemmas in re-branding a university – 'Maybe people just don't like change': Linking meaningfulness and mutuality into the reconciliation. *Corporate Reputation Review*, 23, 92–105.

Leijerholt, U., Chapleo, C. & O'Sullivan, H. (2019). A brand within a brand: An integrated understanding of internal brand management and brand architecture in the public sector. *Journal of Brand Management*, 26(3), 277–290.

Lemmetyinen, A., Go, F. & Luonila, M. (2013). The relevance of cultural production – Pori Jazz – in boosting place brand equity. *Place Branding and Public Diplomacy*, 9(3), 164–181.

Liu, G., Chapleo, C., Ko, W.W. & Ngugi, I.K. (2015). The role of internal branding in nonprofit brand management: An empirical investigation, *Nonprofit and Voluntary Sector Quarterly*, 44(2), 319–339.

Liu, G., Ko, W.W. & Chapleo, C. (2017). Managing employee attention and internal branding. *Journal of Business Research*, 79, 1–11.

Luonila, M. (2016). *Festivaalituotannon merkitysten verkosto ja johtaminen: tapaustutkimuksia suomalaisista taidefestivaaleista* [*The network of meanings and management in the festival production: Case studies of Finnish arts festivals*]. Doctoral dissertation. Sibelius Academy of the University of the Arts Helsinki (Arts Management), Studia Musica 70.

Luonila, M., Suomi, K. & Johansson, M. (2016). Creating a stir: The role of word of mouth in reputation management in the context of festivals. *Scandinavian Journal of Hospitality and Tourism*, 16(4), 461–483.

Luonila, M., Suomi, K. & Lepistö, T. (2019). Unraveling mechanisms of value co-creation in festivals. *Event Management*, 23, 41–60.

Mäkelä, A. (2019). Pori Jazz on kaupungille mittaamattoman arvokas brändi – Suomi-Areenan ja jazzfestivaalin saumaton yhteistyö on kaikkien etu. *Satakunnan Kansa*, 8 June. Available at: www.satakunnankansa.fi/paakirjoitukset/art-2000007095171.html (accessed 10 February 2021).

Pori. (2021). Culture. Available at www.visitpori.fi/en/culture (accessed 10 February 2021).

Pori Jazz. (2021). Introduction. Available at https://historia.porijazz.fi/en/ (accessed 10 February 2021).

Pori Jazz. (n.d.). *Communication Strategy of Pori Jazz*. Unpublished internal material.

Punjaisri, K. & Wilson, A. (2011). Internal branding process: Key mechanisms, outcomes and moderating factors. *European Journal of Marketing*, 45(10), 1521–1537.

Saleem, F.Z. & Iglesias, O. (2016). Mapping the domain of the fragmented field of internal branding. *Journal of Product & Brand Management*, 25(1), 43–57.

Satøen, L. & Wæraas, A. (2015). Branding without unique brands. *Public Management Review*, 17(3), 443–461.

Stuart, H. (2016). Managing a corporate brand in a challenging stakeholder environment: Charity branding. *International Studies of Management & Organization*, 46(4), 228–234.

Suomi, K., Kuoppakangas, P., Hytti, U., Hampden-Turner, C. & Kangaslahti, J. (2014). Focusing on dilemmas challenging reputation management in higher education. *International Journal of Educational Management*, 28(4), 461–478.

Suomi, K., Luonila, M. & Tähtinen, J. (2020). Ironic festival brand co-creation. *Journal of Business Research*, 106, 211–220.

Urde, M., Baumgarth, C. & Merrilees, B. (2013). Brand orientation and market orientation: From alternatives to synergy. *Journal of Business Research*, 66(1), 13–20.

Vallaster, C. & de Chernatony, L. (2006). Internal brand building and structuration: The role of leadership. *European Journal of Marketing*, 40(8), 761–784.

Yildiz, S.M. & Kara, A. (2017). A unidimensional instrument for measuring internal marketing concept in the higher education sector. *Quality Assurance in Education*, 25(3), 343–361.

Yle. (2015). Vapaaehtoisten hurja työpanos Porissakin festivaalien elinehto. Available at https://yle.fi/uutiset/3-8146330 (accessed 10 February 2021).

INDEX

Page numbers in **bold** refer to figures, page numbers in *italic* refer to tables.

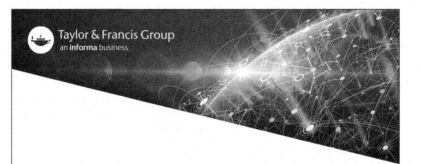

Printed in the United States
by Baker & Taylor Publisher Services